SUSANN BOSSHARD-KÄLIN

WESTWARD

Encounters with Swiss American Women

POSTSCRIPT
Leo Schelbert

They Went Before: Four Historical Portraits
Essay: Women in 20th Century America

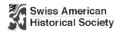 Swiss American
Historical Society

 Musée
des Suisses
dans le Monde
www.penthes.ch

Publication of English Edition of *westwärts*
by Swiss American Historical Society, Washington, DC, 2010
and the Editions de Penthes, Geneva, Switzerland, 2010

This book is *Swiss American Historical Society Publication* No. 29.

Fotos: Annina Bosshard (except of L. Geiser by Christoph Müller)
Selection of Historical Pictures: Leo Schelbert
Graphic Concept and Design: taylormade GmbH, Wädenswil
Layout and Printing: Druckerei Franz Kälin AG, Einsiedeln
Graphic Support: SteckDesign, Zollikon

Translations:
Marianne Burkhard (E. Bollier, M. Burkhard, E. Carney, L. Geiser,
L. Lee, M.-S. Pavlovich, M. Schlapfer, N. Schleicher, R. Schupbach)
Leo Schelbert (all other texts, except own translations provided
by M. Ammann Durrer and M. Bernet)

Copy Editors:
Rita Emch, New York and Wendy Everham, Wilmette, Illinois

Send book orders to:
Leo Schelbert, SAHS Book Editor
2523 Asbury Avenue
Evanston, IL 60201
lschelbe@uic.edu
or
Susann Bosshard-Kälin
Hansenweg 2, CH-8847 Egg, Switzerland
info@susann-bosshard-pr.ch

Foreword

The cultural chain is a chain of women that
connects the past with the future (Mohawk)

People – Women, Men, and Children – Migrate.

They have always gone out into the world – from Switzerland as
well. And almost as many from abroad have settled in Switzerland, be it for a short or a long period of time. It has always been a
country of emigration as well as immigration. Reasons for migrat-
ing are manifold; they may be personal or may be rooted in economic, social, political, or ideological circumstances.

In the 20th century when Switzerland itself became increasingly a country of immigration, Swiss women and men went
abroad nevertheless and, following a long tradition, also to the
United States of America.

A few women representing many have been given a voice in
this book: Did they leave forever? Alone? Was it for their one true
love? In search of adventure or seeking an escape? Some felt they
were foreigners throughout their lives in the New World, others
felt at home. Many were successful, others submitted to an unexpected fate; some found their happiness while others are still looking. They stayed in old age in the new homeland or returned to the
Swiss one.

It was the historian Leo Schelbert who gave me the idea for this
book. He has been living in metropolitan Chicago for nearly forty
years and, after studying at Columbia University in New York,
taught American history for 32 years at the University of Illinois at
Chicago, especially the history of American immigration. He has
also featured the global history of Swiss emigration in books and

articles. In his view, the Swiss abroad – in 2009 some 676,000 people – represent Switzerland's 27th canton. "As written history in general, also the history of migrations has remained largely men's history," he asserts. "Documentary sources of women emigrants are little known, although women achieved just as much as men either by themselves or as mothers and partners." Precisely for that reason Swiss American women were to be given a voice.

Leo Schelbert was taken by the book *spruchreif – Zeitzeuginnen aus dem Kanton Schwyz erzählen* (ready to be told – Witnesses of Their Times from Canton Schwyz Tell Their Story) that I had initiated and attended to in 2004. He inspired me four years ago to undertake a similar project of encounters with women who had moved to the United States in the 20th century.

Each of my fifteen encounters from east to west was unique. In the selection of the time-witnesses I consciously eschewed typologies and was guided by neither geographical nor sociological concerns. During the three years of work, the contacts with these women intensified and wonderful friendships evolved. The time-witnesses portrayed here come from different Swiss cantons, have different familial and occupational backgrounds, and live in different regions. They tell of their diverse experience in Switzerland as well as in the United States.

What emerged is a series of impressions, of fascinating individual experiences as portrayed from a woman's perspective. The life stories feature memories, experiences, and desires, shaped by every day life, homesickness, joy, and crisis. As told and written, they will be shielded from becoming forgotten. In encounters lasting several hours women told me of their experience with great candor in most diverse Swiss German dialects or in English. The fifteen stories show women standing between two worlds, two cultures, and two languages, – but above all people who have shaped their lives and world with a zest for life, with humor, courage, equanimity, and wisdom. I am deeply touched by them and their stories. I thank them for their trust, openness, and kindness.

In the second part of the book four portraits feature the unique world of women from the 18th and 19th centuries. Surviving letters and pictures that Leo Schelbert and others had gathered made these encounters possible. His concluding essay sketches the status of American women in the 20th century and the world in which the women portrayed have shaped their lives.

From the start my project met with genuine interest and much support. My acknowledgements list all the wonderful people and generous institutions without whose help this book could never have been done.

I want to thank cordially above all Leo Schelbert, my wonderful and kind friend and mentor. During the whole project he has laid out the red carpet. During all of its phases he accompanied me on the journey despite the spatial distance. He or his wife Virginia accompanied me on the interview trips across America, and in their house in Evanston they extended their generous hospitality.

Heartfelt thanks also to my husband Jürg who stood by me throughout all the storms of this ambitious project and remained tolerant and truly patient, wise, and supportive. I thank my daughters Annina and Catherina for their joyful accompaniment on my trips, and to Annina especially, for the pictures she took of the women portrayed in the book. As my first reader, Mirjam Weiss always encouraged me and critically reviewed my texts. In the midst of the project Walti Graf Chiriboga passed away whose friendly suggestions were most useful to me. A special thank you also goes to the American-Swiss graphic artist Anna Taylor, who created the book's masterful design, to Rita Emch and Wendy Everham who served as copy editors of the English edition, and to the dedicated translators Sr. Marianne Burkhard OSB and Leo Schelbert who, as the book editor of the Swiss American Historical Society, also monitored the preparation of the English edition.

Thanks also to Doris Stump of the eFeF-Verlag, the publisher of the German edition, to the Swiss American Historical Society, especially its president Dr. Heinz B. Bachmann and to Gerhard Kälin and Katja Schönbächler of Franz Kälin Druckerei AG of Einsiedeln. They were all most helpful in guiding the project to what it is now.

My Swiss American friends, it has been a great honor to share in telling your stories!

Susann Bosshard-Kälin
March, 2010, Egg near Einsiedeln

ELLEN
1926
CARNEY
ERNST

"Our family is like mixed greens of different ethnic groups, says my German friend. My husband David is from Sierra Leone, I am from Switzerland, and my son is married to a Chinese woman. When David and I take our grandchildren with their almond eyes for a walk in Sag Harbor, the whole world meets." Ellen Carney laughs and uses a clasp to put up her long white hair. She wears a light airy summer dress, which she made herself as she has done with her entire wardrobe for decades.

For over twenty years the family therapist Ellen Carney-Ernst has been living with her second husband David, a former UN official, in Sag Harbor, at the eastern end of Long Island. In the 19th century whalers lived on this island near Manhattan, later painters discovered the region, and today stars and starlets from movies and TV – such as Steven Spielberg or Renée Zellweger – have their summer residences here.

Ellen and David live in a secluded modest house that David had built in the 1950s. The glamour that surrounds the regions of the Hamptons – an area of wonderful sandy beaches – does not affect them. "In Sag Harbor, where everyone has everything, we live behind the times. We don't need luxury. We drive a 1983 Chevy, and my Mazda is 16 years old. We came to Sag Harbor long before it became the Saint-Tropez of New York." The Carney's house is like a museum. It is filled to the rafters with mementoes and treasures of its widely travelled owners. Each piece has its history and tells stories from different continents – Asia, Africa, America, and Europe. Mixed among them are many textile creations of the lady of the house. "Yet at times I would like to see only white walls," Ellen says.

The one-story house has a basement that is as long as the house and contains a huge library. "This is David's world. He is a researcher, philosopher, and mathematician. Only he can find his way among these thousands of books about art, philosophy, medicine, politics and literature." The Carney's house has no microwave oven, no answering machine, no swimming pool or manicured lawn. "Status symbols mean nothing to me. Do you know how much we have gotten from the village dump? That's where the rich people discard their good stuff. Lots of books are from there, many of our chairs and our table. Once we saw a grand piano for the taking. And a few years ago I found a Bible from which flew twelve 100-dollar bills. Isn't this decadent? Of course, I took the money together with the Bible."

Ellen Ernst was born on April 10, 1926, in Zurich in the car on the way to the Bethanien Hospital. "The doctors gave me little chance to survive. I was blue by the time my parents reached the hospital. I was transported to the Children's Hospital. My heart was weak as well as my lungs. But I survived, and my parents handled me with kid gloves. I was never allowed to do gymnastics or to swim. I was always 'wrapped in cotton'. Later in life I made up for it. Perhaps my adventurous life was my revenge; that is certainly possible. I always knew – since I was a child – that I was different; I just didn't know how I was different." Ellen was always sickly. "Often I would have a fever and bronchitis for weeks, bronchiectasis. Because of heart and lung problems my parents sent me several times to health resorts, to Adelboden and Ägeri. These days it is again bad with my cough at times."

"I always knew that I was different; I just didn't know how I was different." (1928)

Ellen's parents were never really settled. "Mother was a secretary, and my father came from a family of butchers. Father hated butchering, but mother thought she would always have enough to eat, blood and liver sausage. Father preferred to take pictures of guests in Swiss resorts. He developed the pictures over night, and mother had to deliver them the next day. One of my first childhood memories is from Engelberg where on ice people pushed around what looked like water bottles – playing curling. Perhaps I was about two years old. And I will never forget the woman in Wengen who had her leg in a cast on a chair and ate her lettuce with her hands. Besides living in resorts we also lived in Wollishofen, part of Zurich and in Winterthur where we had a movie theater."

It was only in 1930, when their second child Fritz was born in Altstetten, that the family more or less settled in Zurich. But even then, the family kept on moving around town, to the Weststrasse, the Gertrudstrasse, the Grüngasse and eventually to the Badenerstrasse. "My father moved us and his business to various locations. My memories from that time have faded. My parents did not talk about it much. We did not discuss the past. And we rarely had spontaneous guests and there was never much food on the table. My mother always cooked precise amounts. She did not want leftovers. But we always went on vacations, at a time when this wasn't fashionable yet. We drove to Alassio, to Cattolica, and to the Appenzell during the war. Simply going away: this was different from the families of the children with whom we grew up."

For health reasons Ellen was not able to attend kindergarten. "I remained in my world of thoughts and phantasies. Our parents had little time for us children. Just the other day Fritz said to me on the phone: 'You know, our parents simply left us to ourselves.' But therefore we became independent. This was unusual; it was an adventure. As a child I learned to look around. I observed and drew my own conclusions. As a child I was an introvert."

Going to school turned out liberating for Ellen. "I devoured books as soon as I was able to read. *Emil und die Detektive* by Erich Kästner was my first book. Soon I also read newspapers and the Pestalozzi Calendar, which contained pictures and also some cultural items. I was an outsider, hardly had any girlfriends. I had to stay home all the time. My brother says even today that I was too good as a child. I embarrassed him. He always got the spankings that – actually – I deserved." Becoming a doctor was Ellen's only dream. "Probably, because I was always sick. My doctor impressed me, and especially our neighbor, Dr. Schnabel, an unmarried woman, who had founded the hospital in Lambarene together with Albert Schweitzer. I had a crush on Albert Schweitzer."

Ellen's teacher in primary school realized that this intelligent girl was cut out for the Gymnasium, the college prep school. "He tutored me privately, thus I passed the entrance exam for the *Töchterschule*, the Gymnasium for girls, on the Hohe Promenade in Zurich. Before the war this was unusual for girls from my social milieu. At the beginning we were about 40 students; at the end it was about a dozen that went all the way to the *Matura* [the final exam which guarantees entrance to any university]. One became an architect, another a gynecologist. For the last half year before the final exam I had no report card; I was always sick. Out of the six and a half years of the curriculum I probably have report cards for about four years. My classmates knew what would be expected at the final exams; I had not the faintest idea. I simply took the exams without any extra tutorials. But I did pass the finals with Latin, English and Italian."

During WWII their English teacher encouraged her students to go to the Red Cross Club in the Hotel Eden on the Bahnhofstrasse. "There American GIs on furlough in Switzerland would speak English with us, dance with us. I didn't need to hear this twice. These evenings were fascinating. I met a lot of interesting people. To meet people who would freely discuss topics we were not allowed to broach at home, that was an incredible experience. At the end of my Gymnasium years the war had ended; it was also the end of those evenings – but my fondness for Americans remained."

Ellen's parents did not want to hear about her going to university. "And I had no idea what I could do after graduation. My father took me into his photo shop, which he had opened at the Badenerstrasse in Zurich's 3rd district and in which he had set up a portrait studio. But taking portraits was not my cup of tea. Nevertheless, one day he sent me on a picture hunt with an empty roll of Kodak film. I was to take pictures of people in the Landesmuseum (Swiss National Museum)."

There she met two GIs, a black man from New York and a white one from Philadelphia, they were super models for her. "And once again I was able to speak English. I offered the two a guided tour through the museum. Howard from Philadelphia – who had seen action in Northern Africa and Italy – insisted on getting my address. And soon we wrote letters back and forth and talked about Chinese philosophy. I found this very adventurous."

One day in 1947, a few months after his discharge, Howard appeared on the doorsteps of her family's apartment in the Badenerstrasse. "Self-confident, he announced that we should get married." Howard was an American Quaker who, enraged about Hitler, had volunteered for the Army; he stayed in Switzerland for three months to get to know Ellen. "And he persisted in wanting to marry me. I saw things differently. I felt too young and too inexperienced as I was just 21 and Howard Gillespie was 19 years older. 'You came here to see how you would like it. Now I will first go and see how I would like America', was my answer."

With an immigration visa Ellen Ernst travelled on her own to America in April 1948. "I had asked a saddler to make two large oversea bags – duffle bags – with stable zippers and handles. My father took me by car to Basel. In the train to Amsterdam I met a nice lady who invited me to spend the night with her and her husband, the town-physician of Amsterdam, before continuing my journey toward the Atlantic the next day. In a hotel in Rotterdam, before embarking, I was served something that looked like grubs – shrimp. How would I have known what they were? Still I felt very grown up. I had no fear. And I knew that I would make it, that somehow I would be able to overcome any obstacles."

Where did she find such courage? "Inside. I was firm and secure in myself; I knew what I was able to do. And quite frankly, my savings of 800 dollars in my pocket also helped!" The crossing on the *New Amsterdam* was stormy. "But I was never seasick. The doctor who treated me all my life in Switzerland and who subscribed to anthroposophy had advised me: 'Breathe in when the ship goes up, and breathe out when she goes down.' It worked." Ellen shared the cabin with three women. "One came directly from a concentration camp. She did not say much about it, but told me that a priest on the ship made a pass at her and wanted to sleep with her!

"When I saw the statue of Liberty in New York, I felt as if I were growing some more inside. I felt liberated. But when we docked in Hoboken, I would have preferred to turn around right away. Everything was so dirty and chaotic in this harbor."

Howard met his Swiss girlfriend, but he did not come – as she had expected – with a car. They traveled by train to Philadelphia where Howard lived with his parents – in an old part of the city where African Americans who had come up from the South during the war had settled.

"Everything was suddenly so different. Howard's mother came from one of the first Quaker families of America. Now I was with people who were religious, but not in the way I had experienced in the Swiss Reformed Church. They were not religious in a church going sense. Yet the ways of the Quakers were somehow familiar to me. I understood them in their 'meetings for worship' in which they assembled for silent prayer and experienced these assemblies devoid of ceremonies as divine worship. All this impressed me, and especially the fact that many Quakers think and feel very differently – for me this was deeply religious, a religion without complicated dogmas. Yet I never became a Quaker myself." About herself she says, "Never in my life did I pursue obstinately any firm goal. Everything always moved, flowed. I only had to say yes or no.

"In Chester County, a hilly rural area thirty miles west of Philadelphia, Howard planned to establish a 'utopian community' together with conscientious objectors and their families, a community that did not exclude persons of any racial background. We were a large, extended family and created our own rules in the settlement of Tanguy Homesteads. We simply wanted to 'drop out of the rat race.'"

It was a totally new and fascinating world with professors, librarians, teachers, and nurses and their families. "Interesting people such as Martha Jaeger, the psychologist of the writer Anaïs Nin, lived with us. Exciting. I felt very much at ease. When a five year old girl came to me during my pregnancy and told me how I had made this child and how it would later come out of my belly, I thought that these were truly unusual people!"

The first members of the community lived in an old farmhouse. "Howard and I moved from the beginning into a house of our own; but we had many meals together. Few members of the community owned a car, the women shopped together, and we used vegetables and fruit from our large garden. The men built the houses. I felt at home there. Yet today I know: in reality I do not belong anywhere. I feel at home in the entire world. Wherever I live at the moment, I feel at home, and so also in our settlement.

"Howard and I did get married. And when I became pregnant, they told me: either an abortion or heart surgery. Already at the age of 13 I had heard that I could die because of my heart or my lungs. Therefore I thought that I could die in either case, by giving birth or by having the surgery. I chose what was good for me. I had nothing to lose. Imagine this! And now an old woman is sitting across from you. It is really strange how things happen in life."

Ellen Carney was told that she was the first pregnant woman in America who underwent heart surgery. "I was seen as a special case in the University Hospital in Philadelphia and I became a media star overnight." The surgery was successful, but asthma and coughing have been her steady companions until today. "My lungs could not recover; they were too heavily damaged."

In their utopian community of intellectual leftists Ellen blossomed. "We were different from the average Americans, and I appreciated it. We were looking for a different path, an interior rather than an exterior one, watched each others' children and functioned as nurses for each other. We were almost self-sufficient, created our own little world.

"In 1949 I gave birth to our son Fred, in 1953 to our daughter Hester. For 30 years I lived in this community, until 1978. These were years that deeply shaped me. Howard worked as an engineer in the large harbor of the US Navy in Philadelphia. We participated in political protest marches to Washington in support of black

Americans and protested against the War in Viet Nam." Ellen did not have a profession "until there was a need for a kindergarten teacher for all the children in our settlement. I thought, I would try it and opened a kindergarten for our community that was also open to children from outside. It was great fun. With the children I did everything that as a child I had not been allowed to do myself. We even burned the *Böög* of the Zurich *Sechseläuten* near our creek." [Following an old custom, old man winter is burned publicly one day in early spring when all the church bells toll the summer hour of 6 p.m.]

Then Ellen started feeling a great thirst for knowledge. She went back to school and became an American citizen "so that later I would be able to work as a teacher." As an American with a bachelor's degree, which she had earned at a black college, she obtained a position at a hospital for children with mental illnesses. "I worked especially with autistic children; I was one of the first hospital teachers in the United States, and in our team I had equal status with psychologists and psychiatrists – this was totally new at that time." She continued to take courses and earned a Masters degree in special education in 1962.

"I was one of the first hospital teachers in the United States, and in our team I had equal status with psychologists and psychiatrists."

Yet she continued to be involved in her community. "At Christmas we used to invite foreign students from various universities, mostly blacks. That's how I met David, an economist, who had grown up in Sierra Leone, taught math in America and subsequently worked at the UN Planning Institute in Senegal as well as in posts in the Caribbean and in East Africa. While in the US he used to spend Christmas holidays with us."

When Ellen became ever more independent and earned more money than her husband, he had had enough. "I was too lively for him because I wanted to experience more of life. As visionary as Howard basically was – in his relationship with me he was not open-minded. He did not like the ways in which I had developed and that I paid for our children's college education and our vacations."

They decided to divorce. Howard stayed in the community. And Ellen opened a private practice as family therapist in Paoli near Philadelphia. "I was successful. Once almost half of the Philadelphia Symphony Orchestra came to my practice. I made good money." And: "America gave me a second life, and my heart lived again – both in the literal and figurative sense."

David Carney's wife died, and Ellen visited the widower in 1977 in Dakar where he worked for the UN. "In 1978, the year of my divorce, I married David. My mother got along well with him but said 'if only he were not all that black...' One of the first things my husband taught me was not to be so nosy. 'White people are nosy. Don't ask so many questions!'"

Years with David in Africa followed – an adventurous and fascinating period in several UN missions. "We were in Burkina-Faso, Cameroon, Chad before the civil war. Everywhere I felt at home. Often I came to places where people had never seen a white person. I had to learn that their uneasiness in my presence was not directed at me personally but was simply a result of this unusual experience. Already at age 16 my hair had turned white, though not as white as it is today. This had to do with my illness."

For many years Africa was Ellen's home. "After some time in Maroua, in northern Cameroon, I realized that tourists did not find anything to take back to their children. Thus I began to make toys from shreds of cloth that were not sold on the market. Together with tailors – all men – I created animals, giraffes, elephants, *Kasperli* puppets as well as greetings cards decorated with cloth. As time went by, we were able to hire five to six tailors who sewed the toys. A Dutch organization handled the sales. I was simply spontaneously creative."

In 1984 David retired. "We didn't know where we should live. In his house in Sag Harbor certainly just for a time – but then we stayed forever!" Ellen resumed her creative crafts: "I began with patchwork and quilts, sewed pillows and vests. A neighbor provided me with cloth samples and covers, which she fished out of the containers of various interior decorators in Manhattan. My creations were sold in a store in Sag Harbor and even in some art galleries – until patchwork became very fashionable. Then I stopped. Later I described the memories of my Swiss childhood in a book that I also illustrated."

Today Ellen no longer likes to cook. "Often we eat at the Senior Center where one can get a lunch for $2.50. You have to be at least 55 to go there. At the beginning people there didn't like me, I probably used too many foreign words. But in time they accepted us. Recently I edited a book about the people who frequent the center. They come from Poland, Germany, Ireland – it is a multi-cultural project about mostly simple, but interesting people who have so much to tell if you take the time to listen to them. Everyone has his or her own story to tell. There are so many people here who experienced a lot. Americans are often more profound than we think. They are easygoing. As a nation they think that they are powerful – but as individuals they are sensitive, more sensitive than the Swiss, I think."

Then once more, Ellen looks back farther in her past. "When I arrived in America, the women here seemed different from those in Switzerland. They did what they wanted, were more independent. But they did not have much power. And it seemed they had only little political interest. In America political topics were not publicly discussed. That was somehow taboo at any rate among the people with whom we lived. This only changed in the 1960s."

Ellen is tired. "My lava flows more slowly – though I really was a volcano. I never felt fear. My life probably was somewhat more colorful than the lives of others. Life is a spider's web. Events surface which I had not considered for a long time. Thus there is sufficient material for me to digest. I have no regrets. Of course, there are things that I could have done better. But at the time I did the best I could, I did what I felt was right and necessary."

Does she feel her age? "Yes. David and I are old. We only travel in our minds nowadays. Many of our friends are living in senior's residences. For David, that would not be good. He wants to stay where his books are, he would not be able to part with them. He writes much, philosophical books and political letters to the editor of the local newspapers. The corruption in his home country worries him, yet from a distance he sees the difficulties there a bit less. Africans have a dense social network, here and throughout the world, this is good. David is highly educated and wise. And I like living with him.

"I don't have any great dreams anymore. All is well as it is. Strange, isn't it? Many people say 'If only I had... but I couldn't.' The last time I was in Switzerland five years ago I thought that I would have become a mediocre woman, a *Bünzli* woman if I had spent my life there. Perhaps my life would have revolved around food and vacations. And perhaps I would have died of my illness much sooner. I feel that in Switzerland I would not have had all the opportunities I had here in America.

"Would I have married with my heart problems? I am sure I would not have dared to have children. And I would never have gotten into the circles I did if I had not studied. Thanks to my emigration I experienced a second birth.

"Here in America people deal with life in simpler, more easy-going ways. For me Switzerland was traditional and predictable way back then. Today it may be different. But in my time – everything had its fixed routine.

"When I talk about Switzerland I always say 'at home.' Even today I like to make *Rösti* [sort of hash browns] and *Birchermüesli*. My daughter Hester says that I am still very much connected to Switzerland even though I have lived in foreign countries for 60 years.

"I have little contact with Swiss people here. But every day I am reading the *Tages Anzeiger* and the *Neue Zürcher Zeitung* online. Both Fred and Hester are proud of their Swiss heritage. Both are American citizens but speak Swiss dialect. Fred studied at the University in Basel and is active in Swiss-American events; and he is good at *Jass*, a Swiss card game that my father taught them. Probably it is the first years of life and one's mother tongue that shape our sense of 'home'. Everything else is just sauce for the roast."

Ellen says that she still can delve into each layer of her life; "I have only given you excerpts. I took life as it presented itself; I lived according to the Greek expression *panta rhei* – to let one self be carried along. This requires no courage. The process, the development, was always more interesting and more satisfying to me than the end result.

"I was mother, wife, teacher, therapist and handicraft artist. And with this versatility I was probably little suited for a professional career. Even today I take each day as it comes. This is wonderful. And actually it is even more interesting today than in earlier times. Looking back I see how everything fits together. Is this wisdom? I have no idea! This is the time for me to look back, time too, to check out the apples in the basket and to throw out the rotten ones."

MARGOT AMMANN DURRER 1922

"The first time I ever watched television was at the 1939 World's Fair in New York. For me it was a marvel. General Motors had a great hit with this new wonder of the world. Another popular place at the Fair for the Swiss was the Swiss Pavilion. In the foreshadowing of the Second World War it offered a bit of the homeland. Everyone was very patriotic and one heard Swiss dialect spoken all around. Almost once a week our family drove to the Fair from New Jersey – as a teenager I could join the official events to which my father was invited, or simply went with friends for a raclette or fondue."

Margot Ammann Durrer is the daughter of the Swiss structural engineer and bridge builder, Othmar H. Ammann. She speaks an American brand of her Swiss dialect. The longer the conversation lasts the more extended and colorful her vocabulary becomes. "In my heart I am both American and Swiss; rather than a conflict, this is an asset. Although I was born in America, my Swiss background has made its mark throughout my life."

From her apartment on the 20th floor of a high rise building in Manhattan she has a view beyond the roofs and water towers of the Upper East Side. Summer flowers are in bloom in pots on her small terrace. From somewhere a gentle bell is chiming in the wind and finches are pecking at sunflower seeds in the birdfeeder.

She leans over the railing where a small American flag is fluttering: "I have no fear of heights. I probably inherited that from my father." Back inside at the card table, she lays out a book of the Ammann family of Schaffhausen as well as a scrapbook of her father. The Seth Thomas clock is chiming every fifteen minutes.

"My father built long span suspension bridges here in America. In a symbolic sense I have built a bridge for myself between America and my Swiss heritage through frequent visits to Switzerland, as well as working there for a year – and my association here with Swiss activities and organizations such as the Swiss American Historical Society."

It was only in recent years that Margot got to know details about the private life of her parents. "Mostly I learned these from the 485 letters that my father had sent from New York to Switzerland at the beginning of the last century to his parents and to my mother. My grandmother had saved these letters, often six to eight pages long, carefully bound in red ribbons in bundles according to year. After her death, these precious bundles traveled back over the ocean, returning to my father. His letters to my mother before they were married were saved in a lovely painted wooden box." Margot adds: "It gave me great comfort to read the private thoughts and hopes of my father and also the expressions of love for his parents and my mother. From these valuable writings I also learned of the happiness he and my mother found in their lifetime in America. Letters are like valuable footprints of a person."

While the official papers of Othmar Ammann are kept in an archive at the library of the ETH, the Swiss Federal Institute of Technology in Zurich, Margot has kept his personal papers. "These are always helpful for researchers and reporters to consult for details of his private life. I translated his letters into English as well as the Archive records of the Ammann family of Schaffhausen, going back to 1450. In my eighties, I finally learned, through the patient direction of a friend, the use of the computer's word processor, which enabled me to bring these translations up to the state of the art."

Margot noticeably enjoyed the review of her life. "I have not reminisced on my childhood and adolescent years for a long time. I thought I had forgotten everything! It is wonderful to review my life, scene for scene – as if on stage in a theatre."

But first she turned the pages in her father's album to the description of his first years in America. "In 1904, at the age of 21, father came here to gain experience from the vast engineering opportunities before marrying his childhood sweetheart, Lilly Wehrli and settling down to raise a family and practice his profession in Switzerland. He wrote romantic letters back to Switzerland, and soon he was writing, 'I would like to stay longer in America. But we do not want to spend our youth separated. My dearest, I would like you to come to America.' She answered, 'I will follow you anywhere in the world, but I would like to marry here.' The boat trips to Switzerland and return left only 4 days of his vacation to marry and bring his bride back to America. In the course of the years, new and challenging engineering opportunities kept on presenting themselves, and his planned one-year stay in the United States became a lifetime."

In 1924, after 20 years of diligent service as assistant to several of America's outstanding bridge engineers, he was appointed Engineer of Bridges for the Port Authority of New York, in charge of the construction of his own proposed bridge over the Hudson River in New York. The building of this bridge, today known as the George Washington Bridge, brought him professional recognition and the start of a long career as specialist in long span bridges. Margot remembers walking with him on Sunday mornings to a high point near their home in Boonton, New Jersey, from where he could observe through binoculars the progress of the construction of the New Jersey tower of the bridge. She also vividly recalls him coming home from the office in the evening, going first into the garden and walking around a bit, still wearing his hat and business clothes and street shoes, pulling a few weeds or pruning a few straggly branches from a pine tree. This was how he shed the pressures of the office.

"The several years preceding this appointment were hard times for my parents, living on their savings and hopes for acceptance of father's plans. On May 31, 1922, with my brothers Werner and George, 10 and 12 years old, I arrived as the last addition to the family. 'Our little one does not give us any problem for the moment. She is alert and has a strong personality. She will find her way,' father wrote in a letter to his mother in Switzerland. My brothers added, 'We like our little sister. She smiles at us in the morning.' They were very good to me. I often heard about how

"We like our little sister. She smiles at us in the morning."

they taught me to swim, throwing me into the water even before I was able to walk. Everyone spoiled 'Little Margot'. My childhood was happy and without care. We lived in a house with a large garden, surrounded on two sides with woods and a river. One early memory I have is of sitting with my mother on the terrace while she was sewing. I was her little helper by threading needles for her. I also remember staying with father while he worked in the garden or accompanying him for long walks, with him pointing out certain plants or birds or other beauties of nature. I had a special attachment to my father. He was certainly my first sweetheart. Father gave my brothers and me a lasting example of modesty and honesty. He never pushed us to excel nor ever praised us. He only asked of us that we become responsible, honorable and independent citizens."

"I had a special attachment to my father. He was certainly my first sweetheart." (1933)

Margot then added: "For a long time it was very hard to be the daughter of a famous father. I felt uncomfortable when people praised him to me, or on the other hand, when more was expected from me because of his achievements. In seventh grade at school, in front of the whole class, the instructor corrected an error on my exam paper, saying 'your father has designed the George Washington Bridge. And you cannot even add correctly.' I wanted to fall through the floor. It took time and maturity to overcome this shyness and to find my own personality, my own life. We lived as Swiss, at least that's how I thought of it then. The American children had more toys and fancier clothing, and their parents were less strict than ours. Our meals were simpler and more geared for health, with fresh vegetables and fruit from the garden and eggs and chicken from our own henhouse. In contrast, I had more books, had more vacation trips, more exposure to theatre, museums and later, opportunities of advanced education. I played with the neighbors, taking preference for the boy's sports over the girl's dolls and dresses. Often Swiss friends of my parents visited us. We led a simple life in a small rural town, as was commonplace in America in the 1920's."

At eleven years of age, from one day to the next, Margot had to learn to be independent. "In 1930, my mother was operated for breast cancer. However the cancer had already spread. Mother never complained. I somehow sensed the seriousness of her condition and remember praying for her recovery. After many weeks in the hospital, shortly before Christmas of 1933, she died. I reproached God, 'When I prayed to You to let my mother get better, I did not mean for You to take her away from me.' Her death was very hard for me to accept. Father was busy with his work at the Port Authority and often was in San Francisco as a consultant for the construction of the Golden Gate Bridge. A governess was engaged to manage the household, but she did not understand me, and my brothers were already independent and hardly had any time for me. During this sad time, in which I was very often alone, I lived in my own dreams and fantasies. I learned to think and discover my own interests. I collected stones and stamps. Dolls did not play any role in my life; the games of the neighborhood boys were more interesting.

"My first years of education were spent in a private school. I did not like it there at all. Every Wednesday morning we had to hear a formal lecture about God – and on holy matters such as fire and brimstone. As a child, this was very distressing. My strong protests were heard, and from the fourth grade onward to graduation from high school I could attend public school. Such a change! This opportunity of studying with children of different religions, colors and nationalities made a great difference in my life. To be one of the few of my classmates that could go on to further education left me with a sense of obligation and gratitude." Margot was in the 8th grade when her father remarried. "My stepmother, whom I called 'mother', as indeed she was a second mother to me, was very concerned about my education. She even bought a Latin dictionary to help me with my homework. I had assumed that after high school I would be a secretary in father's office, but my stepmother inspired and encouraged me go on to college."

In her last year of high school, Margot was elected class president. "Today it is big news for a female to have that post," she states, "but in those times both students and teachers were less conscious of role differences. I was used to studying in a mixed classroom. On the other hand it was unusual for a young woman to plan for any professional career other than that of teacher, nurse or secretary. Those who did continue their education were not really taken seriously." Margot failed the College entrance exams in her last year of high school, but passed the following year and was admitted to Vassar College. That year interval was to have been spent in a *Haushaltungsschule, a* domestic management school, in Switzerland, but the outbreak of the Second World War cancelled this plan.

Vassar College, founded in 1861 in Poughkeepsie, NY, was the first all women's college in America. In those days young women usually attended a finishing school, in preparation for marriage. However, Vassar was established with the dedicated goal of preparing women for independence and careers of their own beyond housewife and motherhood. Margot was eighteen years old and living in a women's dormitory on college campus. It was her first time away from home. She dreamed of becoming a medical researcher, "to discover the cure for cancer. Our housemother advised me to get a medical degree before going into research work. I had no idea that this field would be open to women. When I presented this plan of four more years of tuition, father quietly said 'Well, if that is what you want.'"

December 1941: In her second year at Vassar, Japan bombed American ships in Pearl Harbor. "This took away our innocence." Several of her classmates quit their studies and married boyfriends leaving for military service. The rest of the class shortened the four years of study by skipping vacations, many then enlisting in jobs replacing the men that had left for military service. "Life for us suddenly became very serious, politically also. It was a shock. All of us had been born in the time between the wars. We suddenly felt very patriotic. Communication with friends and relatives in Switzerland was blocked. Our only contact with Europe was through the radio. Every evening at six o'clock we gathered around the radio to hear the news from England. Often in the background one could hear the explosion of bombs. On the morning we learned that Hitler had marched into Poland, mother and I went out to the garden to work off our distress. Thinking that father was already in the office, we were very surprised to find him also in the garden, weeding. He had heard the news on the way to the office and was too upset to go to work."

After graduation from Vassar College, Margot began her medical studies in New York Medical College. "A whole new world opened up for me, and soon my goal turned from research to practicing medicine. I had observed that internists were prone to long discussions about medications and electrocardiograms and as I preferred to see some action, I aimed to become a surgeon." After graduation in 1949, she continued her training in the specialty of Obstetrics and Gynecology. This was the ideal field for females to practice. It was less popular for the men, who often were uncomfortable in dealing with women's problems and emotions. Her parents were considering retirement in Switzerland. So after her required training as intern and resident she worked in the Woman's Hospital in St.Gallen, Switzerland. "With this I not only acquired further experience, but I also had the feeling of truly being Swiss. On weekends I was able to enjoy visiting various parts of Switzerland. Then my parents' plans to retire to Switzerland were changed once again when father received an offer for one more irresistible project, the construction of the Verrazano Bridge in NY. With a newly established love for the homeland of my parents, I returned to New York."

But stop! "I almost forgot to mention a very important episode in my life: In 1958 I passed my summer vacation with my parents in Riffelalp in Wallis. There I climbed the Matterhorn. This was not such a great physical accomplishment, as the weather was ideal, I

"..., but I also had the feeling of truly being Swiss." With her parents at Dübendorf airport... (1952)

... and in Montreux. (1955)

had a good guide, and had no fear of heights. But to stand on top of the world, on a narrow pathway of snow looking down to Italy on one side and Switzerland on the other was a thrilling experience that I shall never forget."

And then Margot adds, "on my gravestone, I should like to have three things written: First, 'she once viewed the world from the top of the Matterhorn; secondly, at the age of eighty, she learned to use the computer; and thirdly, she overcame her shyness and learned to share the personality of her father with the public.'" And then she changes her mind and says, "but I am not going to have a gravestone. When I die, I shall go back to my Alma mater, New York Medical College. In dissecting my shell, some medical students will be able to spend a year learning their anatomy. I have specified this in my will and I find comfort in thinking that the full course of my life will come to a close in this final way."

"I will never forget July 28, 1958. Together with a guide I climbed the Matterhorn."

In 1960 Margot opened her private practice in Obstetrics and Gynecology. It was a time of many changes in medicine such as antibiotics, birth control pills, and air conditioning in the operating room. Her first patient was a nurse that knew Margot from her hospital internship. Other nurses and female hospital attendants, as well as their female friends and family members, became the base of her fledgling practice. The new wave of feminism at that time also brought women to her door, saying "we feel more comfortable with a woman physician, she understands us better than a man." Young women who previously never went for physical examinations before becoming pregnant were now coming for prescription of birth control pills. Also, abortions became legal to perform in New York so gynecologists were able to help their own patients rather than send them to Geneva or Puerto Rico and one saw less infections resulting from improperly performed illegal abortions. "I averaged about two deliveries a week and one or two major operations. I enjoyed my profession and my patients. Besides the physical examination I felt it equally important to talk with the patient and to give her a chance to ask questions."

Then Margot switches to another chapter in her life story, "and a very important one." In 1939, her future husband, Dr. Gustav Durrer, a dentist from Luzern, was attending advanced dental courses in America when the war broke out and and he could not return to Switzerland. While working in a dental clinic in New York, he received an "invitation" to serve in the American Army. He obtained his American citizenship and after the war established a practice in New York City.

When Margot returned home after her residency in St. Gallen, she accompanied her stepmother for an appointment with this "wonderful new dentist" that her parents had been praising. "Gusti Durrer really looked so handsome in his white dental jacket and generous smile, but I soon sized him up as the happy bachelor approaching the 40's and thinking, why marry one when I can have many women around? But I really fell for him. Our friendship grew slowly. He invited me to the Swiss Society Ball, and for theatre or concerts. He was a loving and charming escort, but never gave a hint of wanting to share our lives together. Then once, after seven years of dating, he casually remarked: 'Why don't we go on vacation once together?' For me it was quite clear: not without a ring on my finger. That was a cutting moment of decision for the engrained bachelor. Plans were made. We went to Tiffany to buy that wedding ring, but the salesperson was so busy with another customer that Gusti lost his patience; we walked out and went to a friend of his who was a goldsmith. Finally we were married and started a happy vacation that lasted a lifetime."

Marriage to Gustav Durrer was a long, happy and fascinating chapter in Margot's life. "We married late in life but were able to share forty-one years of our lives together. He was a very dear person, treating the cleaning lady the same as he would an ambassador to the UN. He always respected my work and was very understanding when I was called away at night or in the middle of dinner because of an emergency or the delivery of a baby. In exchange, I painfully typed out his lectures and papers on my old typewriter in those pre-word processor days. I never wanted to have children, but yes, I thoroughly enjoyed delivering a healthy screaming baby and handing it over to its mother for care. Although we each had our own profession, Gusti and I were partners – a team. To share an active life together was the greatest gift that I could ever have had."

And then she smiles: "I never looked very much in the mirror. However, shortly after we were married, Gusti said to me: 'What are we going to do about our hair?' I looked him straight in the eye and said: 'We are not going to do anything about our hair.' Later, I compromised by getting a wig but this, of course, was never worn."

Dr. Margot Ammann maintained an active practice and retired at age 71. A few years later, in his eighties, her husband also retired. Suddenly he developed kidney failure, requiring dialysis. "This is a tedious process three times a week, lasting three to four hours and leaving one considerably weakened. Fortunately I had the strength to help him and the time to give him companionship. It was a fulltime project for both of us. His diet was very strict and required careful control. I would accompany him when he went on the wheelchair to and from the hospital and read to him while he had to lie for hours during the treatments. He was always so thankful and how often he would say to me, 'How would I have done all of this without you, Margot?' It was somehow bittersweet.

"In October 2001, two weeks after the attacks on the Twin Towers, Gus died. This was a very difficult time – clouds were over the city and I was enveloped in my own cloud of sorrow. The quick step from life to death was a shock. Suddenly I was alone. However he is always with me. At night before I go to sleep I look at his photograph smiling at me, say goodnight and ask how could I have been so lucky to share my life and love with him. In spite of the great sorrow, I was thankful that he could die in peace and dignity. His heart was slowly failing and intense treatments would have been necessary to extend his life somewhat. It was a hard decision for me to tell the doctor to discontinue dialysis. After three days at home he fell into a peaceful sleep. There was nothing more to do. I realized then how thin is the thread upon which our life hangs – even when we think we are so strong."

Since his death, Margot lives alone. The first time she had to register "widow" as her marital status, she had a shock. But gradually she reinvented herself and soon found that the hours of the day were too short. She found great satisfaction in working as a volunteer for the organization "English in Action", giving practice in conversation to people for whom English is a second language. With an extra bedroom in her apartment, she was able to welcome family and friends to visit and soon she had what she called "a free bed and breakfast establishment." Almost every week one or more guests occupied that extra room, with overflow on the living room couch or sleeping bags on the floor. "I could fill a book with the adventures that these guests brought into my life. I was able to finish the many started projects such as translating the Amman family book into English and the album of father's life and works. Friends and relatives are touchingly concerned about my welfare and although busy with their own lives, always find time to share it with me."

Recently Margot was asked to write an article about feminism in America. "The more I got involved, the more fascinated I became. In my career I had never experienced any incident of discrimination. My male colleagues were always polite and supportive. I strove to do my best, but never had to fight for my rights in my profession. Feminism was not really a theme for me. Therefore I was very astonished when I read Betty Friedan's *Feminine Mystique*, and then later the *Frauen im Laufgitter* of the Swiss feminist Iris von Roten and became aware of their tireless efforts for the cause of women. I see how fortunate I have been. Young women today impress me as being far more aggressive, perhaps because they are in larger numbers and present more of a challenge to the men."

Now Margot leans back in her chair and relaxes. "I stand in the final act of my place on stage. It was a pleasure to bring up so many memories and to peak through the doors into my past." And then more to herself: "I am ready to go on to my next world any time. I take the days as they come and know that in my age 'everything is the beginning of the end.' I hope to be able to keep my independence and to stay in my own four walls, but if fate deems otherwise, to accept the changes with dignity."

ROSA
1928
SCHUPBACH
LECHNER

No sign of jet lag even though she landed in Zurich just a few hours ago. Rosa Schupbach-Lechner comes to Switzerland every year half a dozen times. She is past 80; yet the petite woman with grey-blond hair that comes down to the shoulders looks like 60. Her inquisitive blue eyes seem to ask: What else is there to experience?

The suitcases are not yet unpacked, yet the sprightly woman in a sporty pantsuit is already elegantly offering tea with cookies. "Years ago I came to visit my mother; today I come to meet old friends in Switzerland and relatives in Germany. I feel the need to cultivate my roots in Switzerland and Europe."

This time Rosa Schupbach-Lechner plans to go even farther east to Singapore. "I want to build up my frequent flyer miles in order to keep my gold card from Miles & More," she says playfully. As an economist, calculating comes easy for her, and with a roundtrip-ticket around half the world she will reach the required 100,000 miles without any problem.

There is even more on her program: Before flying back to New York she has dates in Germany. "In my mother's hometown in the Black Forest I will give two talks about my life."

The house of her grandparents is still standing; it's where her mother with her twelve siblings grew up in very modest circumstances. Rosa has preserved lots of mementos of her parents, certificates, pictures that she fetches while narrating her life.

Her mother, Marie Ozeler, came to Switzerland as a maid in 1910. Her father, Florian Lechner, the son of a small gardener in Vienna, trained as a butcher's assistant and later a head butcher making sausages, emigrated from Austria to Switzerland in 1911. He was ambitious. After years as apprentice and journeyman with different master butchers he dreamed of becoming independent in his new home country. In Zurich-Oerlikon a workers' restaurant, the *Dörfli*, was up for rent. Yet he didn't have a wife who could help. He told his colleagues, and one of them gave him a tip about an industrious waitress by the name of Marie who worked in the restaurant at the Klusplatz. She fell in love with the handsome go-getter with his bold dreams. "Mama married in a black dress and high, sturdy shoes. This was the custom for people from the lower income classes at that time. What would she have done later with a white dress and elegant shoes?"

On September 24, 1918, at 6 a.m., after the wedding night the Lechner's small restaurant opened. "My mother had to wait with buying milk and bread until the first glasses of beer had gone over the counter. After the wedding father had not even a cent left. Thanks to his insistence that he had a full wallet, he had been given the first supply of beer on credit."

Hans, their first child, was born exactly nine months later, on June 24, 1919. "At that time Mama had to pay 155 francs and 60 cents for her 13 days in the *Frauenklinik*, the women's hospital. This was a vacation for her." Usually they could not even think of taking any days off. For 7 years the young couple worked 17 hours a day in their restaurant, which did well; the workers from the nearby factories liked to stop at the place of the friendly Lechners.

By 1925 they had toiled and earned enough, and they got an offer to purchase the butcher store next door. "Now mother was in the store, father in the butchery." Their hams and sausages were popular. "On Sundays father would usually go to the farmers in Rümlang or Wallisellen and buy cattle that the butcher helpers had to herd on foot to the small slaughterhouse behind the butcher store." Father Lechner was a good businessman, had a wonderful way with people, and was lucky – with money too. Mother was the soul of the business. In 1926 the immigrants became Swiss citizens.

"Mother was tender and loving. And my big brother Hans worshiped me." (around 1935)

In 1928, Rosa, the only girl, was born as a latecomer into this turbulent business household, nine years after her brother. "Father was very proud of me, Mother tender and loving. And my big brother Hans worshiped me. However, our parents did not have much time for us children. They worked day and night. 'Now it's enough!' father said, sold the butcher store after eight years and retired at the age of 50. He decided dictatorially that we would move to Lucerne." Rosa remembers her kindergarten, her first little friend. "She lived in the same house. I thought they were distinguished people. My friend smelled of perfume and powder. I would want this too, I thought, later in life. At the most my mother would buy lavender-water." The Lechner children felt little of their parents' prosperity. Their motto was "above all, not to spoil them, this is harmful." Father Lechner was restless, felt compelled to set up something new and built a house with four apartments in Lucerne-Mayhof. Still, he found no rest.

"One day he surprised us without warning: 'We are moving to the Ticino!', the Italian-speaking part of Switzerland. My brother was not affected, since he was already doing an apprenticeship. I was in third grade, had many school friends and was abruptly uprooted. Yet I simply adapted and even found it adventurous." Mother had no say in this, and in March 1938 moved, without complaining, all our belongings for the umpteenth time. "This time father rented a four-storey villa in a large park in Castagnola." For Rosa everything was new again, including the language. "It was a wonderful time for me, 'il mio paradiso, my own paradise'. On foot I went to the Swiss-German school in Lugano, swam in Lake Lugano and played for hours in the enchanting park. I did not know what boredom was. Dozens of animals were my playmates – geese, chickens and rabbits." In 1939 oil became scarce. "We lived on only one level in the villa and burned wood in our furnace." Father Lechner eventually abandoned the paradise, and the family moved into an apartment in Lugano Besso. "Even today I remember the loss of the park with sadness."

The family's situation continued to grow worse. "My father had not only had enough of living in the Ticino, but also of living with his family. He left us and rented a room in Zurich Niederdorf. Mother suffered silently and without complaining. One day – I was eleven – she put me on a train to Zurich. I was to bring father back home. Traveling alone was not unusual for me. I was not afraid. And father simply belonged to us." He met the courageous girl at Zurich's main station, showed her the city, and she got to know the various taverns in the Niederdorf. Rosa was able to convince him to return to the family. "I don't know how I succeeded; somehow he himself came to his senses."

But Lugano was to bore him again soon. He wanted to return to Zurich. For Rosa this meant to leave all that she had come to love, to be uprooted again, to go to a new school, find new friends.

"Mother – good-natured as she was – cooperated in everything. She was quite Victorian and religious, was eager to establish a good family life and valued order and etiquette. Pleated skirt, pink blouse – I was always nicely dressed. Pants, certainly not! Mother had my little dresses as well as all her clothes custom-made by a dress-maker."

"I was always nicely dressed. Pants, certainly not!" (1943)

Secondary school (grades 7 and 8) was easy for Rosa. As was the custom for a girl from a good family, Rosa then spent a year in a school for good housekeeping led by protestant deaconesses in Vevey. "These simple women did impress me. I admired them. They were quite strict, but fair, and they treated all of us in the same manner. I liked the fact that they did not just preach their strict rules, but practiced them in their own lives."

Rosa had ambitious plans for herself. "I wanted to get somewhere in life." In 1945 she entered the *Handels-Töchterschule*, a commercial school for female students, in Zurich. "English was my favorite subject, and I learned easily."

In 1948 Rosa graduated first in her class with a diploma from the *Handelsschule* and obtained a well-paid job at the Swiss Bank Corporation. "The transition from school to the six-day workweek was difficult for me. Sitting quietly for an entire day at the desk in the office tired me out. I found it confining." The restlessness of her youth became noticeable. Now it was Rosa who wanted to break away, away from Switzerland in order to conquer the world.

"London was my dream. At age 20 and thanks to my good knowledge of English I obtained a position in the British branch office of the Swiss Bank Corporation. I liked London a lot. Its international character and the business of a metropolis fascinated me." For an admission fee of two shillings Rosa and her Swiss friend Gina once in a while went to one of the dance halls. "One night as I was ready to leave, a man invited me to dance – he was good-looking and charming." It was love at first sight with Mehdi Tajbaksh, an Iranian student of agronomy. The two were soon inseparable. And when he flew home to see his family during the semester break, she followed him. "These were two romantic and adventurous weeks in a different world. Mehdi's home was a large farm on a high plateau in the Iranian mountains." Back in London she began to study Farsi, and the two decided to make their home in Switzerland. "In England I earned a mere pittance, and my friend wanted to continue his studies at the Agricultural School Strickhof in Zurich. We married in 1952 in Zurich. My father did not attend our small wedding. A foreigner as son-in-law and one from the Middle East at that – this was unprecedented and unacceptable to him."

"London was my dream." (around 1950)

This marriage had dire consequences for Rosa. "From one day to the next I had to relinquish my Swiss citizenship. Suddenly I was a foreigner in my own country and experienced discrimination. The Swiss Bank Corporation forced me to quit and to work as a temp. For them I had become a risk, an element of uncertainty. I might have gotten pregnant!" The marriage lasted only three years. "He wanted to return to Iran; for me that was out of the question. I sensed that he was not reliable. Still, I do not regret having experienced this love." In a matter-of-fact tone she says, "the divorce did cost 250 Swiss francs, a third of my monthly paycheck. I have never heard from him again." In the same year Rosa's father died. "I missed him very much, and realized that like a rock, he had always been in my life." She moved back to her mother and took stock of her life. "With regard to love I had not been very successful, but I had a loving mother with whom I got along well and I had a job. Was this sufficient for the rest of my life? Actually,

I had had enough of Switzerland. My negative experiences as a foreigner in my own country left a deep impression on me. I was naturalized again when the law changed, but my disappointment remained – until today."

Rosa wanted to discover something new: Why not America? "At that time the immigration laws were not as strict as later. Due to the system of quotas I could apply for a Green Card."

"Are you ready?" the official in the American Consulate asked. The Consulate's answer to her application for immigration had come surprisingly fast. Too fast! She hadn't expected an answer so soon. "No, I said at first, I can't leave within two months. Mother was desperately unhappy. 'Mommy, I will just go for four months', I comforted her. And I really meant it." Then everything went very quickly. Rosa gave notice, filled two suitcases with clothes, shoes and a few books and on November 12, 1959, flew to New York via Lisbon. In her purse she had 2,000 dollars, her Green Card and the address of a hotel in Manhattan. She thought, "I will use up my money and then we'll see."

New York – breathtaking and exciting. Rosa knew nothing and no one. But she was determined and without fear. "A hotel room on Times Square had been reserved. I didn't know that Times Square at that time was so infamous. I didn't like it there, and after a few days I moved into a boarding house owned by a man from Austria. But he had his eye on me and continued to bother me so that I had to move, this time to another place on West 72nd Street. The room with a heater and a small kitchen felt like a small piece of home."

Rosa Lechner then ran out of money. "I could return home, ask for money from home, or start working." She did the latter and due to her Green Card obtained a position as secretary for a man who sold second-hand office machines. "The office was located on Broadway and 19th Street. My boss exploited me, the naïve young girl from Switzerland. For lunch he gave me barely twenty minutes. I was thrifty and bought a hamburger for 50 cents and a coffee for 10 cents in a coffee shop. The shop belonged to two Polish men who had escaped from a concentration camp; they still had their numbers burnt into their arms. I think they felt sorry for me and sometimes gave me a piece of meat for my evening meal."

When Rosa returned to her office after lunch, her typewriter was often already resold. "I lodged a complaint with the senior boss because he was always late with paying my weekly wages. He got mad and shouted 'you don't have to come to this country to teach us law!'"

Rosa didn't last long there although she was making 90 dollars a week. But she stayed long enough to receive a pair of snow boots from her boss at Christmas. "I needed them urgently in order to survive the first snowstorm in New York."

It was not only the New York winter that was hard for Rosa. "No one told me be careful, don't do that, this is a bad area." Since she was accustomed to a nomad's life from her childhood, she rented one furnished room after another until she finally found a studio apartment on 46th Street between 2nd and 3rd Avenue. "The first thing I bought was a sleeper sofa, and in a junk shop I got dishes and some old pans. Again, I was looking for work."

When Rosa was hired as a secretary at the Caltex Petroleum Company in 1961, the job came with the condition that she must take courses in economics at a college. "This was not at all easy. When I applied at one of the colleges of the City University, I was told that I hadn't even finished secondary school in Switzerland. The admissions officer cited a book that said that children in Switzerland didn't go to school during the entire summer because they had to help with making hay! My grade reports didn't convince her either. I was forced to write to the Department of Education in Washington which eventually confirmed that my schooling in Switzerland was equal to one fourth of the courses for a college degree; and this paved the way for me."

Rosa wanted to stay in America. "The country took me in. No one said that because you are a woman, you can't do this or that.

The decision to continue my academic education brought me significant personal and professional gains. Of course, I could have earned good money as a secretary. But I was fascinated by the academic world. It is also important that each person furthers his or her own personal and intellectual development. In Switzerland I would have had to take all the courses to pass the *Matura* [the final exam that garantuees students entrance to university studies] in order to be allowed to engage in academic studies."

From 1961 to 1967 Rosa buckled down to work and studies without interruption. "From 9 to 5 I worked in the office, in the evening I was at school." Her hard work paid off. In 1966 she earned a Bachelor of Science from Columbia University, in the same year she became an American citizen, and a year later she earned a Masters in Economics and a bit later a Masters in Education. "It was hard. I don't know how I did it. How I envied the people who were able to go home at 5 p.m. while I was taking the subway to attend lectures. I am very ambitious and had the feeling that I could only advance if I earned an American degree."

And what about her free time? "On Saturday evenings a friend invited me to a juicy steak for $4.95. And in the few weeks when I didn't have courses or exams, I visited my mother in Switzerland." From the beginning Rosa had the goal to get to know one new person every day. "Sometimes I succeeded. I was alone, but not lonely. You cannot expect that people approach you first. I always found my way." And then her being alone suddenly was over.

"Edmund Schupbach was my coworker at Caltex, an accountant and very shy. I had noticed him for some time already, but he made no move until he invited me for dinner in January of 1967." Again and again they went out together. "At first we kept it a secret in the office." In April it was clear to Rosa – "he is the one."

During the semester break at the end of 1967 they were married on the campus of Columbia University. "Ed Schupbach was a New Yorker and despite his name had no Swiss roots. He and I scraped together all our savings and bought an apartment for 34,000 dollars on 74th Street between 5th and Madison Avenue, not far from Central Park."

After only six years of married life Ed died of a pancreatic illness. Rosa was 45, a widow, alone again. "I was forced to find a new direction for my life. Should I return to Switzerland? No, that was out of the question. At my age I would hardly have found a job. Mother would have been happy. Yet with work and a college education I had developed my life here, and America had become my home." Rosa had not worked during her marriage, now she worked in various temp positions, then was for a time assistant to a retired economics professor from Princeton, and later was employed by a brokerage firm. "I wanted to be free, to be able to travel, to visit my mother as often as possible. In 1993 she peacefully died in her sleep at the age of 100. Fortunately I was with her when she died."

Though Rosa went to many cultural events, she did not like the evenings she spent in her New York apartment. "This was not good for me; I felt empty and had to find something meaningful to do."

On a Saturday morning she came by chance across a police van with a team that was recruiting volunteers for the auxiliary police in her neighborhood. "Working for the police, why not? I said to myself and filled out an application. A few days later I received a call from the police station of my district; was I still interested? Of course I was."

Five months of education and training followed, a course in self-defense and then the exam at the New York Police Department. In the summer of 1980 Rosa Schupbach was accepted as an auxiliary police officer for her district, which is one of the most densely populated areas of the United States and has 250 regular police officers and 90 auxiliary officers.

"20% of the team are women. In the five boroughs of New York there are about 38,000 regular and 6,000 auxiliary police officers, both men and women. The auxiliary officers support the regular police force. We are not paid and are not allowed to patrol the streets after 11 p.m. without special permission because we do not carry firearms." But they do have bulletproof vests. Rosa has her own bulletproof vest made to measure. "I wear the same uniform as all New York police officers but with a different emblem on the sleeve. We are equipped with walkie-talkies and are connected to Police Headquarters as well as to all the regular police patrols in the area." For her defense she carries on her belt a wooden nightstick, which is 25 inches long and two inches thick. "Using it is allowed only if our own life is in danger, if we cannot flee, or if someone else is in serious danger." In all the years Rosa has provided well over 5,000 unpaid hours of service as auxiliary police officer. She is not only the oldest, but also the most senior auxiliary officer in her police precinct. "I have never been afraid, just like my father. He was not afraid of anything or anybody. But I am never rash. I always keep my eyes open. I am a woman of a certain age; people don't get too close to me. I walk right up to people. Once I am about a foot away from them, they begin to retreat so that there is no need to touch them. This is simply due to my determined manner. Anyone who physically attacks a police officer in New York will be arrested and goes to jail. I patrol the streets either on foot or in a police car, in summer and winter, in every kind of weather. Winter nights in New York are bitter cold! We are also in action at parades and street markets, we help with accidents, and block streets, for example when there is a fire."

For Rosa, the New York marathon is the high point of the year in her police work. "I am usually stationed in one of the Red Cross tents where the runners come down from the bridge on 59th Street. I also help as translator for Europeans who are having cramps, blisters on their feet or urgently need an aspirin or some words that will encourage them to persevere to the end."

A day she'll never forget is September 11, 2001. "Shortly after 9 a.m.. friends from Switzerland called to see if I was still alive. I had no idea what had happened! The shock came a few seconds later when I turned on the TV. A while later a colleague urged me not to go to our police station; he wanted to make sure that I would not be sent to Ground Zero. To be honest, I was grateful to him. A Swiss woman I knew perished in the tower. The mood in New York was similar to that when President Kennedy was assassinated, horrible." Rosa's voice is very low. "The stench of burned plastic and burned corpses and yellow dust lay over the entire city for weeks. For ten days I was on almost uninterrupted duty. Fortunately it was in my district and not in downtown Manhattan. We had to block the street where the Fire House, the Police Precinct, and a Jewish synagogue are located. The people were all on the streets – shocked, traumatized, they wanted to talk. I had to help protect the roadblocks, to calm people, often simply listen to them, to be there for them. I barely had time to go home and get some sleep. We all shared a common destiny; New York has changed since then. The thought that something similar could suddenly happen again is always present in the back of my mind, and will probably never go away. Airplanes or helicopters over the city cause my heart to beat faster every time. 9/11 has changed the life of all of us. But New Yorkers always know how to adapt and how to find the positive in life. I fit in here very well."

Rosa is a dual citizen, but travels with her American passport. "The last time a customs officer in Zurich asked me, 'what are you doing in Switzerland?' – 'I was born here' was my quick answer in Swiss German!"

In her heart Rosa is still Swiss. "I love my mother tongue and I am also participating in Swiss elections and referenda. I see myself as a Swiss living abroad and am proud of that." In the last 40 years she has moved only once, from the 5th to the 16th floor in the same building. She has a two-room apartment with a kitchen, a bathroom and a small balcony from which she can see the trees of Central Park and the high rise office towers of midtown Manhattan twenty blocks farther south. "It is a privilege to be able to live here. It was on the basis of this feeling that years ago I founded the 'East 74th Street Association' for our street – which is less than a quarter mile long – and I am still serving as its president. Our 320 households have a clean street thanks to this association. With the dues that I collect we pay a man who sweeps the street and a gardener who takes care of the trees and the ivy beds around them. Private initiative is indispensable in America. Without it things don't get done!"

Out of gratitude Rosa has also been involved for many years in the Presbyterian Church in her neighborhood. "If we want a church in America, we have to take care of it ourselves. I am grateful for my life and like to give something back. I feel that many things come back to me – in a positive way."

Rosa is involved in the church in various functions and for some years has even participated in its homeless shelter program. "It does take a real effort to spend the night in the lower level of the church looking after up to twelve homeless men by myself. These men of different ages, who are sent to us by the city, are given a roof over their head, a clean bed and a light breakfast at 6 a.m."

She says that she asks herself again and again why she is doing this. "But when I am returning to my apartment after such a night, I truly feel that I did something positive, and that I myself have a little piece of heaven on earth and am fortunate that I did not end up on the street." Volunteer social service is simply part of life in the United States. "Every man and every woman does what is possible within their means."

Rosa is appreciated for what she does and is needed. "At my age people in Switzerland have long been tossed on the scrap heap and pushed aside. In America no one tells me 'you are too old and can go now'. Thank you, America!"

Now Rosa has to leave – Singapore is calling.

LINDA GEISER

1935

Linda Geiser is at home in two worlds – in the East Village in New York as well as in Liebefeld near Bern. When she was 16 years old, she was incurably infected with the "acting virus." To be on stage – that's what she wanted. "At that time, being an actress was a rather ill reputed profession, almost like prostitution. A concerned neighbor advised my mother to keep me at all cost from going to the theater; that would be something indecent, and actresses were loose girls." That was in 1951. Yet theater, the movies, and television are Linda's great passion to this day.

Linda is on a home visit for a few weeks with her partner John. I am meeting the 73-year old expert in the art of living in her Swiss quarters, in the house of her sister Annemarie Bachofner. As always Linda's calendar is full to the brim: a meeting at the studio of Swiss TV, doctors' visits, and lots of invitations to see her Swiss friends. "People are wonderful; I 'collect' them, integrate them into my circle of friends. I am a gregarious person and know almost too many people. Because of time limitations I unfortunately cannot see all my friends every time when I am here, and this I regret very much."

On the streets of Bern people turn their heads when they see the attractive senior woman with her partner who is 20 years younger; they recognize Linda Geiser as the legendary mother of the TV series *Die sechs Kummerbuben* (The Six Boys of the Kummer Family), or as Johanna from the TV soap opera *Lüthi and Blanc*. "John is amused – I believe he is even a bit proud of me. Of course, in New York this doesn't happen."

Linda stops short. "I should start at the very beginning of my life, or even before that. One thing is for sure: Folks in our family were not theater people. My father came from a very strict religious family of Anabaptists. He grew up in the Mennonite town of La Chaux d'Abel in the Bernese Jura. He was the only one of the thirteen children of this farm family who was allowed to attend a school of higher learning. He told us that little by little he had to pay back the loan the Anabaptist community had given him to attend the Teachers' College Muri-Stalden. As a very young teacher in training he met my mother at that college where she was a student in secondary school (6th to 9th grade). Yet they did not really click until later. Mother also became a teacher. Eventually they married and together taught the primary and secondary grades in a tiny schoolhouse in Vorderfultigen."

Linda was born in 1935 in Wabern as their second daughter, four years after her sister Annemarie and eight years before her brother Hans-Beat. And it was quite a sensation a few years later that Mr. Geiser, a primary teacher in the canton Bern, was able to move with his family into a small one-family house in Spiegel near Bern – in the midst of World War II. "Even more sensational was the fact that I had several uncles in America. As a child I would check on the map where Dover, Ohio, was, the place where my uncles Ernst, Werner, Charles, and Willy lived. In school I bluffed about having relatives in America. I remember how the others tapped their foreheads – 'she is nuts!' These brothers of my father had not emigrated for religious, but economic reasons; the small farm in the Jura was too small for the large family."

Linda was born in 1935 in Wabern, four years after her sister Annemarie and eight years before her brother Hans-Beat. (1937)

Religion had no relevance in the teacher's house, but "it was very relevant with *Grossätti* and *Grossmuetti*, grandpa and grandma, in the Jura. Grandfather was rather liberal and did not wear an Anabaptist's hat. Yet I rarely ever saw my grandmother without her blue apron dress. Though she wore it with buttons, not with pins as Anabaptist women still do today in Pennsylvania. And of course we grandchildren had to accompany them to chapel on Sundays. I remember how bored we were and how we secretly chuckled when the text was too bombastic for us. After chapel there regularly was braided bread and tea for everyone at the grandparents' farmhouse. The Anabaptists came with their horse drawn buggies from all directions – everything was simple and modest. My current relatives in Ohio, the children of my late uncles, now have a much more modern lifestyle, they are 'apostates ' as it were."

Linda Geiser's childhood was marked less by religion than World War Two. "Even today I can hear Hitler and Göring yelling in the news broadcast of Radio Beromünster; this filled us with fear. In Switzerland we didn't suffer from hunger, but we needed stamps to buy food. And even after the war had ended, we children wore each others' clothes."

Linda's enthusiasm for school was limited. "After the primary grades where I had been a good student, my parents decided that I should go to the *Progymnasium*, the first years of the college preparatory school, yet I was miserable there. I was no longer interested in the study material, which I found entirely unnecessary. I preferred to dream, to read books, to paint, and I wanted to have a career in theater. What I did take with me from those years is a stock of wonderful people whom I got to know there. I have an entire 'clan of girls,' as I call them, with whom I still have a close connection.

Linda's first day at school. (1942)

"When I had to repeat one class, Mani Matter and Jürg Wyttenbach were my classmates. Mani Matter later became the originator of the *Bernese Troubadours*, and Jürg Wyttenbach a famous musician and composer.

"Fortunately my parents allowed me to participate in evening courses at the acting school even while I was still in school. Margarethe Schell-von Noé directed this department of the Conservatory. As luck would have it, they were preparing a student production in which I was allowed to participate. It was an open-air performance, and I was given the part of a young sentimental girl who was enamored of her teacher and in her lover's grief wanted to jump into the river, the Aare. What a beginning!" Now Linda wanted to join the professional theater.

"Mrs. Schell admonished me that I still would have to learn a whole lot. What for? I already had a first engagement at the newly established studio theater at the Effingerstrasse. Nothing could hold me back now. I resolved to observe in every detail what the experienced actors did and to imitate everything. This worked."

Linda Geiser adds: "However, this does not mean that I did not have to learn a lot more about this profession in the course of the years." Thus it was a settled matter. Linda's father signed her first contract for the *Atelier Theater* under director Adolph Spalinger. "I was only sixteen, and my parents were relieved that I had a firm engagement. They knew: She won't run away from there!

"During WW II immigrants shaped the theater in Switzerland to a significant extent. Many stage artists from Germany and Austria lived and worked in our country. Those who were not able to escape to America gathered in Switzerland. They shaped not only the famous *Schauspielhaus* in Zurich, we also met these extraordinary artists in the theaters in Bern, St Gallen, Lucerne, Basel, Solothurn, and elsewhere.

"They brought with them the great old tradition of theater and revived and inspired theater life in Switzerland. By now almost all of them have died. They are not totally forgotten, yet as the saying goes, 'posterity presents no wreaths to actors,' and most of them were not immortalized in films – to say nothing of television. Thus today we have only one last witness to this era in the great Maria Becker in Zurich who still makes appearances on stage."

For 250 Swiss francs a month Linda Geiser played the roles of naïve young girls – as her specialty was called then – in the ensemble of the *Atelier Theater*. In addition there were salon ladies, character actors, the young heroes – all designations that are no longer used today. "From one day to the next I had to take on great parts for which I had not even been hired. Such a piece of luck! Two actresses were absent; they were talented, but one turned out to be an alcoholic, the other one a hysteric. Thus I was able to play the parts of Eliza in *Pygmalion* by G. B. Shaw, of Jessica in *Dirty Hands* by J. P. Sartre, and several other parts for which I was essentially still much too young.

"These wonderful tasks were the best acting school. It was much simpler for me to play such parts as Wendla Bergman in

Frühlings-Erwachen (Spring Awakening) by F. Wedekind or Emily in T. Wilder's *Our Town*. In this last production Mani Matter played the part of the newspaper boy that I had helped him get when Adolph Spalinger asked me whether I knew a talented classmate who would like to work with our group.

"For three seasons at the theater in Bern I was lucky enough to live with my family, but no one kept tabs on me. I loved the adventurous life in the theater world."

Linda's parents were generous. "The restaurants were often already closed after our performances and thus half of our ensemble walked or drove to Spiegel, filled the Geiser house, and raided the refrigerator – though they brought along wine and other beverages. And as the money for stage sets and props was scarce, our furniture was sometimes kidnapped. Chairs, tables, carpets, dresser drawers, plates – and clothes of my mother – caused sensations in various productions. My sister Annemarie also helped out and we played twins in the Christmas production for children. In time our entire family was bitten by the theater bug, and in 1957 my father even launched an amateur theater, the *Spiegelbühne*, which still exists today."

In 1954 television in Switzerland was still in its infancy. Linda Geiser was full of enthusiasm for this new medium that had already been well established in America. "With our entire ensemble we drove from Bern to the Bellerive Studio in Zurich. We were given a contract for Oscar Wilde's play *An Ideal Husband* in which I played the part of Mabel. At that time Swiss television could not yet afford its own productions.

"On the way to Zurich all our costumes were stolen from our truck. Thus in great haste and agitation we had to organize costumes for the ensemble. The play was broadcast live – the viewers saw each mistake, heard each slip of the tongue! Later I also experienced such TV theater productions in Hamburg and Berlin. They were always connected with great agitation. Oh God! Actors who had trouble learning the text never wanted to do television. This did not bother me; fortunately I have a photographic memory. I look at the texts and then remember them. In general I have little stage fright. Actually it is good to be nervous before a performance because it helps to build up energy and vibes."

At age 19 Linda needed a different environment. "I was advised to get out of the provincial atmosphere of Bern. And after I had auditioned for the *Kammerspiele* in Hamburg for a French comedy *The Stork's Nest*, I was able to sign my first contract myself."

For two years she was at the *Thalia Theater* in Hamburg where she had many parts and was happy until, one day, the boss kicked her out. That hurt. "They said that I had been rude and disrespectful toward a director. I felt that I was treated unfairly, got the short end of the stick, packed my bags, and my family welcomed me home with open arms."

In spite of the disappointment, Linda remained true to the theater. Subsequently she played in two productions in Berlin and soon thereafter was engaged by the *Komödie* in Basel. Offers for television and radio plays were also not lacking. "Then came a dreadful German movie Der *Königswalzer* (The King's Waltz) in which I played Princess Elisabeth of Wittelsbach. Long before Romy Schneider I portrayed the future empress of Austria in this super trashy film that was the first German film in cinemascope. Shooting it was pure torture. The cameraman first had to fly to Hollywood to learn the new technique and returned with an extra thick lens that, fastened to the front of the camera, made the wide screen effect possible. But this also meant that the lights had to be three to four times as strong; we had tropical heat in the studio. Actors and technicians outdid each other perspiring. The result was a film with a cheerful atmosphere." In addition to the films the young Swiss woman found nightlife in Munich very interesting. "I met many colleagues who are friends until today – if they are still alive."

In her private life at that time Linda was happy – and yet not really happy, as she recognizes in retrospect. "I imagined that

Linda Geiser and Dinah Hinz at the *Thalia Theater* in Hamburg. (Fall 1954)

getting engaged and then married would follow. I was very fond of Jürg Federspiel, an author, who was just becoming famous, wrote his first books, and worked as a journalist and theater critic for several newspapers. He was horribly jealous and felt that on stage I had kissed a colleague for too long.

"This led to a huge fight. I didn't understand him and I no longer understood myself. Not just because of this incident. I believe I was in love with being in love rather than in love with Jürg.

"And then I suddenly realized that I did not want to get into a marriage that came with three bottles of red wine per day. So I broke up; my parents were very happy. They had also seen that I was not able to deal with his difficult temperament. Our friends accused me of having broken his heart forever. But thank God, that wasn't true! In the course of his life he went on to meet several wonderful women and he has a wonderful son. I am friends not only with his family, but his ex-wives and ex-girlfriends, too. They remain a part of my life even after Jürg unfortunately died a few years ago."

Love led Linda down unusual paths. "At the ticket counter of the *Schlosspark Theater* in Berlin a young man who was right ahead of me was, in my estimation, an American. He didn't understand what the woman at the counter was trying to explain to him. I intervened and helped him get a seat right next to me for the sold-out performance of Genets *The Balcony*. He felt obliged to strike up a conversation; his name was Peter Mayer, and I found out that he was a student at Berlin's Free University intending to write a dissertation about Klee and Kafka. I told him that I knew Klee's son Felix who was a producer at Radio Bern.

"Peter spoke a funny broken German. His parents were originally from Essen and had emigrated via London, where Peter was born, to New York. After the performance we already were almost friends. He asked me to drive his car from the city's edge to downtown; he would take me on his motorbike to the car. Thus at midnight on the backseat of his Lambretta I clung to a man who had been an utter stranger to me just a few hours before and then followed him in is blue Volkswagen in the direction of Berlin-Center. Crazy...!"

This was the beginning of a great love story and a life-long friendship. "We enjoyed the life in Berlin before the Wall. And I sent Peter for his studies on Paul Klee to [Felix] Klee and said he could stay with my parents. They felt the young American was very nice. Peter returned to New York and I followed him in 1961 after I had played Lisi from Ziberlihoger after the novel *Annebäbi Jowäger* by Jeremias Gotthelf.

Linda visits her Anabaptist relatives in Dover, Ohio. (1961)

"Upon arriving I told him right away that I hadn't come to marry him, but rather because I found that we were the 'couple of the century' in the sense that Jean-Paul Sartre and Simone de Beauvoir were a couple. I did not need a swimming pool nor was I truly keen on having children. Already as a young girl I had the strange idea that I would die if I had to give birth to a child. This is a fixed idea that is still with me today."

For the first few months the couple lived in an apartment in the East Village. "At that time New York was a city without money, a bit run down just like Berlin. Not bombed out, but also rather shabby. We lived between Avenues C and D in Alphabet City on the Lower East Side.

"The area was fairly Jewish then and also Ukrainian. Our neighbors had numbers from concentration camps on their arms; across the street a rabbi had his *schul*; and on the first floor of our house they baked bagels. I attended the acting school in the West Village to learn to act in English. I was the 'key student' in the class of Herbert Berghoff; this meant I was keeping the log and this allowed me to attend the school tuition-free. Later I also had lessons with his wife, the famous Uta Hagen.

"The young women in class envied me for my boyfriend. Peter was handsome, and it was unusual that I cohabited with him. In the early 1960s America was very prudish. It was almost a tragedy if a woman at twenty did not yet know whom she would marry.

She would be seen as lost, an old maid. Many girls were advised to go to college, mainly to find a husband as 'security for life'! Women earned much less than men in all professions. The pill would start to change everything.

"Feminism and emancipation were at first just small trickles, but exploded in the 1970s and 1980s." Linda Geiser was given a part in a film with Rod Steiger. "My first work in film in America! I found out that famous actors behaved simply and naturally. In Germany, for example, you could always feel a difference between those who were already successful and those who were not there yet. Not so in New York. I played with a large touring ensemble that included stars such as Sir John Gielgud and Vivien Leigh, and we all sat down at the same table for meals, unthinkable in Europe."

During a ten-month tour with an ensemble of 50 people Linda became acquainted with the country and with the world of American theater. She had parts in plays by Tennesse Williams, Shakespeare and Gelderhode in Washington. In Akron, Ohio she was in *Who's Afraid of Virginia Woolf.* "The older generation of my god-fearing relatives in Ohio was dismayed at the rough language of the play."

Linda and the six "Kummer boys" at the Rudi Carell TV show. (1988)

In New York Linda Geiser did not break through in theater since the parts she played on Broadway were too small. But still: she breathed "Broadway air"! As a European type the parts of emigrants, refugees, and victims of concentration camps fit her best; in them she was several times quite successful on television. Again and again Linda returned to work in Switzerland. In 1967 Franz Schnyder wanted her for the part of the mother of the *Sechs Kummerbuben* (The Six boys of the Kummer Family), a series that was being filmed for television.

To play Sophie Kummer she remained in the Emmental for six months. A shortened version of the story was also made into a movie; this was to be Franz Schnyder's last film. Linda Geiser had already played in his first Gotthelf-film, *Ueli der Knecht* (Ulric the

Farm Servant) in 1954 and in the two *Annebäbi Jowäger* films in 1961. In both she played rather loose farm girls. In 1957 she had portrayed the very opposite as Anna in *Der 10. Mai* (The 10th of May); this was Franz Schnyder's very successful anti-war film shown at the Berlin Film Festival in 1958.

In New York Linda Geiser alternately fought and reconciled with her friend Peter. "Our relationship was constantly off and on. He thought I should have a super career but still wash his socks at home. He left me, then I left him, and then we were together again. It was exciting.

"We were at the first original Woodstock festival that was called *Hoot-an-Nanny* and was an impromptu get-together. Anyone who knew how to play the guitar could perform. The organizers had posted notes announcing the gathering all over the town. About a thousand people turned up with coke, beer, food, and drugs. The festival lasted late into the night. The mess left behind scared the village elders to such an extent that they applied the emergency brake the following year. The new group of organizers, which had a much better financial footing, had to buy a 3 miles long meadow located 28 miles from the village for the festival which was to be totally rained out, but still became world-famous and a legend."

In 1963 Linda decided to move in with a girlfriend; they rented a small apartment in a red brick house on 5th Street. Both left their boyfriends. The apartment cost 35 dollars per month. The reliable Swiss woman soon earned the sympathy of the house owner, Mr. Trachtman. "From time to time I painted the walls, I organized the plumber when a pipe burst somewhere, and made sure that everything looked nice.

"My landlord thought I was great, 'you are intelligent,' he said. Fine! And after 16 years he said one day: 'Why don't you buy the house? You can have it cheap!' No one from his family wanted to take it over. Thus, in 1979, I bought the red house in the East Village, the old immigrant house built in 1898, for $40,000. At the time this was about 160,000 Swiss francs. I had discussed it with my parents who helped." Linda is enthusiastic about her neighbourhood. "Then the East Village was not as elegant as it is today. It was more of an alternative district with many hippies, but very informal and friendly. And New York was not yet the city of global business. The [World Trade Center] towers were just being planned. South of 14th street there were still cobblestone streets. It was only later that prosperity arrived here too – that entire big bubble which now has burst."

Little by little Linda remodeled the apartments, the old-fashioned "railroad flats" in which one room leads into the next. "In the meantime the apartments have arrived in the 21st century, except my own. The Swiss TV series *Lüthi and Blanc* unfortunately stopped one year too early. I had invested the money I earned from this role in the renovations. Now I have to save again, and thus the four-footed tub still sits in the last room."

5th Street between First and Second Avenue is often used as a backdrop for films. Very close to the red house is New York's most famous police station, Precinct 9, which has been filmed very often. "Our façade is often in the camera's view, or camera people climb up the fire ladder in order to shoot from up above. Then I get 200 dollars."

Linda Geiser laughs playfully. "And it was not just a house that was passed on to me; without this special find I would not have met my current life partner. I was 43 and he was 20. John managed the bar on the first floor in my house. He taught me to play pool with the police officers stationed next door. He showed me pool tricks – and one night he didn't go home. He stayed. My friends, women and men, warned me: This relationship will not go any-where!"

You bet! "John is still here and has been with me for thirty years now. In the meantime he is fifty. A few times I kicked him out and called his mother that she ought to take him back. His mother is two years younger than I am. But he came back. He is from Brooklyn, a world that is totally different from mine and in the evening he smokes his marijuana joint. This is not for me. I tried mescaline once – which was strange. Marijuana does not agree with me and in 1968 I stopped smoking altogether, also regular cigarettes. Many of my friends at that time experimented with LSD and had anxiety attacks. And then it was I who stayed with them through all their panic taking care of them for hours and even days. Smoking, drugs, and alcohol are part of the theater world, but not for me. I can't even drink much. My father says this is to do with our genes – as Anabaptists neither smoked nor drank."

In the 1980s Linda Geiser also established herself as artist-craftswoman in New York. She was among the first people who exhibited erotica. "I made frames for mirrors with scenes from the Kamasutra. I could even exhibit them in the Kornfeld Gallery in Bern together with mirrors that I had decorated with angels. My mother was ashamed for me. After the first half hour all the erotic mirrors were sold, but only two of the angel mirrors!" She also wrote a play about Clara Schumann for the Music Festival in Interlaken (Switzerland) and another one about Heinrich Heine's last mistress. Her "travel tours for women" – *Seeing New York with Linda Geiser* – also became popular in Switzerland.

"For years I explored Manhattan on foot and on the subway with groups of Swiss women – men were not actually excluded! For these visitors Pipilotti Rist's exhibition was as sensational as a blues' mass on Sunday in Harlem, signing the book of condolences for the death of Frank Sinatra in the most famous funeral home, or a performance in the theater during which we were all sprayed with water. Unfortunately the last two tours, which were solidly booked, were canceled after 9/11... though at that time the Swiss would have experienced the people of New York as never before and probably never again. But who knows, I may start the tours again."

Since 1982 several cultural institutions of Switzerland have been renting apartments in Linda's "Red House" where fellowship recipients from various art sections can spend some months. So far 113 artists, both women and men, have been able to profit from the cultural energy of New York. "These encounters with artists are very enriching for me and make me happy. The quiet house helps their talents to unfold and grow in the midst of the hectic, creatively exciting atmosphere of New York. I am hoping that in the coming years many more young artists will spend time here.

"I have found my path. It is only natural that occasionally I am in a bad mood or feel depressed. But on the whole I am a person who is able to come to terms with everything. Freedom is, however, important to me, and I don't like it when people are dependent on me. Yet I am very willing to give of my time. People are important to me, but I want to be able to tell John: today I won't cook. His socks he has to wash himself anyway. I like living with him – I can't explain how we are doing it, but we function well together.

"We live modestly, and as I get older, I am eating less and more simply. I write, talk to myself, reinvent the world anew and then take it apart again. Thoughts dance around in my head; at times they are bats, at times precious stones." Then Linda says almost to herself: "Actually, I should be disconsolate that I have not become famous. As an actress, wouldn't this have been the goal? Strangely, in the course of my life, fame has ever more lost its attraction for me.

"As a young girl I wanted to become a world renowned star – I pinned the ad for *Lux soap* with Judy Garland and Greta Garbo on the wall above my bed: I wanted to be like them, look like them, wear my hair as they did, and appear in ads. Thank God, I lost this kind of ambition. Other values gained importance like having friends, remaining healthy.

"I don't have a good health insurance and can't afford to be sick." Thoughtfully she says, "many of my colleagues have died, but luckily some are still here. I always enjoy to see them again – Stephanie Glaser, Hans-Heinz Moser, Peter Arens, and others."

Does Linda still have unfulfilled wishes? "Several. Let's wait and live. I think that being on stage will be open to me for many years yet – playing character parts, older women with bats in their heads, or very old women with precious stones in their heads. My fondest wish is to play a sharp country woman, a Swiss Miss Marple who unwittingly becomes a detective and turns all of Switzerland, or at least half of it, topsy-turvy."

MARION
1930
SCHLAPFER
BRANDES

"We were born on November 29, 1930. No one had expected me."
On that Saturday afternoon, Marion Brandes was the surprise of
the Rotkreuz-Hospital in Zurich: "I am sort of a miracle," she adds
with a twinkle in her eye. "After the birth of Yvonne, Mother's
abdomen was too big and the newborn infant too small. Was there
a second surprise baby? Ten minutes later I slipped out."

Twins! The routine checkups during pregnancy had never indi-
cated two babies. "My mother was totally overwhelmed by this
situation, and my father was abroad on business. They didn't even
have a name for me. The doctor on duty suggested 'Marion' right
there in the delivery room – as it rhymes with Yvonne."

The brand new father was notified by telegram that his wife
was about to give birth prematurely. On his arrival at the main
station in Zurich, his sister-in-law congratulated the new "Daddy-
of-twins" to which he is said to have responded with irritation
"this is not a joking matter." The Brandes girls were as alike as two
peas in a pod and became inseparable. "As children, most people
could only tell us apart when we smiled which revealed the small
gap between my two front teeth."

Even seventy years later Marion has a vivid memory of
being an outsider: "Thank God, there were two of us." The twins –
daughters of a stateless Polish Jew and a Jewish mother who had
lost her Swiss citizenship when she married him – never felt
that they belonged.

"That we were Jewish was never mentioned in our family. At
home nothing pointed to our roots. In 1937, children in the street
shouted after us 'Jews, you are Jews.' We didn't know what the
word meant! It had to be something really bad, something even
criminal. 'Mami, what are Jews? Surely, that's not what we are,
right?' Mother's face looked worried as she responded 'Yes, it is
true.' For me this answer amounted to a death sentence. If I hadn't
had Yvonne, I probably would have become an isolated and very
lonely child. How often I wished the ground would open up and
swallow me.

"Yvonne and I had a strong need to quarrel and wrangle, at times even intentionally hurting one another, simply in order to get rid of our deep-seated anger and pain. Mother had no time for us. She had to support us tending her store, where she sold custom-made shoes. For her the most important thing was that her twins did not go hungry.

"Father lived only sporadically with us in Zurich. He was denied a residence permit, even though he was born and raised in Switzerland. The official reason given was 'foreign overpopulation'; I believe, however, that 'too many Jews' would have been closer to the truth. Of course, no one admitted such a thing loud and in public."

During the week, Marion's father lived in Vienna and returned to Zurich on the weekend. "Time and again neighbors denounced him to the *Fremdenpolizei* [Swiss equivalent for Immigration and Naturalization Service] when his car with Austrian license plates was parked in front of the house." This painful memory is still visible in Marion's fine face and her large expressive eyes.

"I remember that one day, a police officer came to our door, and he led father away like a criminal and escorted him to the Swiss border."

In school too, Yvonne and Marion were shown again and again that they did not belong. "Who is Protestant? Who is Catholic? And who is Jewish? When school inspectors came, we were always the only ones answering the last question, and the other children turned their heads and stared at us as if we were monsters. And who is Swiss? They all were – except the two of us."

In the summer of 1939 the political situation was escalating in Switzerland as well. War was in the air. Marion Schlapfer-Brandes remembers her mother telling her about the advice a kind officer at the Zurich *Fremdenpolizei* gave to her father: "Mr. Brandes, why don't you emmigrate to the United States of America, the only country in the world that still gives you a chance." "Nobody helped us so that Father could have stayed with us. Mother remained

Marion (right) and Yvonne playing accordion. (December 1945)

silent. She was glad that, as a former Swiss citizen, she and her children were not deported. And in case the Nazis had invaded Switzerland, the officials could have said that they did deport the Polish Jew! We accompanied Dad with his little suitcase to the station for the train to Cherbourg, and we all cried. I never found out how he reached the United States, how he managed to pay for the fare across the Atlantic. Did he have to pay off his passage by cleaning in the hull of the boat? He never talked about it.

"Since all mail was censured during the war, he was never able to contact us during those years. Only much later did we learn that he met other Jewish immigrants on Manhattan's West Side on 72nd Street, somehow scrimped and saved to survive, then was trained as a soldier in a U.S. military camp in North Carolina hoping to eventually get transferred to Germany – and thus be nearer to us. Yet this never happened."

After the war, Marion's father returned as a hero and as an American. "Americans were very popular all over Europe, including Switzerland. Dad had the 'man-of-the-world' appearance, spoke American English, had served in the U.S. Army, looked the perfect gentleman, and talked enthusiastically about his new homeland. Suddenly he was 'somebody' and was allowed to live with us, even received the much coveted residence and work permit, and years later even his Swiss citizenship. Who would ever have thought this possible?"

The "double Brandes girls", the beautiful high school students with their long black braids, received Protestant religious instructions as part of the regular school curriculum. "I was in dire need of a God who would be there for me and to whom I could pray.

Marion (left) and Yvonne in Ticino. (1946)

"On Easter 1947, we were confirmed after we had been baptized the night before. Pastor Hans Frick of the Protestant Church in Zurich Oberstrass showed himself as a compassionate and understanding teacher. He sensed our inner need. I will always be grateful to him for being such a warm-hearted, true mensch. Having received our baptism and confirmation, we finally felt on an equal footing with our schoolmates, felt an integral part of our class." Only at the home of Opa and Oma Kempinski, her maternal grandparents in Zurich, everything was different for Marion: "It was Jewish, though I only realized this much later. Oma's chicken soup simply tasted much better, presumably because the chicken was kosher." On Friday evenings, the Kempinskis lit candles. "Opa murmured something while lighting them and moved his body back and forth. I never asked why he was doing this. I assumed that all this was a great mystery, foreign and unfamiliar, and inwardly I rejected it outright."

After his return, the twins' father took charge of the teens' education and sent them to a school for business administration. He introduced the American way of life via his shoe store, and he imported the first ballerina shoes to the city of Zurich. The store did very well and soon *Chaussures Maryvon* moved from the Augustinergasse to the Pelikanstrasse in Zurich, part of the city's downtown shopping district.

After his return, their father took charge of the teens' education. (1946)

After having graduated each with a diploma in business administration, Marion and Yvonne worked as secretaries and wanted to obtain Swiss citizenship as soon as possible "so that finally we would fully belong. Even though we were born and raised in Zurich and truly were as Swiss as Swiss could be, the immigration officers subjected us to some most rigid examinations to assure we truly deserved Swiss citizenship."

From time to time Marion watches the movie *Die Schweizermacher*, a highly critical satire on Swiss immigration officers "converting foreigners into worthy Swiss citizens". "What the movie shows is in no way exaggerated. I remember an officer coming to our house, walking into our room, opening drawers of our dresser and checking around for any possible foreign items. My sister was asked whether she had an illegitimate child or had ever committed adultery. Such nonsense! And when, at the final examination, I had to give a detailed route description from Schaffhausen to Geneva without, however, passing through Bern,

I felt totally incompetent and failed to give the correct answer." Her sister was quick to counter with a valiant question: "Would a born Swiss know the answer offhand?"

Two years later, they both were in possession of their Swiss passports: "Out of gratitude we volunteered for the *Frauenhilfsdienst*, *FHD*, the women's auxiliary military service. To show our solidarity we wanted to do something practical for our country." For Marion, training and service as a Red Cross driver was a great experience except for the unwieldy military vehicles with their steering wheels on the right hand side of the car. The mere thought of it still revives fearful memories today: "I will never forget how we drove over the Susten Pass in these huge military vehicles, always within a hair's-breadth from the precipice."

"Out of gratitude we volunteered for the Women's Auxiliary Military Service. To show our solidarity we wanted to do something practical for our country." (1951/52 – Marion on the left.)

When Marion came of age, she decided she "finally needed to do something all by myself, without Yvonne. This was a purely rational decision." She moved to Paris and worked for six months at the American Express Company. "My first strolls through the streets of the French capital made me realize how alone I was, all by myself. My shadow was missing and I felt I was only half a person."

Meanwhile in Zurich, their father discovered Yvonne's first love affair. "Father was horrified. At that time women didn't have relationships. Either they were married, whores, or old maids." Daddy Brandes wanted to see his attractive daughters married promptly. He obviously did not trust men. Marion wonders, "maybe he was comparing those men with himself? He was quite a womanizer, which Mother tried to ignore."

Marion, too, was in love, with Adolf Schlapfer who, at their first meeting, believed she was Yvonne. "Father's comment was: 'Either you get married or you break up with Doelf.' If he had known that Doelf had visited me in Paris, and that we had been intimate there! Yet before marrying, I absolutely wanted to spend a year in the United States as Dad had always talked so fervently about that country. I applied for a visa at the American Consulate."

But then everything changed: "Yvonne had to leave Zurich suddenly after father had seen her at a soccer game in a tight embrace with her boyfriend. He exploded: 'How can you compromise me in such a way in Zurich' and simply decided: Yvonne will get Marion's visa! This was possible because of the identical family name and birth date. In 1954, Yvonne left her dental student and took off for New York while I married my boyfriend, Adolf Schlapfer, a junior officer at a local private bank."

Thus America had been reduced to a very remote possibility for Marion. She had only loose contact with Yvonne, but there was enough diversion in her new life in Zurich.

"It was only after my daughter Elena had been born in 1956 that I began to share my life again with my sister in New York through long and detailed letters. And I realized I missed her terribly. Writing to her felt like the past revisited when we shared all our experiences. I told her all the details of giving birth and also mentioned my marital problems. Doelf had been very loving and attentive until we were married. As a husband, however, he did not nurture our relationship."

Looking back Marion says "at that time, one was told that both parents ought to be present at the birth of their child. However, I decided to do this by myself. I did not want to have to sidetrack my attention for the benefit of making a good impression – and certainly not while giving birth to my baby! I always feared that showing any sign of human weakness would result in loss of love. Mother's teaching had been most successful. Her motto in life was: Don't ever look, don't ever hear, and don't ever say anything. I was brought up in this manner, and perhaps this was customary in many families at that time. It took me ever so many years until I realized what nonsense this was."

For Marion's husband, marriage became more and more a straightjacket. He felt that having a child had been a huge mistake; he was jealous of Elena and refused to take any responsibility for her.

Soon he had a string of lovers. "You know, they admire me," he mercilessly told his wife. Marion had to act: "I resented this. I did not want to live this way and I did not have to live this way. Shortly before my 30th birthday, I left the man who lacked all understanding of child rearing, of women, and of human relationships, and who considered himself superior to everyone else."

With emphasis Marion reports that her husband was convinced she would return within a few short weeks and do so on her knees, pleading for unconditional return. "You know, many a woman would feel privileged if I had married her..." he would say sneering. Marion was desperate but remained true to herself. "There was no way back even though Mother felt that I had made my bed and now ought to lie in it. But I could not do that." In her loneliness she often cried when she was by herself while Elena was napping.

"One day my eyes came to rest on a small photo of Yvonne that I had fastened to my kitchen cabinet. 'Come! Join me!', I felt Yvonne beckoning me from the photograph. That same day I sat down and told her in a long letter that I needed to change my life. How would it be if Elena and I came to New York for a year? Spontaneously, Yvonne answered that we could live with her, that she would find a school for Elena, and work for myself."

Then everything happened very quickly. Marion's divorce was finalized on November 2, 1960. Ten days later, with the help of a bridge loan of 3,000 Swiss francs from her father-in-law, Marion Schlapfer-Brandes and her four-year old daughter were on board a Swissair propeller plane on their way to a new life. "The night flight via Amsterdam was the cheapest fare available. When we were already over the Atlantic Ocean, my daughter said 'Mami, look at that daddy on the other side of the aisle, the one with the child on his lap – I always wanted a daddy like that!'

"Only later, when Elena had fallen asleep, was I able to let myself go and cry into the dark. When we landed in New York, I felt empty inside. A door had been slammed shut. Would there be another one to open? I had no idea whether my life in America would be better. I only knew one thing: Yvonne was my fortress and my safe haven. I could rely on her. She met us at the airport where Elena recognized her from far away on the visitors' balcony."

Everything was new! "Even the simplest things were different. The number 7 was written without a horizontal stroke, the number 1 without an upstroke, and in dates the month preceded the day. Of course, these were but minor changes, but they required full concentration nevertheless."

Yvonne, Marion and Elena lived in an apartment with three and a half rooms on 81st Street between York and East End Avenues – "this was a true home for us." Since Marion had a Green Card, she was able within a few days to start her job with the Swiss company, Heitz Inc., where Yvonne had been employed for the past four years. During the day, Elena received excellent care at the Rudolf Steiner School on 79th Street on Manhattan's East Side.

"The little girl flourished like a flower. After just a few weeks she spoke American English, and in the evening she replayed at home what she had experienced during the day in school."

While Elena adapted without any problems, for Marion the change from life in Zurich to living in Manhattan was a challenge. "I would never have made it without the loving support of Yvonne." She takes a deep breath before continuing. "One evening, Elena and I arrived home shortly after 7 p.m.; I had not yet shopped for groceries, hadn't cooked anything, and had not yet given my little daughter her bath – even though her bedtime had already arrived. I must have looked awfully stressed out for Elena asked me softly: 'Mami, do you actually love me'?"

This hit Marion hard. The twins had to get better organized for Elena's sake. "From then on, Yvonne took her to school early in the morning. I began work at 8 a.m. and did not take a lunch break to achieve the required hours. Each afternoon at 3 p.m., I took the bus for 30 blocks up north to pick up Elena from the Steiner School. The two of us went to the park where she would play, climb around, and have fun with other kids. I would read or knit. Finally we had time for and with each other, and I became more relaxed and more balanced."

Marion was the only single mother in Elena's class. "Everywhere it said Mr. and Mrs. and Elena complained, 'everybody has a daddy, except for me.'" Marion was not fazed. "Just a moment; first, you do have a daddy – biologically there is no other possibility. He simply does not live with us. And second, you have something no one else has: You have two Mamis and they even look alike."

Of course, there was not much time for leisure in Marion's everyday life. "For many years my life in New York consisted of Elena, Yvonne, Heitz Inc., and the Steiner School. Yet everything worked out, despite occasional hurdles and struggles along the way. I am very grateful that destiny, or whatever it was, has led me along this road, and that I was able to live in the freedom that life in America gave us during the important years when my daughter was growing up. For a divorced woman with a child this would have been much harder in Switzerland." The intended twelve months Marion planned to spend in New York eventually extended to forty years.

From time to time she had relationships, but nothing really serious. "When a man did not pay any attention to Elena, I was done with him. Many of the men, both single and married, had their own problems. I said to myself: If it is not to be, it doesn't have to be. New York offered me wonderful opportunities, which presumably I would never have had in Switzerland. In America I greatly valued the positive attitude to life itself, as well as the general openness and generosity of the people." The "Brandes twins" lived together for fifteen years, and together they raised Elena who, in 1974, graduated from the Steiner School and attended an American college studying music and voice.

Elena and Marion became naturalized American citizens in 1966. "The officer congratulated me, saying 'today is a lucky day for the United States of America because you have become a citizen.' I was speechless. I was not only congratulated because I became a citizen, but the Americans were pleased that I joined them. It's only a minor comment, but it certainly goes a long way.

"In the winter of 1973, our precious harmony came to an abrupt halt by the saddest of news. Yvonne had malignancies in her breast that required immediate surgery. My 43-year old sister refused both chemotherapy and radiation. Instead she opted for a stay of several weeks at the Lukas-Klinik in Arlesheim, Switzerland, where anthroposophical medicine was practiced. Yvonne looked wonderful when she returned to New York, then within a year suddenly took a turn for the worse. The cancer had metastasized to her liver." Marion did her best: "I tried to be positive, to instill hope, to be supportive."

Yvonne suffered immensely, and the sisters' final parting was incredibly painful. Yvonne died at the end of May 1976. Marion and Elena were with her. "I was shaken down to my very bones. Half of myself had disappeared forever. I had lost my beloved twin sister, my supporter, and my best friend. And I realized that I did not have an identity of my own."

Marion was numb with pain, and it took her months to recognize that from then on she had to take care of herself and find a new purpose of life on her own. "I could not let myself drown in my sorrow, and I stood in front of Yvonne's photo and begged her – 'you promised to help me even if you would be gone. Now is the time; I need your help.'"

Elena was twenty and in college. Marion's work at Heitz kept her going, and after her sister's death she was promoted to vice-president. Yet she knew that the company could not offer her a future, and that she needed to find a new direction in her life.

She did not want to return to Switzerland, as New York had become her life. "Men and sex were not helpful to me. I had to learn to stand on my own two feet. The road from the 'we' to my own unknown 'I' was hard and long and straight uphill."

She read books which were helpful, began to meditate, and in various seminars was shown how to approach people and opportunities without anxieties. Step by step, she learned to take responsibility for her life, to trust herself, strengthen her self-confidence, and be grateful for what she had. "I discovered the method of José Silva's 'law of attraction'which says: You get what you think. This philosophy has impacted my life and accompanied me ever since. A true gift!"

One day on a flight from New York to Zurich, Marion had a conversation with her travel neighbor, a businessman from Germany. With his business connections, he helped her find a fascinating job. "At age 50, I became the executive secretary to the president of Siemens Corporation in New York; in an office on the 4th floor of the General Motors Building with a view of Central Park and the Plaza Hotel. Finally, after plenty of struggles I had learned to believe in my own capacities. And I knew that I deserved this job."

In her thoughts, Marion relinquished any old resentment toward her father and her ex-husband. "In my life I have always received much help, for which I am grateful. Who knows – perhaps my husband as well as my father were precisely the teachers I needed to become strong and independent and learn important lessons for the rest of my life!"

At Christmas 1995, having just turned 65, she retired from Siemens. "Now would be the time to do something new, I said to myself. I was thinking of something that would be difficult to learn and prove a real challenge."

The challenge arrived not long afterwards in the form of an announcement by a former class and swim-team mate informing her of the passing of his wife. "I called W. After a stroke he had been paralyzed on one side, and I promised to visit him in Switzerland. Although I had found him very likeable when we were teenagers, I knew he had become chauvinistic, with political views very different from my own. But could this be my challenge? He invited me to stay with him for a month."

On the first day she checked her watch every five minutes; time seemed not to move. They discussed the possibility of a common future, but she told him very clearly: "I fought hard for my own independent life – not exactly by shedding blood, but at the cost of plenty of sweat, effort and suffering. I shall never give up my personal independence."

Eventually, they agreed that she would stay with him as his companion for five months, then spend a month in New York and come back to him for another five months. "I did not love him, but wanted to be nice and compassionate to him. Thus I commuted back and forth across the Atlantic for almost seven years. His family appreciated my presence. He tried again and again to get my full commitment to share his life and sell my apartment in New York. He said his house was my house. But for me this was out of the question."

In the meantime, Elena had moved to Berlin, where she had become assistant professor at the *Universität der Künste* (University of the Arts) teaching voice. She was married and mother of two daughters.

"During a month in 2004 that I spent with my granddaughters in Berlin, Theresa, a young home nurse took care of W. On my return I could see that in my absence she had become everything to him. At the same time I realized that she was of huge help to me – thanks to her I was able to separate from W."

Marion made plans and wanted to return to the United States for good. "But Elena found it difficult to think of her aging mother alone in New York, so far away from her. Over the last years, she argued, had I not gotten accustomed again to Europe, to Switzerland? Could I not imagine spending the last period of my life in Zurich?

"I had to take a deep breath. In Switzerland, everything seemed so very narrow – and I'm not just talking about the sink that is much smaller in Zurich than in New York, but also about the mentality. I needed more than a clean country and beautiful scenery – I needed the personal freedom that would nurture my further development. In New York, I had learned that I have the right to dream the impossible and that I can make the impossible become possible. There I felt like a human being, and I could believe in my potential.

"Could it be that my next lesson in life was to learn to take Switzerland and its people just the way they are? To learn to not be disturbed by sentences such as 'there is nothing you can do about this', and 'well, this is simply the way it is'? I carefully weighed all the pros and cons and eventually listened to my daughter's advice."

Everybody had been telling Marion Schlapfer that it would be nothing short of a miracle to find a suitable apartment in a senior settlement in Zurich. But she was very lucky. In the *Hadlaubsiedlung*, a foundation of the Protestant Church of Zurich Oberstrass, where Marion and Yvonne had been baptized and confirmed decades earlier, a two-room apartment was available.

Today, Marion flies to New York only sporadically and the apartment in Queens is sold. When she arrives at JFK, she is always happy. "Hi there, it's good to be back home," she says as she shows her American passport to the customs officer. "And he replies: 'It's good to have you back' – as if we were good friends. Yet, I won't ever see this person again."

Leaning back in her chair Marion Schlapfer-Brandes radiates serenity. "I am simply grateful for my life. Even the most painful experiences were hidden learning opportunities. I do not worry about the future.

"I think it was Friedrich Dürrenmatt who once said in a talk in New York, that we don't need to be afraid. That what we are afraid of always lies in the future. But when the future becomes the present, we will simply do what needs to be done, and then it is already past. I am glad that I don't know what will happen in the future. I am in God's hands; he has guided me until now and he will continue to guide me. I am an American with European roots and carry the larger world within me. I enjoy seeing how serenely Elena manages her life. Just recently she said to me: 'Mami, I am so glad that way back then you simply left with me.'"

LILLET
LEE
VON SCHALLEN

1932

"Que sera, sera (What will be, will be) – this is the motto of my life. I pray every night before going to sleep and express my gratitude to God. Somehow I am happy. I cannot change anything in my past anyway."

During our conversations Lillet Lee von Schallen is usually sitting on the front edge of her chair. It is an effort for her to review her life, and she does not want to tell her story in her own home in Johnsburg located at a two hour drive outside Chicago. She prefers to do it in the apartment of a Swiss friend whom she trusts. "Spontaneously she offered me hospitality on neutral ground," she adds.

It was not easy to find the time to interview Lillet Lee von Schallen. The 76-year old woman still works full-time, five days a week from 9 a.m. to 5 p.m. As a travel agent she books hotels and flights for her clients, finds ingenious vacation arrangements. Lillet Lee has to work. Despite her age she cannot afford to retire. "I do not have enough to live on with my small pension from the *Alters- und Hinterbliebenenversicherung, AHV* [Swiss Social Security] and the one from the American Social Security."

And work runs as a continuous thread through Lillet's life. "Fortunately, my job is satisfying even though on weekends I am too exhausted to go anywhere." The elderly woman has lively eyes that however, also communicate a deep sadness. Life has left its traces not only in her face; again and again she has to move, to stretch her spine: She is disciplined, not embittered, just tired. Yet time and again humor and wisdom shine through her narrative.

"I was born on September 8, 1932, in the Castle of Valère in Sitten (Sion). My ancestors were custodians of the castle for centuries. I was born in the castle's attic apartment. My father belonged to the family of von Schallen – he had the right to live in the castle. But by profession he was a baker and construction worker – for us nobility was but a hollow sound." [There is something of a word play in German between the family name von Schallen and the word Schall meaning "sound" and "hollow sound" in the expression *Schall und Rauch* that Lillet used.]

Lillet continues to narrate. "My father married my mother – but not for love. He had had bad luck with women, especially German women; one had even scorned him. Thus he swore to himself to marry the next best German woman who came his way out of revenge. Mother was his victim. The young girl from Freiburg in Breisgau worked as a waitress in Sion. Already on their very wedding day, so mother told me later, he went to see his lover in the evening. Mother had a hard life. She supported us by cleaning for several families in Sion; father was often unemployed; he drank. He had a violent temper, beat mother and us, his five children who were born one after the other – after me at short intervals: Roland, Norbert, Odette and Lydia.

"The apartment in the castle got too small for a family of seven, so we moved to the Place du Midi. There my 8 year old brother Norbert fell out of a window on the fifth floor; he was instantly killed."

In speaking Lillet freely mixes French, German, and English using mostly English when talking about emotional experiences. "Father blew up for the smallest things; he treated my mother very badly. I remember clearly how he tried to stick her hand into the hot fire pit of the oven when something didn't suit him. But my mother's motto was: Say nothing, and bear everything. From the outside no one noticed how bad things were in our home. For a long time, that is. Mother wanted it that way. She was proud, a solid German woman – what happened in the home had to stay in the family. She always said that nothing in life is free. I learned this from her."

As the oldest child Lillet had to be courageous and strong very early in her life. The little girl, barely seven years old, was on vacation at her grandmother's house in Germany when the war broke out in 1939. "Mother called saying I had to come home immediately." Her grandmother put her on the train in Freiburg. "The only train that went to Basel was a military train with a freight car that brought soldiers to the Swiss border. I still can see how grandmother lifted me into the car telling the soldiers: 'This little one has to go to Switzerland.' I sat on mountains of luggage. The soldiers shared their sausages and their bread with me. At the train station in Basel they entrusted me to a Swiss conductor. I had no fear. It was already dark when I arrived in Sion. For hours Mother had waited for me at the train station – she didn't know which train I would be on."

The von Schallen family lived very modestly, even miserably. "It was a matter of course that we children helped. We planted and cultivated two large vegetable plots in Sion. We rarely had enough money. When father once again had no work and we went hungry, I had to go to the soup kitchen of the Capuchin monastery with our milk bucket where we could get something hot for the entire family for free. Before the meal we had to wash our face and hands; and at table we children were not allowed to speak."

Lillet had little in common with her younger siblings; and she had no time for friends. "I had to work, work and work. The only days during which we were allowed to play were the Christmas days and Sunday afternoons if the weather was bad. I hardly had any toys, perhaps a doll. At home we always had to be quiet; we were not to upset father."

One day the family moved from the Valais to Le Pont in the Vallée de Joux located in the Jura mountain range of the canton Vaud. "Father no longer found work in the Valais, and his brother helped to find positions for him and for my mother in the watch factory of Le Coultre."

Lillet abruptly stops. Her face suddenly seems petrified. "I don't know if I should say all this." Yet then something breaks out of her that had been repressed for decades. "Father sexually abused me when I was twelve. This went on for at least two years, out of malice. I was not to say anything to anyone. He threatened that he would beat the living daylights out of me. This was the most terrible time of my life. I think my mother knew it. She was power-less, helpless, and also afraid. Because I was always sick, it all came out somehow; how I don't know and don't want to know. I only remember that the police came to our house, arrested him, and put him in prison for two years."

Lillet continues slowly and in a low voice: "While that time lasted I had only one thought: How can I survive all this?" The scandal spread like wildfire; the 14-year old girl was taken away from her mother and her siblings. "I had finished my eight years of school and was sent to a home for 'fallen' girls in Estavayer-le-Lac. Strange women lived there who had stolen or had illegitimate children. I knew they were bad women, women who had done things that you were not supposed to do. I was the youngest. Why did I have to be there? I had no idea. My maxim was to no longer think about it, not to say anything, and to bear everything."

Lillet pulls herself together: "I had a difficult childhood. Already as a young girl I had to be strong. My mother gave me this strength. She was always able to show us children the good parts of life too. 'You have to be truthful, respect older people, be polite and respect yourselves, no matter what happens.' As the oldest I absorbed everything. I owe a lot to my mother. She said: 'Don't do anything that would harm your family'! It is amazing, now I can speak about my childhood – for the first time after so many, many years."

Mother von Schallen had stayed with the other children in the small town; where could she have gone? At least she had work in the watch factory. Yet she no longer wanted to have anything to do with her husband. After her time in the home Lillet returned to Le Pont and for the first time in her life made friends.

"They were all boys. For a while I was as the only girl in a troupe of boy scouts. I did everything they did, build huts and fireplaces, climbing. I wanted to have fun, and the only possibility to have fun was to do things with the boys. They knew that I was not out for sex. I only wanted their companionship, and they behaved like gentlemen. We used to go to a bar together." And then Lillet laughs out loud: "I could drink them all under the table. I drank one glass after the other, went to the restroom, vomited, and then continued

"I was smart. Let's go...!"

to drink. They could not believe it. They really treated me as a buddy. 'Let us fill up Lillet'! I was smart. Let's go...! I drank a bottle of red wine without any problem. My mother always knew where I went and with whom. When such an evening was coming up, she said: 'Sit down Lillet' and gave me *Rösti* with lots of butter to eat and I also had to chew coffee beans. This gave a good lining to my stomach. Mother was the best. She had a heart of gold. She was my angel."

From time to time Lillet escaped in her thoughts to faraway places where life would be better for her – sometime later. "As a young girl I was already dreaming about America. I wanted to emigrate, away from everything. But I only wanted to go when I would know enough English." Attending a school was out of the question; her mother had no money.

In 1949, at 17 Lillet found a job as a nanny in London through the Young Womens Christian Association (YWCA). "What prospects!" The Jewish family in Landsdown, in the north of the city, proved to be difficult. "The parents were never home and left me to care for the baby who was only a few months old and even slept in my room. They were not only impolite to me, they also never had sufficient food in the house." In the months in London Lillet taught herself English "by reading the newspaper."

One day she had enough. She packed her bags, took the money she had saved, went into the city and bought a newspaper before renting a room in a small, inexpensive hotel. "The porter took me up to the second floor and said I would have to share the room with another woman. In my naïvete I agreed. It was about half an hour later when a good-looking blond woman came into the room and said 'Hey deary'. That's when I felt: Something is wrong here! Despite my broken English I immediately realized that I was in a hotel where prostitutes came to take a rest from their work." Lillet did not sleep that night even though she had put her passport and wallet under her pillow and, as a precaution, had not undressed.

"Through a newspaper ad I found a position as a nanny in Handon outside London the very next day and was able to start immediately. I kept house for the family of the secretary of the American Embassy. Vera, the lady of the house, was pregnant and in poor health." Lillet stayed with the Texans for some months until they were called back home. They were bent on taking Lillet with them, but she had decided to return to Switzerland where she took a job as receptionist in the Hotel des Alpes in Montreux. "But honestly, that was not my cup of tea!"

It was her knowledge of English as well as her courteous and cheerful manners that soon thereafter unexpectedly opened a door to the United States for the 19-year old girl. "I was on a train between Lausanne and Montreux when I struck up a conversation with an older couple; he was a retired politician from the United States, his wife a pianist. They seemed lost. 'May I help you' I asked. I gave them some helpful tips for their trip and they invited me – during that same train ride – to visit them in America, in Redondo Beach near Los Angeles. This was what I had been longing for with all my heart! We exchanged addresses and soon we had a lively correspondence – despite my poor written English."

In the meantime she applied for a job in the Italian Tourist office in Zurich and was hired, "although I could only swear in Italian. But the director hired me immediately even when I told him clearly that I went only to 8th grade. He said I could fill in everywhere." She had some good months in Zurich. "I collected mail, sent it out, was the errand girl, and was paid 1.20 Swiss francs per hour."

Suddenly Lillet glows with joy remembering an episode she absolutely wants to mention: "On one of my train trips from Zurich to Lausanne [Swiss] General Guisan invited me to drink a bottle of wine with him. He wanted to know where I had been at the beginning of the war in September 1939. I told him that the school children were given a free day to greet him, the General, when he stopped in several larger cities, including Sion. I had just

"On one of my train trips from Zurich to Lausanne General Guisan invited me to drink a bottle of wine with him."

returned from visiting my grandmother in Germany where we had had to raise our hand and say *Heil Hitler*. Since I was still young I believed that I had to do this too when General Guisan drove through the city and so raised my hand to a Hitler salute. Guisan laughed as I described this and said it was too bad he hadn't known about my story earlier."

The preparations for America took a year and a half until Lillet finally had her visa for America in her mailbox. "It was December 27, 1956. On the same day I took the train to Geneva, went to the office of American Express, and booked a ticket to Paris, three nights in a hotel in the French metropolis, the next leg to Le Havre and the ship passage to New York." This was the agreement: She was to finance her way, and her hosts in California would pay for her stay.

On January 2, 1957, Lillet began her trip westward with three pieces of luggage. "My mother said, if America is what you want, then go. Good luck and let me hear from you."

Her trip took 21 days. "It was wonderful. In Paris I saw the opera *The Marriage of Figaro* in an elegant brocade dress. With my fake fur and my high heels I walked late at night through the Champs Elysées towards the Arc de Triomphe back to my hotel. The ship leaving Le Havre was actually all booked, but with luck I had gotten a bed in an outside cabin that I shared with a woman who was emigrating from Germany to America. It was an incredibly rough passage. There were 1100 Hungarian refugees on board and most of them were seasick. The cabin steward said: 'Missy, make sure that your stomach always has something to work on. Always eat some small things, crackers or bread'. During the entire 7-day trip I was never sick, not even for a moment. I had much fun on the ship; one man even wanted to marry me. His name was Frankie, he was going home to his family in Buffalo, New York, and took me to dances and also to the bar. Frankie was a perfect gentleman: 'Why do you want to go to California? Why don't you marry me?' But it was no romance à la Titanic. We didn't even kiss. For me, one thing was clear: I am not going to America to get married. I wanted

"...if America is what you want, then go. Good luck and let me hear from you."

to see the country … and perhaps marry some time later!" After arriving in New York, Frankie and Lillet lost sight of each other. Lillet received a second marriage proposal on her trip to the West with the South Pacific Railroad. She was in a first class compartment elegantly dressed as a businesswoman. "I was a sensation on the train: a woman traveling all by herself and coming all the way from Switzerland! Two smartly dressed men sat across from me. One began a conversation and pointed to his neighbor who would like to get to know me. He said that he owned a large ranch in Texas with more than a thousand heads of cattle and was single. Yet Texas as well as marrying were out of the question for me. My goal was and remained California." Suddenly Lillet nervously checks her watch; her boss expects her to arrive at the office on time.

We meet again the following day, same time, same place. She admits that the conversation stirred her up very much. "I sense how my past has returned all of a sudden." Lillet is sitting in the same spot in the kitchen pressing her knees together. For a few moments she absent-mindedly looks out of the window as if she had to go back to search for the thread of her life. "Where did we stop yesterday? – Yes, at my wonderful trip out West. After a trip of 21 days my American friends and benefactors met me at Central Station in Los Angeles and took me to Redondo Beach, to a paradise" – as Lillet calls it – "with kiwi and lemon trees in the yard, with gorgeously smelling bougainvilleas and my own room with a bathroom. It was wonderful." While Lillet had free room and board, she still had to look for work, and she found a job in the service department of the General Telephone Company in Los Angeles. "I was again hired as an errand girl, but after the first half day I was offered a position in sales. I sold colored phones which cost $10 more per month than the black ones. That was expensive, but they sold like hot cakes. I was very successful in sales, yet this did not help my popularity in the team – as a newcomer who didn't know much English and hardly had any experience in sales!"

Lillet had fulfilled her dream: She felt comfortable in America, had fun, earned her own money, and was able to live at the house of her benefactors. "Finally I started my own life."

One day she met Pat at the window of the telephone company. "He invited me for a drink, then for dinner, and eventually wanted to introduce me to his brother Chuck Lee who had just returned from military service in Okinawa, Japan. I was curious and made a date with Chuck. We met again and again." Lillet sighs. "Eventually I slept with him, despite the fact that, as a young girl, I had promised my mother not to have sex before my wedding. A few weeks later I realized that I was pregnant. 'Let's marry' I proposed. I didn't want an illegitimate child. But I never loved Chuck. We married on February 14, 1958, and seven months later our daughter Dominique was born."

In the course of her marriage Lillet had to make the painful discovery that Chuck did not like to work and was also an alcoholic. "We moved to Rochester, Minnesota, where my husband found work as a chef. Soon I was pregnant again and in July 1960 gave birth to our son Norbert Charles. After three miscarriages Samenthia Emma, our youngest child, was born in 1962."

Chuck worked less and less. Lillet stepped in. She doesn't remember all the jobs she had in order to make ends meet. "I was the breadwinner and was able to pay a nanny for the children, but happiness was not meant to be. I knew that I was not to fight with my husband when he had been drinking. He beat me only once. I threatened: 'If you do this a second time, I will kill you even if I have to go to prison.' I know I would have done it. I was beaten as a child; as an adult I did not want to be subjected to this torment." One day when Lillet returned from work she found her husband in the bedroom packing his bags. "He told me 'I am leaving you, I am sick and tired of you and the kids' – 'Okay', was my terse answer, 'you had one suitcase when you married me and you are leaving me with one. Good-bye and good luck.'" From one day to the next Lillet found herself alone with her three children without any support. Dominique, the oldest, was ten, Samenthia, the youngest, six. "I called the children together and told them that their father had left and would not come back. Somehow they were relieved, I could sense it. Then I made it clear to them: We have to help each other. In the following years, whenever we had to make a decision, we had family meetings. The four of us sat around a table and discussed the matter. At that time I realized that we have to involve our children in decisions that affect all family members. My children always had good ideas and proposals about how to solve problems and questions of everyday life in practical ways."

Lillet no longer remembers what she had to do in order to endure in the first months after the separation. Just as so many other experiences of her life she stowed them away in the remote parts of her memory in order to survive. Yet she vividly remembers the significant experience as manager of a restaurant: "I worked as receptionist in a hotel when a stranger offered me a restaurant in the town of Sterling, Illinois. It was closed at the time, but I could have it. The business would be mine if I would take over a $15,000 debt on the building. My children also thought this would be okay, and so I signed an agreement that I would purchase the restaurant and would be responsible for its management. I was able to find the money."

With 85 dollars in her register Lillet courageously opened the restaurant. As a single mother with three children she became the subject of gossip and tales among the neighbors. "The women in the town feared for their husbands. My business was going well. Soon I was able to hire a chef, and quite often we served two- to three hundred guests in one evening. My children all helped – all in dark suits. Dominique helped the chef in the kitchen, Norbert was the water boy providing guests with fresh water, and Samy was the dishwasher. Our steaks were soon popular far and wide. When the children demanded more money for their work, I increased their pay. We were a tight team.

"But of course our family life suffered under this huge commitment to work. Thus, after two years I decided to sell the entire business asking $160,000 in order to build a new life for myself in a different place." Yet things turned out very differently. While negotiating the sale it was discovered that the previous owners had committed significant tax evasion and also had failed to pay social security taxes. Lillet had to pay these back taxes as well as the penalties levied by the State of Illinois. "What a blow! All my profit was gone. With empty hands and three children who were still in school I was facing complete ruin. Where did we go then? What did we do?"

Lillet is desperate. She draws a blank – try as she might she cannot remember how life continued. She is silent, reflects. The sirens of a racing police car are wailing outside. Lillet apologizes again and again. "I am sorry. I only remember that all this was horrible." Silence. Lillet seems lost in herself; at some point in time she continues her story in the more recent past that is more present to her. "For fifteen years I have been working in a travel agency now. I love traveling and have had wonderful experiences; I was in China, Russia, Hongkong and Singapore. My apartment is in Johnsburg, way out in the country. I have to get up at 3:30 a.m. every morning, five days per week. My train leaves at 5:13 a.m. When I arrive at Michigan Avenue in Chicago at 7 a.m. there is enough time for breakfast before I start working in the office at 9 a.m. In the evening I take a taxi to the train station at 4:40 a.m. in order to catch the train and I am back home at 6:30 p.m. My customers appreciate me, and this energizes me. I like being with people. When I am among people, I have no time to think about myself. At my age of 76 I would no longer find a salaried job. I always found a way to surmount obstacles, have always been working. When I didn't know how to do something, I learned it, and thus I succeeded in the world. My children turned out well, are married and have families. I was able to pay for the professional training and the weddings for all three. Norbert was the one who had the most difficulties and needed extra help. He was married several times and has five children. Often he didn't know how to go on."

Returning to Switzerland? "No, this is out of the question. I am too accustomed to the American way of life. My sister Odette calls me every week; we speak Swiss German and French with each other. When my mother was still alive, I flew to Switzerland three or four times a year and took wonderful trips with her by car and by train. Mother peacefully passed away when she was 89; this was very comforting for me.

"I am an American. I think as people here think, but I do not necessarily do what they do. I have adapted to the country. What will be will be! Life will always continue in some way. In my life I regret only one thing: that I had dentures made; they don't hold and are a nuisance. But otherwise God was good to me. I am living a very simple life and am content with what I have.

"Whenever I feel lonesome or am depressed, I am telling myself: Lillet, take whatever comes! Somehow things will work out. I am not afraid of getting older, God knows, I am old! If I were in need of help, that would be bothering."

Dreams? "I have no time for dreaming, at least not yet. I may yet be able to travel by train around the world; I certainly know the most beautiful spots on earth on paper. One time I would like to plan a trip for myself – for me alone! Voilà! From London over the Channel to France, then passing through Switzerland, Austria, and the East European countries to Russia, China, and Australia – from Sydney to Perth and then taking the blue train through Africa. This would cost $12,000 and time – at present I have neither.

"I did not have much luck in my life. I am a survivor. Whenever things get better, I am grateful. But I don't complain. Why should I? I can eat, get up in the morning, sleep at night if I take a sleeping pill, and I still am able to work. What more should I want? A little bit of luxury would be nice, but I don't miss it. Only at night I do feel lonely."

MARIE-SIMONE PAVLOVICH LUDWIG

1944

"GENEVA 4" reads the Illinois license plate on her new car. Marie-Simone Pavlovich has allowed herself the small indulgence of a vanity plate. "Of course, I would have much preferred 'GENEVA 1', but that had already been given out, perhaps to another woman like me who is homesick for Geneva."

She has a mischievous look in her large, hazel eyes. She is a Professor of French at Northwestern University in Evanston-Chicago. Her speech is fast and lively, time and again showing a hidden sense of humor. A clearly audible French accent underlies her English, and she still uses the French pronunciation for her first name, Marie-Simone.

"I have never ever met anyone named Marie-Simone. Back then, in 1944, my mother found that it was fashionable to have a daughter whose name included Marie – there were lots of girls named Marie-Claire or Marie-Françoise, but Marie-Simone, that was special. My mother was an unusual woman, open to the world and curious about life. As I am, I suppose." Her mother, Babette Ludwig-Streiff, daughter of the mayor of Betschwanden, had a desire to go abroad after 12 years of schooling in the canton Glarus. She was not able to train for a profession, but worked for 3 years as a nanny in Finland. There she met her first great love, a medical doctor who was soon to be drafted for the war. As a result, the twenty-three-year-old Babette had to return to Switzerland in 1939. She did not want to go back home to Glarus, so she moved in with her two sisters, Marie and Vreni, who lived in Geneva.

In Marie's house, she met Ernst Ludwig, a watchmaker from Schaffhausen who was twenty-five years her senior – and learned to love him. Without much effort, he soon found work in the French part of Switzerland. The Swiss-German couple married and remained in the city on the Rhone River. On May 6, 1944, their only child, Marie-Simone, was born.

"My first language is Swiss-German. At home, we spoke a Swiss dialect, essentially mixing the dialects from Schaffhausen and Glarus. However, my mother would also teach me French. I loved my mother very much. She was not as boring and conformist as my two aunts. At Aunt Vreni's, you always had roast on Wednesdays, fish – filet de carrelet – on Fridays, and chicken with green peas on Sundays. 'Typical Swiss-German' my mother said in a slightly disparaging tone." When Marie-Simone started school in Geneva, kids made fun of her. "You are a Toto – a Nobody!" Toto was the designated word to mockingly refer to those who spoke French with a Swiss-German accent. This was a cause of shame for Marie-Simone; subsequently she made a pact to give up speaking Swiss-German as soon as possible.

"My mother would also teach me French. I loved her very much. She was not as boring and conformist as my two aunts." (1946)

Marie-Simone had a convivial childhood in the district of Eaux-Vives in Geneva. "My mother made sure that I had dance, piano and rhythmic gymnastic lessons, and that I socialize with other children. Unfortunately, that also meant she would send me to some extremely boring summer camps."

She was compensated for the boring summer camps by being allowed to partake in wonderful vacations with her cousins in Braunwald. "In the valley of Glarus, far away from my French classmates, I could unabashedly speak the melodic Glarus dialect. I had skating lessons on the ice rink in front of the Grand Hotel. Mother invited us for tea in the elegant hotel, and then we returned to the simple farm of my uncle. There was no heat in the bedrooms. I slept with bags of cherry pits that had been heated in the large, tiled wood-burning stove. And I still remember the utterly unique smell and taste of the cheese my uncle fabricated."

There were also wonderful things, such as vacations with her cousins in Braunwald. (Summer 1946)

Marie-Simone recalls how often she was sick as a child. Coughs and bronchitis were her constant companions during the winter months. She still remembers the tiresome stays at the Lenk spa that involved drinking sulfurous water that tasted like rotten eggs. She reminisces, "Really awful and what a pain!"

Marie-Simone Ludwig was only fourteen when her parents separated and divorced. "I wasn't even unhappy. Life became calm, and there were no more quarrels at home." She stayed with her mother, yet the father's child support payments were not enough.

Bit by bit the world of the sheltered young girl broke apart. Her mother Babette had to find work and accepted a position as a private cook for a wealthy Italian family in Geneva. As "Madame Barbara", she created menus and supervised the kitchen crew. "In addition, mother cleaned offices in order to support the two of us. She fought valiantly, but in vain. She became ill with lung cancer and in early 1961 was admitted to a hospital for an undetermined time. Overnight, I was forced to become an adult."

At that time Marie-Simone was a student at the *Ecole Supé-rieure des Jeunes Filles* in Geneva, at that time a high school for girls only. She hoped that her mother would soon recover and return. She was now running the house and getting up early to do her mother's cleaning job in the mornings before school started. "On no account could mother lose this job." But all hope vanished when her mother died in June of 1962. "She must have sensed how serious her situation was and asked her sisters in a letter to look after me if she should die. She didn't want to bother my father with this. One of my aunts refused to take on this responsibility, but at least I was able to have my meals at the house of Aunt Vreni. Yet I never felt comfortable there, and her invitation 'you can come and go as you wish' always felt half-hearted. I felt like an intruder and if I wanted a piece of meat, I had to get it myself at the butcher's. Thus, I soon preferred to go to the parents of my friends where they simply added another plate. *Voilà!* These experiences were difficult, but probably best for me in the long run. I didn't owe anything to anyone, and during this time I may also have developed my uncomplicated French manner of thinking and shed the Swiss-German mentality for good."

One year before graduating from her college preparatory school, Marie-Simone lost her father. "He died of a stroke six months after my mother. I don't know how I managed all this by myself. It was incredibly hard and rather chaotic. I burned a lot of pans on the stove during that time. But somehow, things worked out. And I survived!"

No guardian was appointed for her. A lawyer settled her finances, and she was allowed to stay in the apartment. "Yet I had to take in a lodger, a woman who, with her active nightlife, was not exactly an appropriate role model for me!" Thanks to the help and moral support of her neighbors, friends, and friends' parents, Marie-Simone passed her final exams for the *maturité*, the diploma issued at the end of college preparatory schooling in the French part of Switzerland.

She prefers not to talk at length about the overwhelming sense of loneliness that permeated her life at that time, only to say, "The personal part of my story is mine alone. I learned to respect that boundary very early in life." Fortunately Maître Roullet became a part of her life. "During that first year without both my parents, my professor of literature introduced me to her best friend, Odile Roullet, a well-known Geneva lawyer." Maître Roullet became a positive influence on the young woman. "I liked her and trusted her. We met regularly and I had to talk about my life. Even today, I call her before making an important decision. During my entire life she has been a trusted advisor. When I travel to Switzerland, my first visit is always reserved for Odile Roullet."

In 1963 Marie-Simone enrolled at the *Ecole des Etudes Péda-gogiques* (School of Education) in Geneva. "This was not the education I had dreamed of, but I wanted to be able to stand on my own two feet as soon as possible and earn some money." At the same time she enrolled, together with four other women who had just graduated, as a student of law at the University of Geneva.

"Jurisprudence fascinated me. I was already dreaming of a career as a judge in juvenile court." At one of the many student parties she met an American medical student in 1966. He told her that years earlier he and his widowed mother had emigrated from Yugoslavia to the United States, and that his mother felt studies in a French-speaking country would suit her son. "I liked Branko Pavlovich, he was attractive, and pretty soon he asked me to marry him." Marie-Simone was surprised. "I was young. In my student circles almost no one was married, and we used to make fun of married couples." Marie-Simone Ludwig finished her courses at the School of Education and was hired as a grade school teacher in a suburb of Geneva. And she married. "My husband finished medical school. He wanted to return to America as he felt he had some obligation toward his new home country. He married me, so he would be able to take me with him as his wife."

The young doctor returned to his mother in the States for a few months in order to find work for himself and a place to live for the three of them. He found both in Chicago.

Marie-Simone Pavlovich clears her throat and becomes thoughtful: "I must have been very naïve. We married in 1967, and one year later I followed him to the United States without giving this decision much thought. No longer having an immediate family in Switzerland, I felt like there was nothing really holding me back, yet still..."

The definitive parting came in May 1968. This also meant that she discontinued her studies at the law faculty. Everything happened very fast. Branko Pavlovich returned to Geneva for his young wife, five big suitcases were packed, and "I didn't even finish the school year. I relinquished many of my belongings, not to mention my friends, my students, and of course, Maître Roullet. The latter took the parting with more understanding. One of her sisters was married in the United States, so she knew that one could survive such dramatic changes! Only then did I realize – this parting was for good."

Marie-Simone cried until they were in Le Havre. "I loved my husband, but I was inconsolable as it meant leaving for good!"

After a crossing of five days on the *France*, the young couple arrived at New York harbor. "My first impression of this immense city was: Horrible! New York was dirty, paper flying around everywhere. I could not understand how people could live in such dirt. I came from a country where people looked disparagingly at you if you threw a cigarette butt on the street. And I was frightened by the mammoth skyscrapers." From New York the couple traveled west by train for a day and a night – to a new world. The first months in America were a nightmare for the young wife. "The three of us lived in a modest two-room apartment. My husband worked as an intern in a clinic south of Chicago. He left the house very early in the morning and did not return until late." Marie-Simone had no occupation, didn't know anyone, or anything about life in her new country. And she spent her days in a small apartment with her domineering mother-in-law: "Since lack of room forced my mother-in-law to sleep on the couch in the living room, as soon as my husband would leave for work, she would come into our room every morning and climb into our marital bed, where she continued to sleep snoring loudly." Her husband didn't have the courage to confront his mother. "I was desperate and almost ready to pack my bags and return to Switzerland. I had to change something in order not to fall apart. Mike Kaplan, who worked in an employment agency in Chicago was my savior; even today I remember his name."

The Swiss teacher had good grades and spoke English and French. Within five days she had an interview at the library of Northwestern University in Evanston. "Typing skills were required, but I had none. Thus, one weekend, I plowed through a typing manual for beginners and sat down for the test the following Wednesday." She could have saved herself this drudgery. "You can't type at all, but we are hiring you anyway," they told her at the university. "Actually I never had to type; it was simply an entry requirement. But finally, after these horrible months, I was able to do something meaningful – and to escape my mother-in-law for at least a few hours every day."

At the University Library she came into contact with many interesting people though she had little taste for her work of checking out books and shelving new ones. "Antonia Fodor, my Hungarian supervisor, soon realized that I was not suited for this. She introduced me to various men and women professors as she thought I should study psychology. Yet this was not what I wanted. I had already met Americans who had problems and did not want to deal with their issues." One day she met the Chair of the Department of Romance Languages in the Library. "I immediately spoke French with him, and he invited me to attend some lectures. Some time later he offered me a position as a teaching assistant in his department." Thus Marie-Simone Pavlovich became a teacher of French and a student at Northwestern University.

"At home I could no longer tolerate to live under one roof with my loud and domineering mother-in-law. She wanted me to call her 'mother' but that was out of the question. I had had my own mother, and didn't need another one." When the young couple decided to move, they were met by strong opposition from the mother – "what will my friends think when you simply put me out" – but eventually, they found separate apartments in Evanston.

Her life in America became more normal. "I was now a registered graduate student at Northwestern University. I continued to teach between 1970 and 1972; I also prepared to take my exams in French literature (M.A.)." In the meantime her family grew. "In 1970 my son Ivan was born, and four years later his brother Alexander." Reluctantly, she asked her mother-in-law to watch the children. While she worked and studied, several au-pair girls took care of the children during the day. "In the 1970s, nannies were not unusual in the United States." Marie-Simone was ambitious and wanted to further her career.

While telling her story she realizes under what stress she lived at that time, and how many different roles she had to fill. In 1977 the family moved into a house of their own in northwest Evanston. "At first, the realtor didn't want to show it to me, but I begged her. It was love at first sight. We had to do a lot of remodeling, but the house was large, comfortable, and our home for many years. But I also wanted to finish my dissertation before my third child, Nicolas, was born in 1978." When the boys went to bed, she too would go to sleep. "But I would get up at 1 a.m. to work on my doctoral dissertation." With an iron will she finished her exams, and eventually her dissertation, *Aesthetic and Moral Reflexions on The Farces of the Middle Ages*, was accepted. Her study discussed mainly wittiness and roguery in the little comedies written at that period of time. Veiled humor has great appeal for her, and there was little research on this topic, the scholar says. She prefers not to go into detail regarding the years with her three children. She only remarks, "these were good and fulfilling years."

In the United States, her passion for the French language was unwavering. After having finished her doctorate, Marie-Simone Pavlovich was hired in the Department of French at Northwestern University in 1978, the very year her third child was born. Soon she was called *Madame Dictée*, Mrs. Spelling Bee. In her classes, she loves to have students write dictations, and as *Directeur de la Grande Dictée de la Francophonie*, she has been organizing dictation competitions for the American Association of Teachers of French and for the Francophone community.

In the United States, Marie-Simone Pavlovich is one of only a few Swiss women who are university professors. Would such a career have been possible for her in Switzerland? "No, probably I could not have done it the same way. Had I stayed in Geneva, I don't know if I would have remained a grade school teacher for the rest of my life. In the United States there were always opportunities for me to accept new tasks. As an immigrant from Europe, I had free reign. And I am convinced that in the 1970s things were easier than they are today."

Despite being very busy, and having a fulfilling life in the US, she never really forgot Switzerland. In the 1980s, she joined the Swiss Benevolent Society and in 1989 became President of this charitable organization that was founded in 1872 after the great fire of Chicago. The Society continues to organize events for its members to ensure that Swiss culture in Chicago keeps the honored place it deserves. Francophone culture is very important for her, which is highlighted by the fact that she was president of the *Alliance Française of Evanston* for ten years (1989–1998). For this work the French government honored her in 1998 with the title *Chevalier de l'Ordre des Palmes Académiques* – an order created by Napoleon 1st in 1808 to reward people's contribution to the French language and culture. She was promoted to the rank of Officier in December 2008.

For a third time, everything in her life was about to change again. "After 35 years of married life – 34 of them in the United States – I filed for divorce in 2002. It was a very difficult decision. Most of the time I am very patient, but there comes a moment when I am unable to tolerate things any longer. This also happened in my marriage." She does not want to divulge any details. "For my husband, the divorce was a shock. He probably never thought that I might lose my patience for good." The family home was now too big. Two of their sons were in France teaching English, the third studied in a different state. "I sold everything that I had grown to love." And she did something that, for years, had been unthinkable for her: "I organized a house sale. For two days, absolute strangers walked through our rooms, rummaged through everything, and bought what was left of our belongings."

Her analysis is very sober. "A part of my life was gone. When the house is gone, it is gone. *Fini!* That's it! Something else takes its place; life continues."

She never felt lonely. "Some people, however, no longer invited me after my divorce, presumably because the wives worried about their husbands. This is some sort of American psychosis. But I don't need to have somebody around all the time." After her demanding work at the university during the week, she enjoys being at home on the weekends, inviting friends for whom she cooks, or doing art. "I love colors. When I am painting I try to transform what I see into another reality. I love to see things from constantly changing perspectives. My own creations of collages and wall hangings in my apartment are examples of such alienating effects." Since her emigration from Switzerland, Marie-

Simone Pavlovich has carried a great dream in her heart – she wanted to have her own apartment in Paris, and thus have one foot again in Europe. "It was unreasonable, just a dream." In the summer of 2001, a few months before her divorce, she traveled with a friend from Geneva to the city on the Seine. "My friend consented to come along only on the condition that this time, I would not try to look for an apartment." And then what was bound to happen happened. Marie-Simone Pavlovich found "her" apartment in the 5th *arrondissement* (district) near the *Jardin des Plantes* a few weeks before 9/11. "A part of my heart now also belongs to Paris. I carry a Swiss and an American passport, as do my sons. I do not see myself as an American, but as a European in America. Academic women in America are usually very serious, too serious, and often do not understand my French humor. I like to joke, in my own way." The Professor of French literature has recently been bestowed with the title of *Distinguished Senior Lecturer*, and plans to teach a reduced course load, as she wants to retire gradually. "I greatly appreciate the contact with the students, and because my students are younger, I'm always feeling young also!"

She has by now lived longer in the United States than in Switzerland. "I enjoy returning to my old home country even though I have often experienced bitter disappointments in my country of origin. It really gets to me when a large bank dictates to me how much money I, as a Swiss living abroad, must have in my account in order to be of interest to them as a customer." Without hesitation she closed her Swiss account and transferred her money to Paris. Returning definitively to Europe during the latter stages of her life is out of the question. "This would be difficult. Given that my health is still intact, I hope to spend six months in Paris and six months here in Chicago. Life in a nursing home in Schaffhausen, my father's hometown, is inconceivable for me. Fortunately I have an optimistic nature. My life is stimulating. Something is always going on, or I will make sure something is going on. For every problem, there is a solution."

MARGRIT MEIER SIDLER

1938

Margrit Meier smuggled her first four geranium shoots from her brother's flower box to America. "Thirty years ago these were unknown in Hartland. We passed customs with the shoots wrapped in wet tissue hidden in a coat pocket." Today hundreds of those hanging "Swiss Flowers" adorn the windows of the Hartland Inn. They are a trademark of her inn and a counterpart to the large Swiss flag above the entrance.

On Monday the "House of Swiss Elegance and Friendliness" is closed. Thus the sprightly hostess who talks in the unmistakable dialect of central Switzerland finds time to sit down. "Welcome"! Margrit Meier Sidler is used to being a hostess. For forty-two years the Hartland Inn – 25 miles from Milwaukee in Lake Country – has been her life. "I am 71, and in work I can still measure up to the young. At nine-thirty in the morning I am the first in the shop and at night I am the last to lock the doors before midnight. I am always on the go, take care of purchasing and bookkeeping, watch over the kitchen, and take care of guests. That is my rhythm, and I like it."

The enthusiasm for her job gleams in her eyes. "My daughters are always teasing me and say that I was married to the Hartland Inn. And in some way it is true. Michelle and Monica know how much work such a business demands; therefore neither of them wants to take it over."

To tackle things is nothing unusual for Margrit Meier-Sidler. As a farm girl she had learned it early on in Rumentikon near Cham in canton Zug. She grew up with twelve siblings – eight brothers and four sisters. "We were far and wide the family with the most children. I am the youngest girl. My oldest sister is twenty years older than the youngest brother. And I was the first in the family who was born in a hospital, on March 2, 1938. Before me my mother gave birth to ten children at home."

"We were far and wide the family with the most children." Margrit, front row in the middle. (1940)

Everybody's lending a hand was needed on the 45-acre homestead in Rumentikon, a small hamlet of about a hundred people, without inn, church or school. "Each and everyone had a task – in the stable, in the household, in the fields. The cows, cattle, pigs, and chickens, as well as a host of apple and cherry trees demanded that all did their part. To gather apples is one of my most early childhood memories.

"Father was very strict and would not tolerate disobedience. What he said that was it, no argument. At the table during meals we were allowed to talk only when asked. If he realized we children were nudging each other under the table with our legs, there was scolding. I was afraid of my father. But I learned to adapt and remain silent. I had no choice. In contrast, mother was more easy-going, less heavy-handed; she understood me."

Margrit, delicate and sensitive, also reticent, followed her mother's every step. When folding the wash she could tell her things. "She would defend me when father was scolding. He often angrily observed that I would never become a farmwoman!"

At the Sidler's home eating yoghurt was already common in the 1940s. "A part of our milk went to Hirzel, the large cheese factory and dairy. In return father was obliged to accept yoghurt. In those days that was still rather uncommon. I remember how people envied us for the delicacy." Yoghurt was a desert for the family. For breakfast there was "Rösti", a kind of hash browns, on the table. "I grew up with Rösti. Plaited loaf with butter was served on Sundays only." Even as a little girl Margrit heard from her father that work was the most important thing in life, and math the second most important, "and that we would turn out right only if we obeyed and went to church."

In the 1940s her father bought a car. "It was one of the first in the area. But when my brothers had gotten old enough to drive themselves, father was against it. He just wanted none of it – and so he sold the car without ado."

For Margrit school was a child's play. "I was very adapted. The strict nuns of Menzingen who taught primary school in Niederwil impressed me but little. I was used to a hard regimen! But when father was against my attending secondary school,

I objected. Luckily, my mother stood up for me and I was allowed to ride my bike to the high school in Cham some kilometers away. After that I would have liked to become a teacher. The teacher training seminary Holy Cross was not far away. But father was against it and had the last word. I did not dare to contradict him."

It was also the nuns who organized a trainee post for Margrit in Fribourg. "I acquiesced, went to the Maison de la Providence which was a convent, a hospital, and an orphanage in the poorer part of the city of Fribourg, to help with cleaning, laundry, and ironing. In return I received free French lessons from the nuns and twenty francs pocket money per month."

After a year in French-speaking Switzerland, Margrit faced the decision: What now? "I did not want to work at home. Father had told me long enough that I would never become a true farm-woman. That as a 'shade plant' – a girl who liked to avoid the sun – I was not made for working with cattle and in nature. Well, perhaps he was right. The sun easily burned my skin. And I far pre-ferred office work from making hay.

"In the meantime one of my brothers had become a station-master of the SBB, the Swiss Railway System, in Grenchen. He wrote to me about a business that was seeking an office girl apprentice. Father was amenable because it did not cost him any money."

She would talk to her mother about her secret wish to one day manage her own hotel. "Already as a child I had a dream that later in life I would receive guests in a hotel and entertain them. I imag-ined that to be wonderful. I remember how I saw pictures of hotels in magazines. That impressed me."

During her first months in Grenchen Margrit stayed in the loft of her brother until she could rent a room in an attic from a widow. "I liked the work in the office of the factory that made golden encasements for watches. I had no trouble to master the three years of apprenticeship. I was adaptable and industrious. I had little contact with my landlady. But in the restaurant 'Gärtli', Little

Garden, I began to wash dishes to eat for free. I became friends with the owner's daughter and soon I felt at home there. I got to know the 'Fasnacht', the merriment days before lent, and I could dance. Dancing was wonderful. I had learned dancing at home from my brothers. When father was away, we would push the furniture of the living room to the walls and dance to folk music from the radio. Despite our strict upbringing we Sidler kids managed to have a lot of fun. Whenever we get together, we have many interesting stories to talk about."

After her apprenticeship Margrit went to work for a travel agency in Grenchen. "The traveling virus had gotten a hold of me. I dreamt of trips to faraway continents, and in addition I liked one of the bus drivers. He had a motorcycle, and that was superb. But nothing serious developed because my brother Johann, a mechanic who had emigrated to the United States, needed my help."

Being keen on traveling, that was welcome. Margrit took half a year's leave and in November 1957 left for Amercia with her sister-in-law and Johann. "Due to his contacts my brother was able to get me a visa within a week. Finally I was able to get to know a new world."

But she did not like New Jersey very much. "Everything in America was so big, out of proportion. And there was so much uncultivated land where only brushwood was growing. I could not understand that one did not cultivate the land as one did back home."

During the months in the United States, Margrit looked after her little nephew Richard in an apartment in New Brunswick. "I was often bored. Just to babysit was not that exciting. I saw little of the country, and I was daydreaming about discovering America later on my own."

Margrit eventually returned to Europe on the *Hanseatic*. "I wanted to experience a boat ride on the Atlantic. Although it stormed vigorously for three days, I was at the table for every meal."

For a short time she continued working at the Grenchen travel agency, but then successfully applied for a position as hotel secretary in Champfèr in the canton Grisons. The new position brought her a step closer to her childhood dream.

Life in the hotel of an elderly Dutch lady-director was wholly to her liking. "In the morning the boss only took a quick look at the office, otherwise I saw little of her." Margrit was the only secretary and, besides free board and room, earned 400 francs a month. "I took the reservations, checked in guests, and wrote the bills."

After the death of the owner two years later, the hotel was closed and Margrit had to look for a new job. She found the idea of a summer season at the Hotel Alpenblick in Braunwald enticing. It was to last two years. Margrit loved her work as a hotel secretary there and made many friends in the Glarus region.

Then she becomes quiet. "Then, suddenly, in one blow, my life changed." She swallows, fights tears. "My mother died in 1961, wholly unexpected, during my time in Braunwald. She, who had never been sick before. It was an enormous shock for me, the worst that could have happened. The pain is still with me. I was very attached to my mother. I completely lost the ground under my feet, I lost my homeland, and I felt very lonely. Except for my two youngest brothers all of my siblings were married. There was nothing anymore to keep me in Switzerland. I wanted to travel, to go abroad. It was not for nothing that my friends had given me a thick atlas for my twentieth birthday.

"One day Elisabeth, my Braunwald office mate, came in running. In a magazine she had found an exciting ad: Near Lands - end in Cornwall, England, a small hotel on the canal was looking for people taking on service and reception. We applied and got the positions. "It was a hard school. As employees we had meager salaries and little to eat. Luckily, the guests used to receive some cheese with their evening aperitifs. What was left over we would hide in tablecloths and dug it out at night. I wanted to move on. Southampton, London, Jersey were places where I further worked for some months in hotel business. I think that I lived mainly on fish and chips for the year and a half in England." America remained the dream of the young woman from canton Zug, and so she applied for a visa.

Meanwhile her father had called his youngest daughter back to Switzerland. "Although I was over twenty, I obeyed, with little enthusiasm for sure. And I was clear about one thing – as soon as I would get the visa, I would emigrate. I took on the household for the widowed father and the two brothers."

Quietly Margrit looked for a job in America in the ads of the Hotel-Review. When after a year the desired visa finally arrived and she had signed on as a waitress in a first-class hotel in Madison, Wisconsin, there was nothing to keep her back any longer. "I did promise my brothers that I would come back and help them in the office of their newly established transport business. Sometime, whenever!"

In Southampton she boarded the *Rotterdam* bound for New York. "I had arranged with my brother Johann that we would meet on May 20, 1964, at the port of New York. Everyone else was met but myself. For hours I sat there, abandoned on my large ocean chest, and waited and waited. I was not afraid. I knew Johann had never been on time his whole life! Finally, shortly before it got dark, he did arrive." For a few days Margrit was his guest before she flew on to Milwaukee. Three elegantly dressed gentlemen met the Swiss at the airport. "They were a German physician from the town, a Swissair steward, and the head chef of the hotel where I was to work. They were on their way to a party – did I want to come along? What was I to say? I had no choice. Thus I enjoyed my first evening in the Midwest at a barbecue in Pewaukee on one of the many lakes of the region with the Swiss family Good. That evening was also the first time I came in contact with a Martini. Thank God I drank it slowly."

After the party, the young cook brought Margrit to the Park Motor Inn, her new place of work, directly on the town square in

Madison. "My driver was Max Meier, who was very attentive to me. I found him attractive."

Margrit did not suffer from homesickness. Her days were far too exciting. She worked in the Café Corner, then in the more refined Heritage Room, at the front desk, in the bookkeeping office, and soon everywhere in the hotel where someone was needed. She was viewed as efficient, helpful, and cordial, and the guests liked her. "Management wanted to send me to a larger hotel in Des Moines, Iowa."

But meanwhile Margrit had become a close friend of Max Meier who was eight years older and now working as Food and Beverage Manager in Green Bay. "He came to visit often, and we dated. But I think he didn't take the relationship too seriously. I heard that he was also dating other women. After three years in the United States I considered returning to Switzerland. I felt that Max wasn't quite sure what he wanted. Furthermore I still had to keep that promise I had made to my brothers."

But things were to turn out otherwise. "One day Max called me, sounding serious. He needed to talk to me right away. On the sofa in my little apartment he proposed. 'Would you marry me? I like you, you're pretty, and kind.' He then put the ring of his mother with a small diamond on my left hand. To be honest, I was perplexed. I had not expected that. And of course I said yes. I thought to myself, perhaps I am actually the best of all! We then decided that our wedding should take place on August 26, 1967."

Suddenly things became hectic. "A few weeks after the proposal, Max called me with excitement. Would I also manage a restaurant with him? A friend had tipped him off that there was a restaurant for sale in Hartland, Wisconsin. Together we took a look at the place. I did not particularly care for it. On the other hand, such an opportunity would not turn up again any time soon. The restaurant, a historic 19th century house, had first been a beer brewery, later a hotel, and was one of Hartland's special points of interest. It was also supposed to have a large patronage, we were told. In addition, it was centrally located, and for me the best asset was its wonderful bar.

"The area around Hartland with its hills and lakes reminded me of Switzerland. Only the mountains were missing. Max signed the contract by himself without my signature. But I was his partner from the first hour on. Max had many good friends who lent him money. We both also contributed all our savings so that we could have our own business."

The young couple now had its hands full. At the Hartland Inn in Hartland, they had to clean up, make purchases, and arrange things; the wedding preparations turned wholly marginal.

From one day to the next the two faced an unexpected problem. "The Catholic pastor of the village of 800 people would not allow us to live unmarried in the Hartland Inn. We proposed that Max would sleep on the left side of the 11-room apartment on the upper level and I on the right side. But the clergyman found that wholly improper. And so – until our wedding – I spent my nights at the house of the Good family on the lake. Every night Max would bring me there after cleaning up the restaurant and came to pick me up again in the morning." Margrit smiles. "It was ridiculous. Nobody believes such a thing nowadays!"

On the evening of June 17, 1967 – three months after the purchase – Max and Margrit opened their Max Meier's Hartland Inn. Many came out of curiosity. Everybody wanted to look over the new owners from Switzerland.

Not everyone was welcoming, though. Margrit remembers: "One woman from the village came towards me and said: 'What are you thinking? This is Hartland. You will never make it in Hartland!'" But the couple was young and enterprising. Such threats would not intimidate them. "Let's see how it goes was our guideline.

"We had to prove that our menus were tasty – fondue, veal cutlets, and the Swiss Geschnetzeltes." The Meiers brought a European style to Hartland. "At the end of the 60s, people in

America were used mainly to beer and liquor. We introduced the culture of wine to the region. One could also get wine by the glass, perhaps a Fendant or Dôle from Switzerland."

To this day the business is called Max Meier's Hartland Inn, although Margrit has been managing it by herself since the death of her husband fourteen years ago. "Max always wanted that our restaurant would be called Max & Margrit's Hartland Inn. I found it simpler that only he, the chef, was mentioned by name."

And like a late declaration of love Margrit adds: "Max was simply the best. He was good looking and fun. He always had a joke ready. He got along well with everybody. And he used to stress in front of guests all the time: 'I have one partner only, and that is my wife.' We got along well, were a team. He was in the kitchen, I with the guests. Often he would come out of the kitchen and say to me: 'Go sit down a bit; I will take care of the guests.'"

Besides the demanding life as new restaurant owners, there was also the impending wedding. "My brother and sister-in-law arrived from New Jersey, Max's brother from Hawaii. Otherwise no family members were able to come. It was a merry feast with many of Max's friends. He was the president of the Swiss Club of Milwaukee at that time and knew a lot of people. Understandably we didn't have time for a long wedding trip, but at least I could now officially move into the Hartland Inn."

After the first months in business Max and Margrit realized that to succeed, they also had to cater to the American taste. "The people of Hartland, almost all related to each other, let us know without a doubt that we were outsiders; they had not waited for us in any way. We were the only Swiss in the village. But we didn't give up.

"We were the only Swiss in the village. But we didn't give up." (1987)

"Besides our typical Swiss specialties we started carrying BBQ Ribs on Thursdays, Fish Fry on Fridays, and of course sandwiches. Luckily, people who lived on the lakes and knew Max's culinary arts from before when he was a cook at the University Club in Milwaukee, did not drop us either."

Finally an article of a gastronomy critic of a regional newspaper made the Hartland Inn popular. "He wrote enthusiastically about our kitchen. And almost from that day on we were sought after. When we opened, often there were already guests at the door. On December 2, 1967 we organized our first Open House – a tradition we still maintain today. On that day guests are served free of charge; the first year there were about thirty; today we regularly have about two hundred people."

In September 1968 the first daughter, Monica, was born. "I worked less in the business. But we soon had to realize that I was also needed in the restaurant. We were still living in the large apartment on the upper level then. After the birth of our second daughter Michelle, we decided to buy a house on the outskirts of the village. The children should be able to grow up in the green." Soon au-pair girls from Switzerland took care of the two girls so that Margrit could again put more work in at the Hartland Inn. The children went to the local school and used to have lunch with their parents at the restaurant.

Today Margrit observes with some regret: "Perhaps, I did indeed not have quite enough time for our two children. But Max needed me also. Without my help, the business would not have flourished. And our two girls were easy to handle."

The early 1980s brought some difficulties. "After the expensive addition and renovation of the restaurant for which we had to borrow much money from the banks, interest rates doubled in the shortest of time. We reached our limits and did not know whether we could keep up the restaurant. At the same time, a worker at the bar had been cashing in for himself. It had been a long time before it came to our attention. Max had fully trusted his long-time friend – until he had to realize that dismissal was the only way to go! That was probably one of our biggest disappointments. We calculated and calculated. But, actually, we had no choice. Had we given up, all would have been lost. And Swiss don't do this – give up and simply declare bankruptcy – do they? I cannot understand

how Americans can do it without further ado – to declare themselves unable to pay and to start over again somewhere else." In
1984 Margrit decided to become an American citizen. "Max had
been a citizen for a long time and he told me: It is important that
you are an American, too. Should I die before you, you would lose
the liquor license.

"I am not sorry to have become an American citizen; I am
happy here in the United States, although I have remained Swiss
at heart. I can adjust well to the mentality here. I think Americans
are generally friendlier than Swiss and not as reserved. They do,
however, talk about very private things quickly. That is not quite
my line. At work I find some of the young people sometimes less
reliable, also more superficial. Max and I, we started with much
solid effort, with a typical Swiss approach of reliability, quality,
and exactitude."

"I am not sorry to have
become an American
citizen, although
I have remained Swiss
at heart."
(Hartland 1985)

In 1993 Max Meier became seriously ill. He had to have a heart
operation, received a triple by-pass, and shortly after, physicians
diagnosed cancer of the prostate and also Parkinson's disease.

Margrit is unable to continue talking. She apologizes, takes out
a handkerchief, and wipes her eyes. "In 1998 my husband died. I
was immensely sad and felt totally abandoned. I found myself all
alone with that large business. Many thought that the widow had
to give up, that the restaurant would be up for sale cheaply – that
the Hartland Inn could be had for a song!"

But Margrit Meier showed strength. "I decided to continue for
the time being and took the restaurant into my own hands. The
chef, who had been with us for fourteen years, gave notice two
weeks after Max's burial. But somehow, with the help of good
friends, I managed. With a lot of effort and new good cooks I could
keep up the standard. Luckily, my daughters also helped. Monica
and Michelle supported me in many ways. This makes me very
glad; it takes some of the burden off. But both now also have heir
own lives and positions. Michelle still works with me part-time
and is helping me with all kinds of different jobs and decisions. I

am very fortunate to have an excellent chef in the kitchen. He is very hard working, reliable, and prepares great food. Thanks to a great staff – some have been working for me for many years – the restaurant is still going strong and our wonderful guests and friends keep coming back.

"Honestly, gradually I could also imagine selling the business. It would be beautiful if a young Swiss chef would want to realize his dream of having his own restaurant in America. If need be I could also be of help. I could go on seeing my guests. But I would not have to shoulder the whole responsibility any longer.

"I don't want to complain. But I would not be as tied down anymore. I could travel again. I would like to go to Brazil, to the Dominican Republic, or to Australia. And also for a longer time to visit my many relatives in Switzerland." Margrit returns from her dreams: "Max used to say: 'Now we have made our bed. Now we must sleep in it.' In America much has become possible for us. Max and I, we stood by each other; we hardly ever quarreled. What counted for me was to do my tasks as well as possible. I was used to that from home. America gave me much self-confidence."

MARTHA BERNET 1927 ZUMSTEIN

She deftly adjusts the controls of the studio soundboard: "Good afternoon, it's time for our Swiss folklore program on station WEKZ. I hope you find time to listen." Radio broadcasting has been a part of Martha Bernet's life for fifty years. Last year, her coworkers at the station gave her a trip to Switzerland. "You are our calling card!" they said.

On the homepage of the local station, WEKZ, Monroe, Wisconsin, she is called "everybody's Swiss sweetheart." Martha is one of the gang among the mostly young studio crew. And no one would guess her 81 years as she bounds up the studio steps. "Our program is the last Swiss radio program in the whole country. I'm on the air six days a week from 1 to 1:30 p.m."

She began with 78 records in the 1950s when her predecessor, who was in a serious traffic accident and suffered a heart attack, asked her to fill in. "I never thought I would enjoy it as much as I have." And after the 45 and 33 records, it is now her own CDs that she plays for homesick Swiss six days a week.

"I always record two weeks in advance. I announce each piece in Swiss-German and then translate, although terms like 'Mischtchratzerli' prove somewhat difficult. At the close of each broadcast I sign off in Swiss-German 'Sisch wider alls für hüt. Ich hoffä, z'Programm heig Euch gfallä. Uf Widerlose, morn zur gliiche Zyt. That's all for today. I hope you enjoyed the program. Goodbye until tomorrow at the same time.'" Martha Bernet's broadcast area reaches far beyond Monroe. "I receive messages from Texas, Chicago and even Seattle from people who hear my folk music on their PCs. Oh, how I'd miss radio if I couldn't do it anymore."

Martha Bernet invites me for coffee and cake in her "Swiss chalet" in Monroe.

Permanent red geraniums decorate the windows, and near the entrance stands a tall spruce tree she received decades before, smuggled in as a present from Switzerland. Her brother had sneaked it into the United States, she explains in her broad Bernese accent. She has lost none of her mother tongue.

"I have been over there 35 times. I say over there when I mean going to Switzerland. It's a wonder that after 60 years, I'm still at home in both places." She explains proudly how every day before breakfast she logs on to the *meielisalp.com* webcam. "That way I know how the weather is there. The *Blick*, the *Berner Zeitung*, and the *Oberländer* are my daily online news."

Actually, Martha resisted using a computer for a long time. "Ten years ago at dinner with my children, I made a remark that I was becoming dumber by the day; that I was not exercising my brain enough. And before I knew it, there was a computer in the house along with lessons from my oldest son. And today, what would I do without e-mail and the World Wide Web?"

An aerial photo of Lake Thun hangs on the wall behind the corner table in the kitchen. "Because the photo didn't fit in my suitcase, my nephew cut off Interlaken. The important thing is that Leissigen is there." Wherever one looks, Martha's house is rich with Bernese decorated pottery, Albert Anker paintings, and carved furniture and cows.

"I will not fly to Switzerland any more. As I walked down the path past my family home one last time, and when finally the lake disappeared from my view, there was certainly a pang in my heart. But I said to myself, 'Martha, you have always been able to persevere. You can do this, too.' You know, I am also an American. My former school friends in Switzerland have all moved away; the old people in the village have passed away."

Martha returns to her life story. "I was born in Leissigen on Lake Thun on April 16, 1927. I grew up with two sisters and two brothers. I was the youngest and the spoiled one. My oldest brother was 18 when I was born. It was as if we had two families. My mother always said, 'Thank God we had you three later; that's how I stayed young.'" Father Ruedi was a mechanical technician and the village civil registrar and notary; mother Frieda, a lady's dressmaker.

"I was born in Leissigen on Lake Thun on April 16, 1927."

Then Martha smiles. "Don't ask me what I had for dinner yesterday, but I still remember so much from the past." Her eyes flash

mischievously. "For example, when I was six, I pretended to leave home. Mother said, 'I don't want you anymore. Child, if you can't behave, then leave.' I promptly walked out in my messy apron to the train station and got on the next train. I told the conductor I had to go to my aunt in Müntschemier. In Bern, I knew that I had to descend the platform stairs where a woman in a blue frock would be standing, a 'Friend of Young Ladies.' She would bring me to the train. I didn't need a ticket yet, and when we reached the station, the conductor brought me to one of these ladies who, sure enough, waited with me for the connecting train to Müntschemier.

"This was still possible in those days. No one suspected anything since I was so self-assured and knew the way from trips with my mother. But my aunt was shocked when I appeared on her doorstep. 'Where is your mama?' 'She didn't want me anymore. Perhaps you still want me, auntie?' I wanted to give my mother a scare. But the tables were turned! She sent a basket with my clothes, and didn't come for me for three weeks."

Back then there was no kindergarten in Leissigen for the precocious girl. "However at the age of seven, I was finally able to enter the first grade with Miss Frutiger. I still talk with her regularly on the phone. In the meantime, she is 92 years old. Back then she was such a young teacher; that was wonderful. For me, learning was always easy."

Martha's childhood was affected by the war. "It was a big upheaval. We always had soldiers quartered in our house throughout those years. We planted fruit and vegetables at three different locations in the village. Vegetables and potatoes were growing in every flowerbed. There was very little fat in our house because of rationing. Everything was boiled. No more buttered hash browns, and only one quart of milk instead of four. There was a quarter pound of butter per person per month: one pound of sugar, one pound of flour and a quarter pound of coffee or tea. I remember it very well. We preserved or dehydrated what we could. Instead of chocolate, we ate slices of dried apples and pears. There was no fresh bread for sale, and we never saw rice for the entire war. Despite that, there was always singing in our house and we never went hungry."

"Mädi," as they called the youngest one in the Zumstein house, learned how to play the card game Jass from soldiers. That would earn her a scolding from the teacher that she would never forget. "Was that unfair! One morning the teacher in the ninth grade approached me menacingly with his signet ring shining on his hand and said, 'Martha you were playing Jass until midnight. I know that for a fact.' 'No, teacher, I did not. Every fool knows that soldiers have to turn in by 9:30.' There was a big to-do at home. I was supposed to apologize to the teacher for my smart remarks. But I couldn't. I hadn't said anything wrong."

Martha taught herself to play the accordion. "I retreated to the topmost floor of the house where no one would hear me. I searched for the notes and sang and yodeled along. Here this accompaniment is called 'cording.' It wasn't long before I was able to recognize the different keys. And then one summer day, when I had opened the attic window, I heard a neighbor say to her husband, 'Turn on the radio. They are broadcasting folk music.' I must have played pretty well."

After graduation at age fifteen and a half, Martha moved in as a maid with a family in the French part of Switzerland. "Under the auspices of the 'Friends of Young Ladies,' first in Peseux and then in La Chaux-de-Fonds, where besides doing housework, I learned to eat escargots, snails." Rather than a maid, Martha wanted to become a home economics teacher. "But my father felt that it would be unfair to my siblings to underwrite such an advanced education. Fritz became a mechanical technician, Elsbeth a seamstress. They only required three years of training. I would have had to attend school for four years in Bern." So at sixteen, Martha was only able to attend secretarial training in Interlaken. "Twice daily, I rode the train from Leissigen to Interlaken and back. That these

Rather than a maid, Martha had wanted to become a home economics teacher. (1941)

train rides were to determine my future was the farthest thing from my mind." An angry argument about an open window in third class on the Bern-Lötschberg-Simplon (BLS) train was to be the start of her love story.

"The young BLS conductor reprimanded me for opening the window to the frosty winter air for a better view of Lake Thun and to let some fresh air into the stuffy compartment. 'What are you thinking? You should be ashamed of yourself! We have the heat on!' And he slammed the window shut. I found that rather rude, and only back at work in the office with time to think about it, did I realize that he had been right. Sheepishly, I apologized to him the next day on the train. After that, we always greeted one another especially cordially. I liked him, and we occasionally had a short chat, but we remained proper and formal, Mr. Werner Bernet and I. Bit by bit, I learned more about his life. Out of a clan of 17 children, his father with wife and children migrated from Grindelwald to Wisconsin, USA, where the father, Christian, worked in a cheese factory. The children, Werner and Trudi, attended school there until their father became ill in 1939. On the recommendation of his doctor to take a year off to recuperate, they decided to visit Switzerland. Werner intended to return with the family to America in the fall of 1939 where he had a four-year scholarship to study forestry. The mobilization for war on September 1 preempted his plans. As a Swiss citizen, he was required to enter basic military training. After completing his service, still during the war years, he learned French in the French part of Switzerland. Then out of 300 applicants, he was given one of six desirable positions as a conductor on the BLS Railroad.

"One day, at age eighteen, during my second year of secretary schooling, shortly before Interlaken, Werner asked me, 'what are you doing Sunday?' He invited me up to the Kleine Scheidegg. It would be nice, I thought, but I would have to ask my mom if she would pay for the ticket. The hike through the Bonera was unforgettable and romantic. Under the Eiger [mountain], we agreed to address each other informally. 'When people know each other so well, they don't call each other Mr. and Miss anymore. I'm Werner and you are Marti.' Then he kissed me. Yes, under the Eiger. When I look at the webcam picture, I think, yes, under the Eiger."

In 1946 the Bernet family wanted to return to the USA. "I was finished with my training. Werner and I we were still an item, as they said back then. But it was clear from the beginning for him that he wanted to return to the US. 'If you don't want to come with me, then we should end it now.' I assured him that I wanted to come along.

"Suddenly, word came that if we married within six weeks, I would be allowed to go along. Otherwise, I would have had to wait for another two and a half years for a visa. I was overwhelmed being just 19. One had to be twenty in those days to sign one's own marriage certificate. Our parents conferred about the whole situation. Finally dad said, 'If he were the same age as you, I wouldn't sign. But, he is ten years older than you and no longer a young lightweight,'" she recalls.

"Werner knew nothing about any of this, and I wanted to surprise him in Spiez where he had an hour layover between trains. 'Werner, we have to get married right away.' He looked at me wide eyed. 'But not to me… .' And I laughed at him, and said, 'Not that… we have to get married so that I can come to America with you!'"

In haste, they were married in November of 1946. "I had no time to put together a dowry. In any event, it was said we couldn't have taken it with us." Then everything came to a halt. "Every time we would have been able to go, Americans were given preference. It turned to winter and then to spring, and Werner's parents took over management of the Niesenbahn Restaurant for the summer season. I did not look for a job, but waitressed in my in-law's business. Our visas would have expired on October 2, 1947."

Werner had had enough. At the beginning of September he decided to appeal to his godfather, his father's cousin, Federal Councilor Nobs, a member of the Swiss government. Then at once everything went very quickly. "On Wednesday he called, and by Thursday morning at 10 a.m., we were both in the *Bundeshaus* [Federal Capitol Building]. At 2 p.m., we had the transit papers." By the following Sunday, everything had to be packed and ready to travel. Fortunately, the restaurant lease had already been terminated. "But a mere four days was a bit abrupt. Dad said to me, 'and the accordion, don't you want to take it along? One never knows.' When I think of how much joy it has given me in America! I packed my clothes and a few souvenirs: a little book with birthday greetings from my classmates and my drinking cup. But the accordion and my husband were the most precious things I took along." On that Sunday along with 16 large trunks, the six members of the Bernet family – parents-in-law, Martha and Werner, and his recently divorced sister with her young child – emigrated once again to America, first by train to Genoa, and then aboard the SS Marine Shark over the ocean towards New York.

The departure from home was difficult. "The morning of our departure, we attended church in Leissigen and visited the cemetery. My oldest brother had died in May 1946 of kidney disease. I can still hear my mother at the grave lament in a thin voice, 'Here in the grave lies my oldest... and today my youngest is going to America.' That was very hard for me. I reproached myself for abandoning my mother.

"Father was less demonstrative, but as I was already standing on the train platform, I heard him shout, 'you'll keep on singing, won't you. Then everything will be alright.' And that proved to be so. As I looked out the train window, I saw how mother collapsed in my father's arms. One can never forget a scene like that."

On the Atlantic, Martha was violently seasick. Thankfully, she remembers little of the six days on the open ocean. "When we arrived in New York, I was fortunate that I didn't have to be vaccinated. My doctor had forbidden it, because I had had my appendix removed just three weeks before our departure." Werner and Martha intended to move to Colorado into the mountains. But the mother-in-law was drawn back to Wisconsin, and Werner did not want to leave his parents by themselves. In Juda, Wisconsin, he took a job in a cheese factory. He wanted to make Swiss cheese again, Emmentaler.

"And me, the spoiled secretarial student, had to scrub, cook and do laundry, and work like a slave. In March, a year and a half after our wedding, our first son, Hans, was born. Life was difficult, no fun at all. I had to bite my tongue often. I couldn't speak English. We were out in the country. The summers were unbearably hot and humid. We had no air conditioning. We struggled. I weighed just 89 pounds. Werner said, 'If you go down to 85 pounds, we're returning to Switzerland.' But I wouldn't get that through my thick skull. I could already hear people gossiping, 'they wanted to go to America, and now they've had to come back.'"

"I said to myself, 'it will get better'." By fall, her appetite had returned and she slowly improved. "It built character. I learned a lot. If you have the will, you can persevere. I simply tried to pull myself together. But I was homesick, and cried when know one could see me. There was no way that I wanted Werner to know how much I was suffering. And outside there were the cornfields as far as the eye could see, cornfields only. I imagined that beyond them on the horizon were mountains. But there were none. I cried and cried."

The little family moved to Jordan Valley. "There we had a house to ourselves. I no longer had to work so hard, so I could spend time with the little one and soon with my second baby, daughter Käthi." But Werner was looking for something of his own. "He bought a cheese factory in Dutch Hollow. Again there was much heavy work. But this time we were working for our own benefit. I enjoyed making cheese. When the children were still small, we would place them in a large cheese kettle padded with a blanket. They played in there. Today they would say, 'That's child abuse; you can't do that.' But things were good."

The Bernets produced Emmentaler for a large company in New York. "Four wheels a day, about 200 pounds apiece. Learning by doing, I became a cheese maker's assistant. Getting up at 4 a.m. became my routine. I washed 84 centrifuge plates every day. One day, I asked myself how other maker's assistants quenched their thirst. They drink a beer. So that is what I did down in the cellar. I became so tired that I fell asleep right on top of the cheese press. 'Want a beer?' Werner would tease me for years to come."

Son Peter arrived in 1956. "I worked until the day he was born. At ten past five p.m. I arrived at the hospital, and at six o'clock the 10 pound boy had already arrived."

At the end of 1956 Martha traveled with Peter back to her former home for the first time in nine years. "And I flew for the first time in my life. It was a terribly long, 22-hour flight. From Chicago Midway four hours to New York, and after a long wait for the Swissair plane, we finally took off. Because of a snowstorm we had to make an unscheduled landing at an American airbase way up in Greenland in minus 40 degree outside temperatures."

The weeks at home were wonderful for Martha. "My parents always said that it had become so quiet after my departure, that no one made them laugh anymore. I travelled very little and stayed mostly in Leissigen with my son. The high door thresholds were great fun for him. There was nothing like that in America. And I savored the time with my parents. If anyone wanted to see me, then they should come to me, I thought."

Upon his little family's return, Werner picked them up at the new O'Hare Airport in Chicago. Far and wide there was no hint of a huge terminal building. "There was just a little shed where Werner drank a cup of coffee until he could walk directly out onto the tarmac to hug us as we descended the stairs from the plane."

The economic situation for small cheese factories in the early 1950s became more and more difficult. Large tanker trucks were enlisted to haul milk to larger processing centers. "We sold the factory, and Werner worked for a time on his cousin's mink farm until a small specialty store in Monroe was offered to us. We jumped at the chance, and soon 'Bernet's Cheese and Sausage

Shop' was open seven days a week. I became a member of the church choir and finally had the opportunity to sing again." In 1952 Martha was one of the founders of the Swiss Club of Monroe with over 400 members. "The club doesn't exist anymore. Everyone has passed away. In the 50s and 60s, many West Europeans including Swiss came to the area. Now, we are just about the last ones remaining."

In good times the Bernets imported 10,000 cowbells a year for their store, Tobler chocolates, and Knorr soups. "I was the first one to bring *Aromat* to Monroe. The sample shipment of 24 tins was a runaway success. Now, *Aromat* is found all over the USA." They offered brätzeli irons, scythes, and music boxes, but cheese and sausages were their specialties. Martha loved the business. "Our little shop was located behind a bar and grill. In 1957, we paid $25 a month rent – including heat and water. We had the opportunity to move up to the main shopping square in Monroe, but we did well where we were." Then came another boy, Ruedi, in 1959. And businesswoman Martha traveled regularly to Switzerland in search of items for the shop.

In 1973 Martha and her husband won a trip to Switzerland.

In 1973, they won a trip to Switzerland: "From the Tobler Chocolate Company. Not for our large sales volume, but because we had a particularly attractive chocolate display in the shop. We had ourselves photographed in front of the display." Werner in his Swiss cow herder's jacket and cap, Martha in her Bernese Sunday costume. For the first time, the two vacationed together, and closed the store for a whole week. "That was something, our 40-strong travel group. In Bern, we were put up at the Bellevue Palace Hotel in a room with silk comforters and crystal chandeliers hanging from the ceiling. But the beds were so soft that I decided to sleep on the floor. When I awoke at 5 a.m., Werner was not in the bed – he was on the floor too. We had a wonderful time. In the evenings I wore floor-length evening dresses. Werner held the chair for me like a gentleman. 'Just don't expect me to do this at home...' he grinned with a wink. I was just happy that he knew how to do it at all." At the close of the 1970s, a singing quartet asked her to join them. "That's how I became a member of the *Edelweiss Stars of New Glarus*. In the 80s and 90s, we appeared throughout the region; we were well known. We appeared at First of August festivals and on holidays to sing and yodel. Having a woman who helped to cover for me in the store... life was good."

In 1983, the Bernets sold their business. "Werner was 65. The entire following year we traveled: to Switzerland and to visit my daughter, who in the meantime was living in Canada. In 1984 after a memorable August 1 celebration, my husband simply didn't wake up. That was a shock. He lay dead in bed. He was hardly ever ill. He had had a heart attack. He simply stopped breathing. He left me without saying adieu. That was hard. Only later did I remember how at the first of August festivities, he had sat on the stair watching me play accordion... as if he were saying goodbye. My sister, who was visiting at the time, said on the way home that night, 'Werner is still in love with you like he was back then.' That is how he said goodbye.

"It was hard, very hard. Our anniversary came, no Werner; his birthday, no Werner. Christmas – Werner missing again. I simply couldn't believe it. It was five years before I was again able to say that I enjoyed life. But I can never forget him. Even 25 years later, I still sit at the kitchen table and look at the empty chair, and I long for him. Thankfully, I already had my radio program.

"No, I could never have married again. Naturally, there were days when I could have sent him to the moon, without a return ticket. You know, that happens in any marriage. But I miss him so."

Life went on for Martha. In 1985, she spent a month in Switzerland with the *Edelweiss Stars* at the National Yodel Festival and many other appearances.

"Maintaining Swiss culture here in Wisconsin is difficult. I am eighty. I won't be here much longer. Trudy Thomman is 84; Margrit Affolter is 85. They came to America the same time I did. I could speak Swiss in every store on the shopping square. But the traces of Switzerland are slowly disappearing. You see that in the telephone directory. It used to be that 80 percent of the names were Swiss. Now they're gone. When you visit Monroe now, the Swissness is mostly a facade.

"On the other hand, I feel that I am also an American. I have friends and was in the church choir for 44 years. Our church is only active because we members contribute to it. We employ two ministers and have a budget of $400,000 a year. I belong to the altar committee and to the group that prepares communion. At home in Leissigen in one of the oldest chapels in Switzerland perhaps 20 attend church on a Sunday. Here we have three services every Sunday. Eight hundred people attend. Why? It certainly isn't that we are closer to God here. But churchgoing is a social event. Between services there is coffee and cake, cookies and cheese. We exchange the latest news with one another."

Martha's thoughts turn to her children, visibly with pride. "Hans will soon be 60. He studied to become a teacher, but today he is a manager for the cataloguer, The Swiss Colony. Via catalog and online, they sell cheese and Swiss specialties throughout the USA. Kathy is 58, married to a Canadian hockey player; she had lived for several years in the Northwest Territories way up in the arctic. Peter lives in Washington and is an analyst. And Ruedi is a physical education teacher here in Monroe.

"I have a joyful disposition, even if now and again it is hard. I always sang and laughed. People often ask, 'Martha, do you have any new jokes?' Werner was more of a pessimist. I always told him that he should have a hobby. His answer was, 'I have one, you!' He supported me with the radio business and the performing. He told me, 'it wouldn't have been possible without you.' It is true; we always pulled together. I have had an interesting life and still have many dear people around me. Once a week, I play *Jass* with three others. We are two men and two women. And of course, the men assume they are the better players."

MARIANNE BURKHARD

1939

"Welcome to a place apart... a place of renewal and hospitality" beckons the invitation in the unusual pamphlet. St. Mary Monastery in Rock Island is located out of the way in the country side, about 160 miles west of Chicago. Small roads lead to the monastic community. The neighboring town is called Milan, and after a last, long, stretched-out curve, the modern building fits harmonically into the landscape of wooded hills and a small lake.

We are the guests of Marianne Burkhard – of Sr. Marianne. The Benedictine sister wears a skirt and a blouse. Where are habit and veil? "As American sisters we do not want to distinguish ourselves in our external appearance from the outside world," she says and leads into the house which corresponds more to our idea of a modern conference center than to a monastery.

Sr. Marianne has come to the motherhouse for a few days. "In Europe nuns live mostly in cloistered monasteries. When Benedictine nuns came to the United States in the 19th century, they were engaged as teachers for German speaking immigrants and lived where the people lived. And later when they had built their own monasteries, the sisters often lived in smaller houses near their schools and returned to their motherhouse only during the summer. I am living with three of my sisters in Peoria, the diocesan See city, in a house owned by the community. Even though I am not living here, St. Mary Monastery is my main home – here is my stability of heart." The delicately built woman with short grey hair seems reserved, almost shy. One can sense a monastic modesty. She speaks slowly, not without emotion, but with careful deliberation. In accent free Zurich dialect she talks about her life, which took a very different turn from what she had imagined when she was a young student of German literature in Zurich in the 1960s.

Marianne Burkhard, born 1939, comes from an old Protestant family in Zurich. "My father was proud of the fact that our ancestors were already recorded in the registers of 1340. Ever since the Reformation, the Protestant, Zwinglian heritage was greatly esteemed in our family."

She is a *Zuriseemeitli*, a girl from Lake Zurich: "As a child I often sat reading near our house at the lake or, daydreaming looked toward the high mountains of the canton Glarus or toward the ever more gentle hills surrounding the lake in the west, in the direction of Zurich. I felt that I was at the intersection of two worlds and think that both of them gave me much."

Marianne is a Zuriseemeitli, a girl from Lake Zurich. Here in a rowing boat near Feldbach. (Around 1943/44)

Her mother, born early in the 20th century, came from the canton Glarus: "She was happy to leave the narrow valley between the high mountains when she married my father, the son of an agronomist and a member of the Swiss House of Representatives." Marianne's brothers, Paul and Eduard, were eleven and nine years older; "I grew up virtually as an only child."

Mother Burkhard was religious and anchored in tradition; gracious living was important to her. "I always knew: there was our family and then there were other people. But my parents were congenial, did not look down on others.

"My childhood friends came from a modest family and were welcome. For my mother it was important that we played at our house, not somewhere else." And above all, she wanted a good education for her youngest daughter. "She herself would have wanted to go to the university, but in Schwanden, where she grew up, her mother did not see the need to have a daughter with a university education."

After grade school in Feldbach, attending the Gymnasium for girls, a college prep school in Zurich opened the way into a new world for Marianne who was eager to learn the way into the world of knowledge. "This world fascinated me, especially literature." One of her classmates was a Catholic and knew early on that she would enter a convent. "With certain wistfulness I thought that if I were a Catholic, I could also consider such a decision." From childhood on all things Catholic with their rituals and mystical connection had a mysterious attraction for the Protestant girl. "The atmosphere in the monastery church of Einsiedeln fascinated me. My sensitivity for spirituality always existed hidden under the surface, though it was not nourished." After finishing the Gymnasium she wanted to study literature."

She joined the ecumenical group of Pastor Vogelsanger from the Fraumünster in Zurich. "His sermons were fascinating. I found it unusual that a Protestant theologian would even preach about Mary. Thus I again came in contact with the Catholic Church. My mother had little interest in Catholicism, she saw Protestantism as intellectually progressive while Catholicism seemed close to superstition."

She fell in love. "But my friend and I were not really compatible. In my early life I always thought I would marry some day. This would have been my goal had I found the right partner. Yet at the same time there was always also a feeling that perhaps this may not be my path. In my 20s I struggled with this emotional back and forth. I had several relationships; sometimes I broke up, at other times it was he who said it was over. She smiles. "This was difficult at times. Yet remaining single attracted me also."

Her studies helped her to get over lost loves. After having finished her course work at the University of Zurich she wrote a dissertation about the Swiss writer, Conrad Ferdinand Meyer. "His wife, Luise Ziegler, was the sister of my paternal great-great-grandmother. My parents had been personally acquainted with Meyer's daughter, Camilla." Marianne had an intuitive under-standing for Meyer who had married late after having gone through a long and difficult personal crisis before finding his creative voice. "I knew from my own experience how important it is for the old Zurich families that their children stay within the customary family framework."

After getting her doctorate in German and French literature Marianne Burkhard thought she would teach in the Gymnasium, but the editor-in-chief of the daily newspaper *Zürichsee-Zeitung* in Staefa unexpectedly offered her a position as newspaper editor. She learned the journalistic craft from the bottom up and was the first woman among the paper's editors. Though she was responsible for the cultural section, "I wrote about all kinds of things with the exception of sport and fashion." On Fridays and Saturdays she took the early shift. "The paper went to press at 7 a.m., this meant that I had to be in the office by 4:30 a.m., for by that time all the news from the United States had arrived over the wires and needed to be sorted for possible inclusion in the day's paper."

Soon Marianne Burkhard was mentioned in the list of editors, but she also experienced some opposition among colleagues. "An older editor later told me that he had serious doubts and had no idea whether a woman in the editors' office would work out at all!"

For many years Marianne Burkhard was the first and only woman among the paper's editors and responsible for the cultural section. (1964)

During her time as a journalist at the newspaper she also discovered a budding interest in politics. "At the beginning I was not for women's suffrage in Switzerland. Yet suddenly I woke up and realized that I understand politics as well as my colleagues. Thus I began to revise my traditionally conservative views about equal rights."

Her main love was her work reviewing plays. She would attend the first performance in the evening in Zurich, write her review at night and take it to the office – 15 miles away – early enough that it could appear in that day's paper. She remembers the hectic pace in the editorial office: "I learned to write fast. Finding a good title often took longer than writing the actual text." Working on the editorial team was the antidote to her academic work during her studies. "When you write a dissertation, you are all by yourself in your little room.

"Yet as time went on I realized that I missed scholarly endeavors because the newspaper work did not provide me with the possibility of devoting more time and a more intensive study to a specific topic." In high school she had studied French and Italian in addition to the mandatory Latin, but now also felt the desire to learn English. "If I wanted to see myself as an educated person, not knowing English in the second half of the 20th century was certainly a deficiency." Marianne Burkhard contacted a professor at Yale University who had written a book about C. F. Meyer. "He recommended that I look for a larger university in the US, which would have a good library if I wanted to do some academic work."

In the spring of 1968 she had to choose from a long list of positions in German Departments in the United States and Canada: The University of Illinois in Urbana-Champaign offered her a position for the fall semester. "I was ready to expand my world. And I thought that in the United States, women in academia would have an easier life."

She planned to stay in America for a year or two. "But soon I realized that Switzerland seemed too narrow for me. This certainly also had to do with my family and their very definite ideas on how my life should develop. Yet in the United States I was free. I was who I was – without the burden of family expectations."

She never really suffered from homesickness. "Right away I felt comfortable living in America. Here I was able to shape my life without having to satisfy some ideals that were not my own. This felt good." She learned English rather quickly, especially with the help of the works of African Americans. "I devoured these books."

After three or four years Marianne Burkhard knew that she wanted to stay in the United States. "My mother never came to visit me. The ocean was like a psychological barrier, and perhaps she did not want to see what I liked better in my new home than in the old one. I didn't feel it would be right to try to persuade her to come. My father had often remarked that America had neither cathedrals nor old castles. My objections that the cultures of Native Americans were much older failed to make an impression. For my parents America was a foreign world." During the summers Marianne Burkhard went back to visit her Swiss home. "As time went by this became more difficult because I no longer fully belonged to the world there."

In Urbana the young Swiss woman was Assistant Professor in the German Department of the University of Illinois, a large state university with about 35,000 students. She taught German language and German literature, published articles and gave presentations at conferences in the hope of being promoted and given tenure. "As a woman I still had fewer chances but nevertheless I worked harder. At this point I experienced discrimination personally." When she came up for tenure, the lifelong position, she was rejected for flimsy reasons, a rejection she did not accept. "Although I probably could have found another academic position at a different university, I found the rejection unfair, a discrimination against me personally and against women generally."

She began to fight. "Since I did not have a family to take care of, I dared to go out on a limb." She became more and more interested in the legal and procedural aspects of her case. "It got to be a long and wearing, time-consuming process. I had to go from one university committee to another to defend myself."

Thus she discovered a pugnacious side in herself as well as a flair for the law. At first she hoped that her appeal would be resolved in six months. But the multiple evaluations and committee negotiations eventually lasted for two full years. She won her case and was promoted to Associate Professor of German with tenure. Shortly thereafter, in 1978, she published a second book on Conrad Ferdinand Meyer. At the same time she felt a certain emptiness.

"I realized that my spiritual life had fallen by the wayside. In academia people do not talk about religious matters. Scholarly research is the main criterion as well as the number of publications." This was no longer satisfactory for Marianne Burkhard. "Perhaps I should do something for my inner life after having won my case? But I did not know what this would be. Sometimes I told my friends, perhaps I will do something entirely different in my life." She toyed with further studies perhaps in psychology or law.

"I told my friends, perhaps I will do something entirely different in my life." (1980)

At a workshop for teachers of German she met John, a lay Franciscan. "With him I had long discussions about religion. He told me: 'You remind me of some of the good nuns who taught me in school.' Utterly dismayed I asked: 'Why do you tell me this?' A bit later he sent me a rosary. For me the Catholic Church was a real problem; women can't even be priests!" From that time on she felt drawn to attend Catholic Mass from time to time. "I didn't really know why. I began to read the Bible again and corresponded with John. At some point he wrote saying: 'You can't wait until you find the perfect priest and the perfect church. Don't you realize that God is always much bigger than any church?' This statement hit me like a thunderbolt out of the blue. Why hadn't I ever seen that? It didn't make sense to get upset about the Catholic Church. But where should I go with my longing?"

Marianne began to search. "On a Monday morning in 1983 I went to a small simple Catholic Church in Urbana. I liked it and registered for an introductory course in Catholicism that was offered at the parish. Only later did I realize that the priest at St. Patrick's was one of the very best in the entire diocese. Yet how would I tell my mother that I felt at home in a Catholic parish?" With a practical and sober common sense she said to herself: "We'll cross that bridge when we come to it." In January 1984 her mother suddenly died. "My first reaction was: Now she understands everything, she needs no more explanations."

In the same year the faithful Protestant Marianne Burkhard became an equally faithful Catholic convert. At the Easter Vigil 1984 she celebrated her first communion and her confirmation. "When I became Catholic I realized that now I belonged to a Church which at least offers community possibilities for people who do not feel called to marry. But I want to emphasize that I did not convert to Catholicism in order to enter a religious community." Yet she doubts that she would have converted in Switzerland. "I experience the Catholic Church in America as very open, uncomplicated and welcoming. On Sundays churches here are filled with people, from babies to great-grandparents. The Church is alive. And American Catholics who were outsiders when they immigrated to the United States, were poor farmers and factory workers, have worked their way up over generations. Today they are educated, prosperous, and no longer a marginal group. The Catholic Church in the United States is much more attractive to me than the one in Switzerland." Marianne Burkhard still was a committed professor of German in Urbana, even spent a semester as a visiting professor at the University of Notre Dame in South Bend, Indiana. "I felt that I was being sent there, but I didn't know for what."

There she met a Benedictine sister who helped her to learn to pray. "I didn't really know how to pray." Through her parish priest in Urbana she met Sister Audrey who invited her to visit her Benedictine community in Nauvoo, Illinois. "It was incredibly beautiful there, almost idyllic; because of a dam the Mississippi river is very wide and reminded me of Lake Zurich. I felt that this was a landscape of my soul." After Christmas 1985 she again spent some days in the community. "And when I got into my car after New Year's Day, I knew: I cannot leave here any more."

The Swiss Professor was by now 47 years old, taught German and German literature, was the proud owner of a house, earned a good salary, and had opportunities to advance in academia. She was a US citizen and well established. Still, she missed a deeper meaning in her life. "Monastic life attracted me more than ever. Several of my friends were concerned about what would happen with my education, my scholarly activities, if I buried myself in a monastery."

In August 1987 Marianne Burkhard entered the Benedictine community of St. Mary in Nauvoo as a postulant. Nauvoo is a small town in Illinois on the border of Iowa and Missouri, two hours from any larger town; it is also the town which Joseph Smith, the leader of the Mormons, had chosen as refuge in 1839 and later built up into the main see of his church.

Marianne Burkhard sold her house and all her possessions. She took a few things with her: a book shelf, two small oriental rugs and a small painting of Luise Bodmer-Escher, a great-great-great-relative who belonged to her father's ancestors. "I have always had an anti-consumerist attitude. Money and possessions were never very important to me. I was always attracted by the fact that Benedictines try to live a simple life."

In the monastery she worked as receptionist and in the house cleaned stairs. "I was by no means unhappy. For Benedictines there is no work that is more valuable than another." Obedience, subordinating herself was, after decades of independence, much more difficult. "There were, and still are, situations which require struggling that can be wearisome. People can be difficult. Again and again we have to let things go. Since I have been in the monastery, I have never been bored intellectually. Earlier I saw knowledge and faith as absolute opposites, but here I have learned that intellectual knowledge is less important than wisdom.

"When I look at the older sisters who have less education I realize that by living the Benedictine life they have gained a deep wisdom of which I had not been aware. What I was looking for in religious life is an integration of knowledge and wisdom. And I have found the possibility of achieving this in a religious community rather than in an academic one."

As if speaking to herself she continues: "Probably, there was a monastic element in me since childhood. As a young woman I often thought I might become the director of a school with which I would entirely identify. It has always been important for me to be fully involved in something. I also became aware that my 'enemies' are often my own wishes, desires and ideas in which I am stuck. I would like this or that – to have it my way and preferably right now. Often we feel certain in knowing what form the solution to a problem should take, yet at times there is no actual solution. Inside us, however, something is being loosened making the situation less wearisome. When I am able to deal with my inner difficulties and 'enemies' I no longer feel the need to revolt."

Did Sister Marianne feel a clear call to enter the monastery? "Yes – but realizing its nature took a long time and is difficult to express in words. There was something, first not very clear, a sense, an inner longing that stayed with me and never disappeared. The fascination the Catholic Church had for me as a child, vacation experiences I had in Italian churches full of incense, the beautiful vestments of the priests, the entire atmosphere. For me coming from Zwingli's Church which is almost devoid of sensate liturgical elements, all this was fascinating, a child's dream. But there was a deep inner longing that did not let me go – and one day I knew: I cannot not do it!"

She never regretted her decision to enter the monastery "even though this life is not always easy. I know that in order to grow spiritually, I have to pass through some dense, dark woods." Citing the Rule of Benedict she says, "it is important for a Benedictine sister that she truly does seek God, sincerely and consciously striving 'all the days of our lives.' For me this is a deep desire. God is always present to me in some way, everything is connected to God, and everything that I do is worship, is service, is in Benedict's words, opus Dei, 'work of God'." To some extent she also sees herself as a feminist "though not as one who mounts the barricades. I am the type who wants to work within the system. I have never had the feeling that I should be able to be a priest. I am not called to the priesthood myself, yet I would welcome it if this calling would be open to women," she says.

"I see Jesus as a sort of feminist. What we read in the gospels about women is quite amazing. For instance the story of his encounter with the Samaritan woman: by addressing her directly, Jesus breaks two taboos at once. A Jewish man did not speak to a woman in the public square; Jews did not speak with Samaritans who no longer lived the Jewish faith nor fully accepted its laws. And Mary Magdalene was called 'the apostle of the Apostles' and legend says that she went all the way to France. Spiritually and intellectually she was an equal of the Apostles."

In 1990 Sister Marianne made first profession, promising to remain a sister of St. Mary in Nauvoo for at least three years. At that time she worked as coordinator of religious education in a parish, more or less enthusiastically. "It was the position to which I had been assigned by our Prioress." Shortly after her profession the Bishop of the Peoria Diocese asked several religious communities of women, including the sisters in Nauvoo, whether they might have a sister who would want to study canon law, the law of the Catholic Church. "He had the intention to educate a sister for the diocesan Marriage Tribunal because sisters were able to work five days a week in the office while priests always have two or three additional jobs besides working in the Tribunal."

The prioress in Nauvoo proposed Sister Marianne "being fully aware that I had not yet made my perpetual monastic profession." Sister Marianne met with the Bishop, letting him also know she was a convert. "I only had to promise that after my studies, I would work for the Diocese for 8 to 10 years. Then he would pay for my studies."

Half a year later Sister Marianne – who was now over 50 – registered at St. Paul's University in Ottawa, Canada. In 1993 she returned after four semesters with a Licentiate in canon law and began to work in the diocesan Marriage Tribunal. Two years later she made her final profession as a Benedictine sister of St. Mary Monastery. In the Tribunal she worked first as Defender of the Bond and then became a Judge, the first woman to have either function in the Diocese. "We have to carry out a delicate task. In our Church a marriage is only ended by the death of a partner or by a canonical process that declares it to be invalid. Canonically there is no other solution for people who want to remarry in the Catholic Church. Thus we try to find out whether in a particular marriage something essential was missing from the beginning, which then allows us to declare it as invalid."

Is this still appropriate today? "This is the doctrine. Only an Ecumenical Council would be able to make any changes. The Catholic Church never said that people are not allowed to divorce, but that after a divorce they are not allowed to remarry in the Catholic Church, and if they remarry civilly, they are not allowed to go to communion. People from all classes and of all different ages come to us to petition for a declaration of invalidity." Marianne Burkhard tries to speak with all petitioners personally – she knows about their struggles. "It is easier to find certain details in a direct conversation, and I always have a lot of clarifying questions."

Each case that receives a positive decision has to be confirmed in a Second Instance Court that functions as a sort of quality control. "Our formal annulment cases, about 120 per year, are usually confirmed." Yet only 10 to 15% of all divorced Catholics submit their cases to an ecclesiastical Court. "These people come to us because they feel downgraded to second-class Catholics. And after a new civil marriage they would like to return to full participation in the sacramental life of the Church."

Sister Marianne finds her profession fascinating. "It has a certain detective aspect, and the life stories which I hear are impressive in so many ways. We especially like to help people who needed much time before approaching us. As judge I am now interpreting real-life stories instead of interpreting literary texts.

I think it often does make a difference that a woman is looking at these marital stories and not a man. While I have never been married, I have seen many marriages from close up and have talked with women friends who are, or were, married. I suspect that as a woman I am more sensitive to the difficulties that arise from details in the everyday marital relationship."

Marianne does well in her work, and in 2004 she was promoted to Tribunal Director. "People say that in the United States there are a large number of annulments. Many people here take the religious consequences of a civil divorce very seriously, while I think that Catholics in Western Europe no longer care. Negative decisions are often difficult for me; then I can only pray, 'God, You need to help these people; I did the best I could.' And I believe that God has ways of helping people which we can't even imagine."

In the meantime the monastery's boarding high school for girls in Nauvoo was losing students and in 1997 St. Mary's Academy had to close. What next?" In a careful, democratic process, which lasted about two years and involved all the sisters, the community of Benedictines decided to sell their buildings in Nauvoo and to look for new buildings or for a place to build in the area of the Quad Cities, 100 miles north of Nauvoo. "In an area where our sisters had taught for decades in the Catholic schools, we were seeking a quiet place for ourselves and for all the people who want to come to us for retreats."

On the 125th anniversary of their foundation, on October 15, 1999, the entire community came to the edge of Rock Island, to the 90-acre property that they had purchased.

"We blessed the land. We all took part in planning our new monastery, making many suggestions. Of course they could not all be incorporated. We had a building committee, and I can say that it was the community that directed the building process. In 2001 we were able to move into our new monastery – a modern, practical building with much light, looking out over the wooded, undeveloped hill of our land."

How would Sister Marianne describe herself? "I have always had the ability to empathize which I could use well in my literary studies and which I use both in my work and in community life. I am an introvert and rather reserved. I like to listen. At times I have to tell myself not to wait for too long before saying something."

She smiles. "I am very interested in people's lives. I have a deep desire to help people, to show them how God is working in their lives. And I have learned to be patient, which was often very difficult. Anyone who tries to grow spiritually learns that we can find meaning in things or events that at first seem hopeless and devoid of meaning. Perhaps there is not much exterior change, but there are ways to reconcile ourselves with life, they are being shown to us, and we are given the grace to accept them."

What about returning to Switzerland? "No, I am staying in the United States and in my community. And for the time being I am working in the Tribunal. In addition I have a long-term research project. First I thought I would not begin until I 'had time', yet I might have to wait a long time for that moment," she adds. "I am researching the spiritual history of the Benedictine sisters who came from German-speaking countries to the United States in the 19th century. I am looking for German books which the founders of our monasteries brought with them from their monastery in Eichstätt. In some archives of our monasteries there are manuscripts written in the old German script, which soon no one will be able to read any more. The lives of these monastic pioneers fascinate me. Just think about it: These women came from a cloistered monastery in Germany – and some from Switzerland – to the United States and had to find their way establishing a new community in the midst of the huge woods of northern Pennsylvania. They were successful in transplanting their Benedictine life and adapting it to an entirely different situation and laid the basis for most of the communities of Benedictine women that still exist. And a little later Benedictine nuns from Sarnen, Maria Rickenbach and Melchtal also founded American daughter houses – they all did it with much patience, trust in God, courage and perseverance."

To return for good to her old home country was never a possibility Marianne Burkhard considered. On the other hand she always made sure to keep her Swiss dialect alive. "I have always paid careful attention to my language; I didn't want to lose it as it was my profession, and Swiss German is my true mother tongue. I consciously use German when I write my diary. I am also very aware of how much my home country means to me: Switzerland shaped me, and without it I would not be who I am. This is important to me. Yet in order to realize myself I needed more. The landscape of my childhood is always present in my heart. That is sufficient."

ELSBETH BOLLIER BÜCHE

1924

Red letters spell out André's Confiserie Suisse on a brick house on Main Street in southwest Kansas City. A Swiss flag flies in the hot summer wind. Elsbeth Bollier is a handsome woman with lively, mischievous eyes who wears her white hair pinned up; she welcomes us at the entrance to the store. At the age of 84 she still works every day in the family business – as she has done for almost 55 years. Right now she comes from the kitchen where she cut 30 lbs. of chicken meat for the lunch menu. "Wherever there is an urgent need, I will help out. Our employees sometimes tease me: 'You are a tough old cookie and you can be bitchy!'"

Elsbeth Bollier laughs heartily. "This is not untrue! I was always strict. When I expect something from people and know that my expectation is on target, there is no other way. But I'm also one to have fun with."

This morning there is a constant coming and going in the shop. Customers wave, exchange a few words with her. She seems to know them all by name. In the display windows Engadiner Nut Tortes lure, Grand-Cru Truffes, Chocolate Almonds, sandwiches with ham, salami, Tilsit and Emmental cheese, small cheese tartelets and small Matterhorns made of chocolate butter cream and cake finished with white fondant snow. The tea room is furnished like the main room of a Swiss chalet, and the menu might include Chicken Vol au Vent, Bratwurst, Raclette, or other typical Swiss dishes. "We also serve Swiss fondue but do not sell alcohol. At the very beginning we were advised not to offer alcohol because criminal organizations might extort protection money from us. In the early years customers could bring their own wine and we charged a nominal $0.50 per bottle for service."

In authentic Basel dialect Elsbeth Bollier tells us proudly that by now the second and third generation of the Bolliers work in the family's business: their son Marcel and his American wife Connie manage the business and Elsbeth's grandson René joined them a few years ago. Yet Elsbeth is the CEO and André's Confiserie Suisse is her life. "I am happy that at my age I am still able to work.

Nowadays, my workplace is mostly the office. All the bills go across my desk – just as on the first day in October 1955."

Elsbeth was born on November 2, 1924, the only child of Fritz Büche, a postal employee in Basel, and his wife Rosa Büche, a ladies' seamstress. "In my early years we lived close to the Ciba factory. As a child I saw many of the workers drink some brandy before work and again when they went home, probably as an antidote to the chemicals with which they had to deal in the chemical industry!" Grandmother took care of the household because Elsbeth's mother was busy in her dressmaking shop. "From early childhood on I developed an independent nature and a healthy self-confidence that I may also have inherited from my father. He always told us how he had been among the first workers on strike in Basel. He was not a 'red' and never participated in demonstrations or protest marches, but he found it unfair that workers had no vacation and their working days were far too long. He fought for the 48-hour workweek. Because of his participation in the strike the postal service did not promote him. My mother was the more vivacious, more energetic of the two; she would occasionally give me a slap in the face. She also made sure that, as an only child, I had opportunities to be among people. Already in kindergarten I was allowed go to the studio of Radio Basel to recite poems in the programs of radio pioneer Haussmann. For me this was nothing extraordinary and did not impress me in the least. Important for me was playing hide and seek, being outside, swimming in the Eglisee and reading. I was playful, not particularly interested in school. I had lots of girlfriends with whom I have never lost contact.

"At the age of 14 my mother wanted to send me to a boarding school in the French part of Switzerland. As this was out of the question for me we agreed that I would spend a year with a family instead. In the house of the Forestier family in Jogny sur (above) Vevey I had an excellent time; I was never homesick." With boys of the same age Elsbeth attended the village school, learned French easily, and enjoyed being educated in a free manner. "I fed the chickens and pigs, sometimes butchered a cock, helped with cooking, served as attendant at the gas station, and in the fall I helped harvest the grapes in the vineyards of Madame's relatives. 'Mimi, come have a glass of wine' was part of my life at fifteen." Elsbeth smiles, "in the vineyard I had my first kiss because I had left out one plant – this was the customary 'punishment'. I remember him well – his name was Ferdinand, he was from Chardonne."

After her return to Basel the bright Elsbeth Büche had good grades in the Oberrealschule (10th to 12th grades) and would have been accepted at the teachers' college. "But my father did not want an educated bluestocking; as he said, he preferred a secretary, especially since I would marry soon anyway and have children. A position in an office at that time was something special, thus I had no reason to oppose his plan."

Her father found work for his daughter in a firm that sold office machines. "Was that ever boring! In the middle of the war I left and went to Bell, a large butcher firm. As most men had to do military service, I was able to take on much responsibility when I was just 20 years old. In the train station of St Johann I controlled the Bell trains and their loads all by myself and in between I served as the main receptionist. I did this until someone called my attention to an open position at Singer's, which at that time was the largest pastry shop in Basel with 16 branch stores." Elsbeth never did an actual apprenticeship, but thanks to her diligence she worked her way up, attended evening courses and soon was responsible for the personnel.

"I made more money than my father, and it was part of my job to bring the employees their pay envelopes. When I had to bring his first pay to a Mr. Bollier, who had just joined the firm, I asked him for his employee number. 'I don't have one, I am part of management' was his somewhat uppity answer." The handsome pastry chef, who had moved to Basel from Lausanne, soon set his eyes on Elsbeth. "I liked his French charm, but I did not let it show.

Instead I avoided him and had another office employee bring him his pay. One evening, when I was in the streetcar on my way into the city, a man next to me said that some crazy guy was running after the streetcar – could he possibly be running after me...!"

"In time we went out with each other. I liked André; I was never bored in his company. He was entertaining, had a flair for art and created the most beautiful pastry decorations that I had ever seen. Once I even walked with him on foot from Basel to Aarau – he was a triathlon athlete. And he asked for my hand in marriage because he thought that we got along well. My father was happy and wanted to arrange a large wedding in 1948, but then he died of a heart attack two months before the wedding; thus, we only a small wedding – too bad!"

The newlyweds moved into the large apartment with Elsbeth's mother. "Mother was as dominating as a general. I was used to her regime, and André accepted it with equanimity. We knew it would only be a temporary solution." André was ambitious and very capable; he had even written a book entitled *Swiss Confectionery: An Illustrated Manual for Progressive Pastry Chefs*. Elsbeth helped him with the pictures for the book that became a classic in the field of pastry production.

Soon the committed professional received an inquiry from Spain. "Chocolat Tobler was looking for a specialist in developing chocolate candies. But they hired a Spaniard, and a position at the Côte d'Azur did not work out either. After the war the French did not like to pay salaries to Swiss – their argument was that we had been profiting from the war."

Therefore a letter from André's brother Robert in the United States arrived at the right time. "Come. Here in America you will have a future," he wrote. In the meantime Elsbeth was the mother of two small children: Marcel was born in March 1950, Denise in December 1952. The family now lived alone in the large apartment of Elsbeth's mother who had moved out because the apartment had become too small.

Then came a shock for the family. "Our pediatrician told us that Denise had cystic fibrosis, that from birth her pancreas was not correctly developed. Yet we had no idea that the doctors did not give her long to live. My mother knew, but didn't say anything in order to spare us additional worries. Denise suffered from constant diarrhea, she could not digest food; I cooked a special diet for her. It was a very difficult time for me. I also missed my work at the office; somehow I felt dissatisfied, hemmed in. My husband had an interesting profession while I was always at home. I was not fulfilled; I missed the contact with people."

For Elsbeth America was the desired challenge. The dream of having their own business, of the many opportunities in an immense country – enthusiastically described by Robert Bollier – convinced Elsbeth and André in 1955 to pack their suitcases, to sell all their furniture, and to emigrate.

"My husband was the driving force, and I said: 'Yes, let's try it!' To tell the truth, I was reluctant to say goodbye to our nice home. I knew that the summers in Kansas were very hot, yet I dreamed of another world where there would be new opportunities for me as well. I was rather naive then, America was a dream, and we were young and adventurous."

Elsbeth still has the letter to her mother in which she described their trip to the United States. She quotes: "Dreams of America... to travel to the States with two children, to give up a good position in Switzerland while not having anything in hand seemed a bit crazy even to ourselves. These were probably the thoughts that accompanied us while we were traveling along the Rhine, and looked with some nostalgia at all the lovely small towns and villages that we would not see again for a long time. Around noon we drove to the harbor in Rotterdam and the landing place of the *Holland-America Line* where we boarded the *New Amsterdam*. We loved life on the ship. Our stomachs were greatly challenged as the selection of dishes was huge. As soon as we were on the open sea, one person or another was at times absent, and the faces of passengers often had a slight greenish tint. Our steward advised us to take some good brandy, and thus we were spared of seasickness. We do not know whether this was the result of the Dramamine pills or the brandy. I had a hard time to leave the ship because I sensed that now the great change was imminent. We arrived in the port of New York at sunrise, and though we knew the sight well from movies and photos, we were quite impressed."

"We loved life on the ship." (1955)

With twelve pieces of luggage and their two children the Bolliers arrived in hot Kansas City in June 1955. The first few weeks they lived with Robert Bollier and his wife. The heat was especially hard on little Denise who soon had to be taken to a hospital. Elsbeth suffered because of her sick child and because she felt homesick, "yet I didn't really know what I was homesick for." In retrospect she realizes: "Fortunately, I seldom had time to reflect."

André worked for five or six weeks as a pastry chef in a Jewish country club, but he wanted to establish his own business as soon as possible. The family moved into a small house in the city. "Then we rented office space on the first floor of a house on Main Street, in a quiet part of Kansas City. Swiss people who knew their way around had advised us to get established in this part of the city." With some Swiss workers from Kansas André remodeled the rented space into a store – they painted the walls, installed electrical connections and set up the store. They did it all in just a few weeks. "We were full of hope. André brought with him excellent professional training and experience. We had no money, but we wanted to establish a business that would be just like one in Switzerland with regard to the quality of its products, its appearance and service. Mr. Brändli, a Swiss hairdresser whose salon was close by, loaned us the first $5,000 for the store. I will never forget that – he did it with a handshake. In the meantime he is 88 years old, and I still have him cut my hair out of gratitude and friendship." At the end of October 1955 Elsbeth and André Bollier opened André's Confiserie Suisse. "We had many Jewish clients from the very beginning; they came because we were Swiss and because they knew André from the country club. From the first hour I worked in the store, in bookkeeping, in the bakery – wherever I was needed. When the store opened at 8 a.m. I was there, six days a week. André made everything that we are still offering today: pastry, confectionery, and chocolate in every kind of form. We were the first *Confiserie* in Kansas City. Fast food had just become established in American minds and kitchens and for many, fine food simply meant beer and barbecue. Chocolate and chocolate candy, *Pralinés*, were neither known nor popular though pastries, *Patisserie*, and cakes were." With a smile Elsbeth says: "Even then it was said that Americans were overweight, and in this respect our smaller Swiss cakes fit much better!"

Elsbeth and her husband worked hand in hand. "I know that without me we would not have made it." At home she engaged a Black woman to help with the children and the household. "Of course, I had a bad conscience that I worked so much outside the home, especially with our sick child. Often I took Marcel with me early in the morning, and on the way I told him all kinds of stories that I invented myself. We walked to the store, very unusual in America. At the beginning we only had one car, which my husband needed to use."

Elsbeth remembers well how they had to count their pennies in the first years. "In winter when it snowed, not many people came to the store. Marcel washed the baking sheets in the kitchen. And when he saw that the cash register was pretty empty, he offered to shovel the driveway for our neighbor and put the 25 cents he earned into the register!

"But somehow we always made it. Our earnings were invested right away back into our business – for instance, into one of the first air conditioning units which was important for our chocolate. I never had more than $15 per week for groceries for our entire family. Fortunately we could bake our own bread, and we stuck together, we were a team. Yet it was clear: André was the boss and I was the boss behind the scenes. André began work at 4 a.m.,

"We stuck together, we were a team."

later at 5 a.m. Neither of us was crazy about money, we only wanted to establish a good business and a work place with a good atmosphere."

Denise's health declined more and more, no one could help her anymore. Her doctors were powerless against her illness. "Our little daughter died when she was five years old. A mother's worst experience is to lose her child, horrible. Denise died in my arms, and we were so far away from Switzerland. But I had to function, and I believe that in such moments we are given the strength to carry on. At that time, and again when my husband died of cancer at the age of 64, I thought that I could not let myself go and show my sadness, or young people would no longer come to us. My motto was: Elsbeth, pull yourself together! The deaths of my child and of my husband were the worst times in my life." Elsbeth takes a deep breath as if she were again trying to repress all her life's difficulties.

In her thoughts she returns to their everyday life of long ago. "André's" was doing very well. "As time went by we were able to hire people, people from Switzerland, too." People talked about it: The "Confiserie Suisse" was unique and its chocolate delicious! The Bolliers worked hard for their success with Elsbeth always out front. "What was our recipe for success? Perhaps friendliness. It was important to know regular customers by their name. We also began to send chocolate and chocolate candy all over the country as we are still doing today. We hardly adapted our recipes and products to an American taste. Our chocolate candy and our cakes, the chocolate bunnies and Santas are the same as those in Switzerland. The recipe for the Napoleon is Swiss, only the fondant color is different, pink as they like it here." What does Elsbeth like to eat? "I love our croissants, the whipped cream Glacier Torte and the Engadiner Nut Torte. But actually I prefer salty things to sweets. "

Elsbeth was pregnant again. "I felt panicky – would my third child be born healthy?" In October 1958 came the birth of a healthy girl, Brigitte. The family's joy and relief were immense.

"My sister-in-law was a great help to me. She watched the little one because I had to be in the store. Every light cough of the baby scared me. But fortunately there was nothing wrong; the little girl developed beautifully and soon crawled back and forth behind the counter. Thus I was closer to the children when they needed me.

"I was happy. I had really taken root in America and loved being a businesswoman. I could have said I wanted to stay at home, and we simply would have not been as well off. What a gift it was that later we were able to purchase a beautiful house with a yard just a few minutes from our business."

The Swiss Club in Kansas had an important function for the Bolliers from the very beginning. "Shortly after our arrival we celebrated the 1st of August with our compatriots. Thus we quickly met a lot of people. In the 50s about 250 people gathered at such celebrations. You sensed that they needed each other. The people coming to the United States today no longer have the same need to stick together. Among the Swiss we found our first friends. It was wonderful to speak only Swiss dialect for an entire day. My husband also began to invite more and more guests and business people to dinner in our home, and thus I often had to be in my own kitchen after the store closed. At times I cooked for up to 150 people because my husband was the Honorary Swiss Consul here for 15 years until he died in 1985.

"After his death the then Ambassador of Switzerland in Washington asked me, 'Wouldn't you like to take on the office of Swiss Honorary Consul?' But I declined politely. 'You need someone who is younger,' was my answer. And I didn't want to push myself to the front. My son Marcel then accepted this task."

In 1964 the Bolliers expanded their business again. They purchased some land farther up on Main Street and built their own place "so that we would not only have a modern and practical establishment, but also a sufficient number of parking spaces. This is very important for Americans since they do not like to walk all that much."

But André was restless, a kind of a gypsy type. "Whenever he made small marzipan animals, we knew, 'he wants to leave again'. He began to establish franchise stores so that he could travel – about ten times a year he was on the road to visit the 'André's' in Denver, Houston, Menlo Park, and St. Louis. We had up to six such stores; they were managed by Swiss pastry chefs and trusted former employees. While André was on the road, I took care of our business in Kansas City by myself. After André's death we dissolved most of the franchise stores, now there are only two other 'André's', one in Denver and the one our daughter Brigitte manages here in town."

Elsbeth kept a close connection with Switzerland. "In the mid-70s I did dream about selling everything in America and to begin anew in Switzerland. I would have liked to return home. I thought it would be nice to have a pastry shop with a Tea Room in Chardonne, in the French part of Switzerland. Our son Marcel was now a pastry chef himself and with his American wife Connie had worked for several years at Sprüngli on Paradeplatz in Zurich and at Monjonnier in Lausanne. In 1975 the two became partners in our business in Kansas City. At that point it was clear for my husband: 'We are staying in America'. He made the decision, and I accepted it. My husband was the decision maker and I backed him up. When questions arose, I usually said 'talk to my husband'. But I was his partner and was the one who looked after the money. He let me know how much he appreciated me. If I just think of the flower arrangements that he would send me! But we also could have great arguments together.

"I had my own career in our business – I believe that when you are competent, you can make your way anywhere. I was willing to do anything – except making pastries and being a wait-ress. In my generation it was custom that the husband determined where to go, and I didn't know anything else. My daughter Brigitte laughs at me and says that her father was an old school type who let his wife work. This is not entirely correct. But I never minded to contribute my part. I always wanted to give my best and expected others to do the same. I think André and I were successful in America and we worked hard for that success. For us America was a dream come true. We remained a family that did not really adapt to American customs. *'Il n'y a point comme nous* – there are none like us'! This has been a standard phrase in our family for decades and it requires some tolerance of our daughter-in-law and our son-in-law. My husband and I became American citizens in the 80s, our son Marcel was not able to do it together with his parents and he still is not a citizen.

"I don't look back – I prefer to look forward. I experienced dark periods, especially after the death of Denise and when I became a widow. Fortunately my work has always helped me get over my sorrows. This was also true in 1998 when floods ruined our entire production space; we survived this, too. The rain had poured down for two days, the sewage system was totally overwhelmed and our entire production, the decorations for Christmas, including boxes of raw chocolate and all our production machines were sub-merged in five feet of water. We faced complete ruin. My son wanted to give up, but my daughter-in-law and I said: 'We will continue – let's go and roll up our sleeves!'

"I, too, had some sleepless nights then. We cleaned for days. But somehow we made it, thanks to the wonderful support of many people, and not least thanks to our Swiss suppliers and Swissair that flew in new supplies at low cost. In December, before Christ-mas, we sold chocolate again – it was hand-made because our machines were still being repaired in Switzerland. This experience brought us together as a family anew. It was good that we didn't lose heart; we simply worked overtime and we all pulled to-gether."

Elsbeth Bollier smiles: "I am very content with my life. I'm in good health and grateful that the new generations take pride in the business and are fully engaged. Why should I complain? Will I travel to Switzerland again? Perhaps. Until now I have gone 42 times. With my daughter Brigitte I will fly to Albuquerque for a few days of relaxation. I have four great-grandchildren and five grandchildren. I have never taken myself too seriously, and this has helped me as well as my sense of humor. I never wanted to be more than what I am. And I know my weaknesses, yet I have to fight with myself to be patient with others who cannot think or are lazy."

Then she searches for words: "I have high expectations of myself and of others. However, for people who believe they are superior, but have nothing to back this up – for such an attitude I have no sympathy. I was never envious of people who earned more and could afford a larger house. But when I meet people who have greater knowledge – then I sense that I have missed something. I was born in a time when it was even unusual for a woman to work in an office. For a while I had toyed with the idea to study history here in America. The only thing I truly regret in my life is that I was not able to study when I was young. Knowledge, yes knowledge is of great value.

"I never gave up, and I never felt sorry for myself. In America I learned that it is not the problems that count, but the opportunities to dare doing something new.

"With a husband like André I would emigrate again at any time. Now I am often alone in the evenings. Then I taste one or two pieces of our chocolate candy and am grateful that I am still able to live in my own house, where I want to stay as long as possible. Once I had made a deposit for a senior's residence, but then reclaimed my money. I want to be independent and work in our business as long as I can. And if there is a mistake in a bill, I am stubborn and strict even today; then I do complain. If I had my say with the personnel, I probably would be more consistent with the employees. I was always strict with our employees, but I liked them and still do. Therefore they call me by my first name or Mutti, Mama or Mom. I believe I am a basic woman, as they say here – a woman rooted in the soil who does not give in."

NELLY
1927
SCHLEICHER

Nelly Schleicher moved from Paradise Street into one of the 320 senior's apartments in the Villa Monterey. A high wire fence surrounds the community in the southeast corner of Las Vegas. "In this labyrinth of buildings it is not easy to find me. I will meet you at the entrance gate."

Her welcome is warm, her handshake soft. She speaks with a low and trembling voice. "Please do bear with me, I am having problems with my lymph glands." Later she will mention in passing that, for two years, she has been suffering from bone marrow cancer and has been in and out of the clinic and specialists' offices; that fortunately the cancer is presently in remission and does not grow. With a limp she climbs the stairs to her modest one bedroom apartment.

The deep blue sky over the glimmering city of Las Vegas and the palms surrounding the swimming pool right around the corner do not hide the fact that Nelly Schleicher, at 82, seems tired and has been deeply marked by life. "Here in the Villa Monterey I feel comfortable and secure. I am a restless person. In the last decades I was drawn to move west, from New York to Denver and beyond. Now I don't want to go any farther; Las Vegas is my last stop. I will probably die here. The urn with my ashes is to go back to Switzerland; I would prefer to be buried in a forest cemetery." She repeats: "Yes, I would like best to find my last resting place under a Swiss pine tree. That would be lovely."

Nelly Schleicher from Zurich was born in 1927 into difficult circumstances. "We lived in a small apartment in District 4. Finances were tight, and welfare workers were often coming and going. My father always had his head in the clouds and had little sense of responsibility; again and again he had difficulties in finding work. And while my mother was cheerful, she was also overextended. By taking in work, such as sewing for a small clothing company, she tried to make ends meet for our family of six. When she was barely 23, she was forced to give us children into foster care. Yvonne, my oldest sister, and Elenora, the youngest were in a foster family in Lachen, canton Schwyz, my younger brother André and myself in a family in Dällikon, canton Zurich. I can still see clearly how a woman, who was a complete stranger, carried me away. It was night, and we were in a dark street in an unknown town. I was so afraid. The foster family also had three children of their own. We knew that we were the strangers. People in town called us 'Schimmeli' [*Schimmel* means a white horse] because we both had such light blond hair and looked like twins. When we wet the bed, the foster mother threw the wet sheet over our head and as punishment we had to stand in a corner of the room. Never was there a hug, never a tender word. In our hearts we were starving from lack of love. And I still believe that my brother and I suffered from malnutrition at that time. Usually we had light coffee and some pieces of bread for breakfast. We rarely saw healthy and nutritious food, fruit and vegetables. The two of us were never allowed to have seconds at table. Oh, how often were we hungry!

"The foster family also had three children of their own. We knew that we were the strangers." (Around 1932)

"I remember a nice neighbor lady who once in a while would give us a cookie. I believe she felt sorry for us."

Nelly sighs, "isn't it strange that I still remember all these painful things? We experienced very little that was good. When the family had company, we had to leave the living room. On Sundays we were always by ourselves; the family's outings did not include us. André and I played in the sand box and built castles in the air. Usually my brother took me by the hand as if to protect me; we depended on each other." Nelly Schleicher rubs her eyes and restlessly moves back and forth on her chair. "An evening of Saint Nicholas (December 6) was the worst experience of my five years in Dällikon. I can't remember that we were insolent; we had no opportunities to be so. We were always threatened with 'be good, or Saint Nicholas will take you with him.' And one day St Nicholas did come. André and I were trembling with fear and found no place to hide. I don't know why, but this stranger did indeed put us into a bag and put us down outside the door. I can feel it to this day: We were petrified, were not even able to cry. We were sure, now he will take us into the forest, and we will never ever get out from there! It was cold, and much time passed before St Nicholas finally came back, untied the bag and let us go saying 'today I will turn a blind eye for the last time, but never again!' This experience haunted me throughout my childhood."

Nelly leafs through her written memoirs. In the days and weeks before our conversation she took the trouble to search for her childhood memories and to write down some key words. "When I began first grade in Dällikon, I was a delicate, skinny girl. I was told that I was overly sensitive. Still, I have good memories of my first year in school. A neighbor lady gave me a slate, a slate pencil and a small sponge. Finally I was allowed to learn something. I loved school."

One day their father was at the door to take his two children with him. "To my surprise our foster father cried and hugged André and me when saying goodbye. Had he somehow become fond of us, after all? My brother and I were then separated. I came home to my parents in Zurich, he to the foster family in Lachen, whilst my older sister also returned home to Zurich. I don't know the reason. I missed André greatly. For many years he had been the only person to whom I related; he had been my all. I didn't really have a relationship with my older sister, only in time did we get to know and love each other." Nelly had to find her way around Zurich in a new environment. "I got lost on my way to and from school, was fearful and insecure.

"Unexpectedly and without preparation I was told one day that I had to go to the doctor. He had me breathe ether – I cried and then lost consciousness. Only afterwards was I told that I had undergone a tonsillectomy."

The next two months, which she spent recovering in a children's home in St. Peter in the canton Grisons, were a ray of hope for the pale city girl. "It was winter, and at the age of eight I was, for the first time ever, somewhat spoiled. I was even allowed to ski. But Christmas was a difficult moment again; I was the only one among the children who did not find a package from home under the Christmas tree."

That very same Christmas night Nelly developed a high fever. She had contracted German measles and had to spend the next three weeks in an isolated sick room. "Still, I have good memories of this time. I had enough to eat and people treated me kindly."

In January 1936 Nelly returned to her parents' house where the atmosphere was often depressed. "Those were the years of the economic depression, and father had to eke out a scant living with various jobs.

"Beginning in May 1939 my parents worked at the *Landes-ausstellung*, the 'Landi', the Swiss National exhibition; father was in a section that showed machines, mother was selling sweet specialties in a booth. From time to time she brought us some small chalets made of chocolate which we felt were almost too beautiful to eat. We children had a free pass to the exhibition, and the 'children's paradise' was wonderful – a land of milk and honey. I was able to move around freely, to drive in small play cars through landscapes with lots of flowers, and I could play in a store with real cash registers and little coins."

On September 1, 1939, everything abruptly changed. "My entire 6th grade class was at the *Landi*. At noon the loudspeakers announced that everyone had to leave immediately, that war had broken out, and that the men would have to report for military duty within a few hours. Our teacher was a lieutenant in the Swiss Army and was forced to leave our class right then and there; we had to find our way home alone on foot.

"Then followed the years with black outs night after night, air raid warnings, bomb shelters. I can still feel the fear that you never forget, can hear the deep noise of bombers flying over our house. Incendiary bombs were mistakenly also dropped on Zurich. From our windows we could see the flickers – by the time the sirens began to wail, the bombs had already fallen, and we were not yet in the shelter." Every year three girls from low-income families were given a tuition waiver to attend the Catholic *Sekundarschule* (grades 7 to 9) for girls near the Central, a square across the river from the train station. Nelly as well as two of her sisters received such a waiver. "My parents would have never been able to afford this private school. The teachers were nuns who were good to us, but strict. I went to and from school four times a day, which was very hard. I often had to run most of the way, and when I arrived in class I was out of breath and my face was beet red. Before leaving for school in the morning I had to clean the stairs in our apartment house, and after the noon meal wash the dishes. By that time my mother worked in an office, and my father was a traveling sales representative, but there was no happiness in our house."

After the required nine years of school Nelly, at age 15, was sent as an au pair girl to a family in Lugnore in the canton Fribourg. "I had enough to eat, but had to work hard in the house and on the farm. Nonetheless I felt at home there." After her return to Zurich Nelly wanted to become a pediatric nurse. "My parents opposed this, not only because of financial concerns, but also because of my delicate health."

Thus she worked for weeks or months as helper in various bakeries in Zurich. During that time life at home totally collapsed; the parents got divorced. "I got sick, had pains in my joints, swollen feet, rheumatism, and was given injections, which made me depressive. Fortunately, by that time I had a boss who was very understanding; Mrs. Olivier took me under her wings. I felt at home in this baker's family, watched the children, and took them for walks. Mrs. Olivier gave me some of her clothes, even a gabardine coat which her seamstress took in for me. It was then that I learned to appreciate beautiful clothes."

Fate was merciless. From one day to the next Mr. Olivier was diagnosed with tuberculosis and sent to a sanatorium. "Shortly afterwards I also had difficulties with my breathing. The diagnosis was pleurisy and an infiltration in my right lung. I had no reserves and collapsed." She spent months recuperating in Tesserete, canton Ticino, Arosa, canton Grisons, and at the end on the Appisberg on Lake Zurich. Much of the time Nelly had to lie in bed to regain her strength. During this time she knitted a huge number of sweaters and socks in order to earn some pocket money. She was twenty when, in spite of her anemia, she had recovered to a certain extent. She found work as a shop girl in a large bakery, and she fell in love.

She spent months recuperating in Tesserete (Ticino), Arosa (Grisons) and at the end on the Appisberg on Lake Zurich. Much of the time Nelly (second from left) had to lie in bed to regain her strength.

"It was at the ball for Zurich's festival of *Sechseläuten* [following an old custom, old man winter is burned publicly one day in early spring when all the church bells toll the hour of 6 p.m.], on April 25, 1949, in the *Kongresshaus* (conference center). A young man invited me to dance." Nelly Schleicher laughs for the first time. "Siegfried always said that he fell in love with me the moment he looked into my eyes. We danced through the night, and then met almost every evening. Siegfried and I planned to marry, 'in two years' he said. He had artistic talents and worked in a fashion shop as window designer. I still have all his letters with their wonderful, romantic statements. He was my first great love. But his parents did not accept me as daughter-in-law. Presumably I was not good enough for him and on top of it, I was a Catholic. This was a deadly blow for me. I was desperate and lost twenty pounds in just a few weeks. The only thing I wanted to do was to leave, so I decided to emigrate in order to forget my grief."

In 1950 a customer at the bakery helped Nelly find employment in Malmö, in the south of Sweden – in the elegant house of a distinguished family. Soon she waited at table dressed in a uniform, learned customs, and to speak Swedish. She earned 175 Swedish kroner per month. "For me that was a fortune!"

Nelly remained shy and reserved, blushed, and was embarrassed when people spoke to her. But soon she was able to read Tolstoi's *Anna Karenina* in Swedish. After a year, however, she wanted to leave and looked for a different position that she found in Stockholm. And ten months later an ad in the newspaper

Dagbladet caught her eye: An American family in Syracuse, New York, was looking for a nanny. "I was restless which I probably inherited from my father." So she left Sweden, even though the family in Stockholm wanted to take her along for their vacation at the North Cape, and a young Swedish student who was working his way through the university had fallen in love with her. "My, was I stupid then! I should have taken my time to get to know this friend better."

In an elegant suit and with two suitcases that contained all her belongings the 25-year old Nelly Schleicher flew to New York via Newfoundland in August 1952. In her purse she had 50 dollars, the Green card for the United States, and a contract for two years. Her host family had paid for the flight, an expense she would have to pay back in installments. "I didn't know a word of English. At the airport in New York I used my hands and feet to let people know that I had to find my connecting flight to Syracuse. A nice black man carried my suitcase through the airport."

In the family with three children and a golden retriever there was much work to do, and when the housewife realized that Nelly was a good cook, she also asked her to take care of the kitchen. Nelly was homesick.

"To sweeten my life a bit the couple once offered me a ticket to a movie. This was something totally new for me. I dressed in nice clothes – what a waste! What I found was a noisy crowd, popcorn scattered all over the place, and constant munching and gum chewing. All this was very confusing to me; I don't even remember what movie I saw. And when the show was over, I hardly could get up – I was stuck to chewing gum!" Nelly thought that Sweden was much more civilized and more orderly. And the climate did not agree at all with her, "it was so humid." But she did not want to go back. "My pride would not have allowed it. People would have asked what I had seen, why was I coming home so soon?"

But after a year in Syracuse Nelly had enough, so she took the Greyhound bus to New York where she could stay with a friend from Sweden. "I had very little money and survived by babysitting and doing day care." The young Swiss woman went from one job to another, from a screen play writer to a widow and then to a baby, moving with her suitcase from one furnished room to another. She laughs: "I could write a book about furnished rooms, just like in Erich Maria Remarque's *Shadows in Paradise*. In the house of an impoverished Russian Countess I even had bedbugs."

In the meantime Nelly was in her late twenties. "At that time I still thought that, some day, I would marry and have children." Again and again she fell in love. "Peter, a Swiss immigrant, whom I met in New York, lived in the shadow of his successful father who was building hotels in Germany. He had little vitality, didn't want to marry. But he had a wonderful singing voice, was a gourmet, and I liked him a lot. We went out together, he invited me to eat in restaurants. Later Peter returned to Switzerland; we remained friends until his death a few years ago."

The young Swiss woman went from one job to another, from a screen play writer to a widow and then to a baby, moving with her suitcase from one furnished room to another. (1956)

At the Cambridge Business School Nelly obtained new skills, business English, typing, and shorthand while still jobbing as babysitter, so that she could afford the tuition and a room. She lived from one day to the next and from hand to mouth. "Often my food came out of vending machines. For 25 cents you could have a little dish of baked beans and a few slices of sausage. A cup of coffee with milk was 10 cents. Even today I love those baked beans. And on my way home I passed a bakery where I bought straw-berry tarts for 50 cents."

Nelly did not feel lonely in New York. Again and again she met interesting men. "At a party I made the acquaintance of a German psychiatrist named Hans whom I found fascinating, but he was also cruel to me. He said 'you know I would like to meet a girl from Park Avenue, a rich girl.' In this respect I certainly was not the right one! I had nothing! He was looking for a new position, so I typed forty letters for him and addressed them to various hospitals. And then he abandoned me for a pianist from Cuba – precisely on my 30th birthday. I thought it was the end of the world."

Nelly did not feel lonely in New York. "Again and again I met interesting men." (1956)

Later she became friends with a Lebanese psychiatrist; "but he wanted to marry an American so that he would be able to stay in the country. I suffered physically and emotionally and made an appointment with a woman psychiatrist. One session cost 15 dollars. That was quite expensive for me, but I needed help. And then, honestly, I was unable to utter a single word, and the psychiatrist neither said nor asked anything! I stopped after six weeks, and somehow life continued."

Nelly drinks some water as if she wanted to wash down these experiences. "I am a tree that cannot put down roots. I would have loved to live with a man – with or without marriage – instead of having one adventure after another. Though, sometimes I myself did not want to enter a firm bond. It is strange: My greatest desire was for a family and children. The longing was always there and I never gave up hope. At the same time I was also afraid of it, since I did not want it to be the way it was with my parents."

Thanks to her schooling in clerical work Nelly found a position in the department of public relations of a pharmaceutical firm. When the department was dissolved two years later, a friend gave her the name of a surgeon at the Sloan-Kettering Cancer Hospital who urgently needed a secretary. "In spite of my age my credentials were rather modest. But I was lucky: 'Honey, the job is yours!'" Having obtained the position for a trial period of three months, she kept it for the next twenty years. "I typed manuscripts, copied diagnoses and surgery reports. 'Europeans are reliable, ' said my boss, Dr. Brunschwig, a medical doctor from Texas and a pioneer in the area of American cancer surgery. At first it was difficult, but interesting and educational. Every night I crammed until midnight, read articles written by doctors and learned medical terminology." Nelly was promoted to Statistical Research Assistant. "I loved the job and the team of which I was a part, as well as all the people with whom I had contact. And the patients liked me also."

Nelly moved into her own apartment, ten blocks from the hospital on 77th Street between 2nd and 3rd Avenue. "Finally I had put down some roots. And Dr. Brunschwig believed in me. Later I also worked in his private practice when his secretary was on vacation, although I felt somewhat insecure there. 'Try it' he said, and it worked very well."

The United States had become a part of home for her, and thus she decided to become an American citizen. "When I was given the document, the Judge said to me, 'that's what we need, people like you, nice people.'"

Nelly did not have much of a private life; she lived for her job. And by now she was able to start saving some money. After Dr. Brunschwig's death there were big changes as the old hospital was demolished and the administration totally restructured. With this her old restlessness returned, the feeling that she had to tear herself away from what had become a rot. So: let's keep going west!

The United States had become a part of home for Nelly, seen here in the summer of 1957 in Miami Beach.

"Colorado attracted me; I knew the area from vacations. In 1979 Denver was still a small town. The move there was a big change for me – and soon I missed New York and the amenities of a large city.

"I was 52 years old, once again alone with my few possessions, and my dream of having my own family and a husband who really loved me had slowly, but surely come to an end." She found work in the recording department of a cancer hospital, but on lousy conditions. "I earned very little, but was glad to have an income at all – and time! I enjoyed attending concerts in the newly built Concert Hall. Once Daniel Barenboim and Vladimir Ashkenasi were on the program – and since the Americans there knew little of these two artists, the tickets were very reasonable!"

Her inner restlessness never left Nelly. She no longer remembers how often she changed her lodgings. "Dozens of times," she says. "In the Denver Public Library I happened to pick up a book that described Las Vegas as a wonderful place for older people, with a comfortable dry climate and reasonable living expenses. Thus after ten years in Colorado I packed my bags again and moved to Las Vegas." Who knows, perhaps she might even find work and a comfortable life in this growing city in the middle of the Nevada desert? She soon had to admit that in her profession as medical secretary she had little opportunity in the harsh world of Las Vegas in spite of her excellent credentials. "Here money is king." Shortly after her arrival she took a temporary position in the Golden Nugget Casino. "I had to earn some money because the small pension I had from my work at the New York Memorial Cancer Hospital paid only 162 dollars per month, and I had very little in savings."

In retrospect she says: "Working in hospitals was not very lucrative, and in my experience Americans are very ambitious, for them money is all-important. Somehow I was never able to get ahead financially. My assets are in my mouth – in the crowns and bridges that dentists have put in."

Nelly rented a one-bedroom apartment at a reasonable price on Bonanza Street in downtown Las Vegas. Its address was telling. "It was a bad neighborhood with many alcoholics on the street. Robberies were part of the day though nothing ever happened to me because I was a senior, but on the public bus someone stole my wallet with 90 dollars."

Her last employment was in the gift shop of Cesar's Palace. "Crazy! There I actually sold toys for 800 dollars and tuxedos and dress suits for 5-year old boys for incredible sums. And I had a basic wage of 5 dollars per hour." She rented a tiny apartment on Paradise Street "although it wasn't a real paradise," and for a while watched the children of her Lebanese neighbors. "This was at least fun for me and also paid 5 dollars per hour."

Telling her story has been tiring for Nelly Schleicher. She is visibly exhausted from reliving all the difficult experiences of her life. "But it feels good that someone is interested in me.

"Was I ever happy? I don't know nor do I even think about it. There was much that was positive, and this sustains me. I don't feel lonely, but I do feel a sense of emptiness when I think about my life. Basically nothing that I wished for has ever come true.

"When I feel depressed, I simply take the bus up to the strip, where all the casinos are, all that bustle. Or I meet with Trudy from the Swiss Club and we go out to eat. Trudy prefers a restaurant to the casinos. She has a car, I don't. Together we also go on short trips. With Marilyn, an American, I go to a buffet lunch in one of the casinos every few weeks. There was a time when the food there cost next to nothing if you also played. Then the smaller casinos used to sell two-for-one coupons for their buffets. This is rare today. Even for the casinos the times are not very good!

"I have to watch every penny. I am an immigrant who, in contrast to many others, never became rich in her new country. But in the United States I have done good work that was appreciated. And while I was not lucky in love, I was lucky in meeting many people who were nice to me.

"I regularly talk on the phone with my sisters in Switzerland and with my brother in New Zealand. My niece Christine means much to me, and my friend from my time in New York, who is back living in Zurich, is 'my angel in disguise'. This friendship has an extraordinary value for me.

"My story is difficult, I know. When something beautiful happens, I am glad, and when this is not the case, I am no longer bothered. I need a lot of sleep; then I do feel good. Fred, one of the residents here, says that we are not to regret anything, not to look back, but to look only forward. He is an expert in the art of living, a bit eccentric in some ways, I think. But I do like him. His concern for me is touching. But it doesn't have to be a romantic thing any more."

MARGRIT MONDAVI BIEVER KELLENBERGER

1925

"For a start, let's go to the winery." To talk about herself pleases 83-year old Margrit Mondavi Biever Kellenberger far less than to lead people through the winery in the heart of the Napa Valley, the Robert Mondavi Winery in Oakville, California. Everywhere on the rounds she is being cordially greeted be it by the Mexican workers in the cool wine stores, the young employees in the shop, or the receptionist. You sense that the small, dainty, but energetic lady, whose face is creased with laugh lines, remains in command here.

Since the summer of 2008, when her 95-year old husband died, Margrit Mondavi lives alone. "If I am in doubt, when I'm not clear in my mind about something, I ask him, 'Bob, what shall I do'? But I actually know. He had told me: You must continue what we have begun." Robert and Margrit Mondavi – a touching love story and an entrepreneurial dream-team: He the visionary pioneer in the cause of American viticulture, she the creative patron and promoter of art and culture.

Her life happens here in the winery – for forty years already, thirty of them as the wife of the noted owner of a vineyard. "Now I am the last Mondavi in the business." And she continues diplomatically: "Unfortunately the two sons of my husband were not as engaged in the business as their father. All has been sold. I cannot change it. It is a pity. Luckily the new owners continue to manage the business in the way of my husband. And as long as I am healthy, I can be active here."

Margrit Mondavi, the grand old lady, is still to be found every morning after nine o'clock in her office. Together with her assistant Karen she weaves the cultural threads – organizes concerts, festivals, or exhibits in case she is not somewhere else speaking as "Ambassador of Wine" about art, culture and wine in Washington, Boston, even Italy. She continues to do so perhaps more than ever after the death of her husband.

The Napa Valley, America's most important viticulture region, shows style and elegance. It is not quite an hour by car from the pulsating metropolis of San Francisco, an idyllic oasis. "The area has many similarities with the Toscana, the gentle hills, the olive trees, and vineyards. But meanwhile there are as many tourists here as in Disney Land." In the Robert Mondavi Winery, a bright sprawling building with a high tower, one feels like being in a monastery. All is clear and simple. Beyond the bow windows in the courtyard extends a vista of the well-tended lawn all the way to never ending vineyards that touch the horizon.

"One hundred and eighty years ago there were twenty-one mission stations between San Diego and Sonoma built by the Spanish Franciscans. When building the winery, our Californian architect, Cliff May, borrowed the Spanish-Mexican colonial style of the 18th and 19th centuries."

Margrit Mondavi talks perfectly and without accent in a dialect of eastern Switzerland. Only occasionally terms come up in English when a technical matter is at issue. "After the repeal of prohibition in 1933, this winery was the first in the Napa Valley, but was built anew in the mid-1960s. It was seen as being ultra-modern. Specialists and visitors arrived from all over the world in order to view the technical innovations. Our vineyards, close to Highway 29, where the Cabernet Sauvignon, the Chardonnay, the Sauvignon Blanc, and the Pinot Noir are thriving, are called 'To Kalón', in Greek 'highest beauty'."

The Mondavi Empire covers hundreds of hectares. And each vineyard has been given a letter of the alphabet, so that U-grapes do not end up in the vats of Z-grapes.

Margrit Mondavi knows the details as precisely about fermenting as about separating and pressing, about the noble vats made of oak that some years ago again replaced those made of steel. "Today the winery is an attraction; 150,000 to 200,000 guests visit us here every year.

"It was different in the beginning. Americans had yet to learn what wine meant as part of a way of life and pleasure. It was the emigrants from Italy, France, and Switzerland that brought along the culture of wine from their home countries."

In the room bathed in light where concerts and events of all kinds happen, there is not only a black and white picture of the immigrant family Mondavi, who migrated in 1905 from Sassoferrato in Italy to America, that commemorates the past, but also a large color photograph of Robert and Margrit Mondavi. It was they who transformed a small business into an international firm of world renown.

With purpose and vigor Margrit Mondavi leads us into the garden. In the Napa Valley with its ideal climatic conditions everything grows: herbs, tomatoes, beans, eggplants, melons, and, of course, Margrit's favorites, wild strawberries. "These are less known here."

And Margrit confesses that besides art cooking is her great passion. "In 1976 we started a cooking school here and therefore laid out this garden. We invited chefs from France – Michel Guérard, Paul Bocuse, Alain Chapel and others. They each cooked for us for a week, and we organized large banquets. They got to know Californian wine and we French cooking. We had realized that wine is best appreciated together with a meal. It was around the same time that our friendly contacts with Baron Philippe de Rothschild were established – and the creation of 'Opus One', the prestige wine of the Napa Valley made after the prototype of a 'Premier Cru Classé' of Bordeaux: The fruitful collaboration between our two vineyards."

Margrit insists that she wants to be photographed in the midst of the vines that surround the garden. "It is my favored place. The grapes are not ripe yet; they still need a few weeks until harvest time." It is time, however, to eat. Margrit drives her Mercedes to a chic restaurant in the little town of Oakville. During the light lunch, served with Fumé Blanc – of course from the House Mondavi – Margrit talks about Copia, the American Center for Wine, Food and the Arts, an interactive museum in Napa which she and her husband had helped initiate. "For me that unique center is a dream come true."

A counterpart to the winery is the Mondavi's home, built by the same architect in the same modest style, high above the Napa Valley on top of the Wappo Hill that once served the Wappo Indians as their meeting place. "Omnia vincit amor" – love conquers everything – Robert and Margrit Mondavi had ordered to be chiseled on the wall of the attractive villa. Great love it was indeed that united Margrit Mondavi, from the canton Appenzell Ausserrhoden, with Robert Mondavi, the grand-seigneur of Californian wine culture.

"My children think that I should not live here by myself – not only because of the raccoons which come all the way into the kitchen, and the coyotes which at night are slinking around the house. So now I am looking for a woman to share the house with me and also look after me a bit."

In the garage stands her red twelve-year old Ferrari that she only rarely uses. "It is not easy to drive and built low. I can't get in and out so easily anymore." And with a rascal-like blinking of the eye she adds: "I still have a passion for fast and beautiful cars. Just to hear the motor... The splendid Cabrio-drives with my husband along the coast to Los Angeles – they are unforgettable to me."

Margrit Mondavi sits down on the white sofa in the living room, together with her small lady-poodle, and hesitantly starts to talk about much earlier times. Switzerland? Her roots? All this seems to be far away, and yet: "Memories remain. I was born August 2, 1925 as Margrit Kellenberger in St. Gallen. But my parents, both citizens of Walzenhausen, canton of Appenzell Ausserrhoden, moved with me to the Ticino, the Italian speaking part of Switzerland, when I was nine months old. In the Ticino, the weather was nicer, less foggy. They were both bohemians who loved the Côte d'Azur, also the exotic. In the Ticino there were palm trees and beautiful flowers. It was far more lovely there than in German-speaking Switzerland. My father Ernst had lived in Paris for some years before as a banker. And my mother was artistically gifted and like father had an urge towards adventure."

"We grew up as children of the Ticino." Margrit (middle), her mother and her siblings Victor and Vera in the garden in Orselina. (1931).

In Orselina little Margrit was considered a *Zücchin*, as Swiss-Germans were teasingly called in the Ticino, although she soon spoke perfect Italian and its local dialect, just as did her two siblings. "My brother Victor was born three years after me, and Vera in 1929. We grew up as children of the Ticino."

Margrit's mother never learned proper Italian. She lived at home for her family. "And she cooked like an angel. She could make wonderful meals out of nothing. And she was artistically truly gifted. At Christmas we didn't have just a Christmas tree, but always also three little decorated trees, one for each child. And everything at home was nicely arranged. I am sure, had she been allowed to have a creative profession, she would have gone far. She was knitting, crocheting, embroidering, had a maid, and much time. Mama always had a golden-brown tan; that was her pride. In our garden she took sunbaths like the people on Monte Verità. When the grandparents came to live with us, also we, the children, suddenly had to wear bathing suits at the pool; gone were swimming and sunbathing in the nude".

"When the grandparents came to live with us, also we, the children, suddenly had to wear bathing suits at the pool." (1933)

Going to school was a daily fitness training for Margrit, five hundred steps up to the village Orselina and then five hundred down back to her house on the sunny slope. Twenty children of all public primary school grades were taught in one room. "A wonderful time," Margrit calls it today. In the Gymnasium, the college preparatory school in Muralto, she was one of the few girls. "Father said, what do you, a girl, want to do at university? That's something for Victor. Therefore studying for the Matura, the final exam for university access, was no topic. Instead, after the mandatory nine years of school I helped my father in his office. He had meanwhile established a small business that produced homeopathic medicines. Coming from the Appenzell, where natural remedies were big as with my father, he cooperated with a spa in the village Wald. His business flourished. With us the physician was the 'biggest enemy'. He was consulted only if life and death were at stake or if someone had broken a bone. When we had a

"Father said, what do you, a girl, want to do at university? That's something for Victor." (1947)

cold, mother would put a pillow cover filled with hot onions on our chest; we would smell of onions for quite a while and had to miss school."

Margrit grew up in a world that was natural and one with nature. "Father would drive with his homeopathic medicines to the markets of Ascona and Locarno. I remember that the people from Monte Verità, a community that pursued an alternative lifestyle according to its own laws, came with a donkey to make their purchases. They looked funny in their special clothes. My parents had an open home and a heart for people less privileged. During the war Mama was also cooking for Polish and German refugees. It was an artistic household, always somehow joyous. But father hated the Nazis. He even taught us children how to shoot. He made a target himself, drew Hitler on it, and in the chicken coop we had to aim at his moustache. My brother was good at it, my sister also. I myself never learned it properly, I trembled, missed, and was labeled a coward."

Alone in father's office, Margrit found her job boring. Therefore, for two years she attended the arts school in Minusio and learned how to paint and make frescoes. "That was my passion; I wanted to further my education in art."

In the midst of the war, in 1944, her parents sent Margrit to a boarding school in Clarens, canton Vaud, in order to learn French. One day she had to serve the manager of a jewelry store whom she knew as interpreter. "I explained the beauty of a music box that played yodels to an American who wanted to buy a Swiss souvenir for his sister. Which one would I choose, he asked me. My Lord, surely none! I thought. Of course, I could not let him know that so directly. I selected the least kitschy."

To thank her, the man invited the young woman to a cup of coffee and told her of his assignment as captain of the US army in Holland. He was on a week's furlough. "That's how I got to know Phil Biever. He also visited me in the Ticino later. Father did not like that at all, and he forbade me to go out with him. Phil returned to Holland, and I thought that I would never see him again. But he wrote to me almost every day. As a member of the Allied Forces, Phil had come to England and over Normandy to the continent, had stepped over dead bodies, had seen the bombed out cities, and witnessed the war at close range.

"Only today do I realize what he saw in me: I was something like Heidi, untouched and blond. I was living in a peaceful country, was someone who did not have to struggle, unlike many people in Europe. The circumstances were absurd, were they not? For me it was an adventure. Hollywood! Phil was very good looking, like a movie star. He was a lovable man from a good family from North Dakota, a teacher of physics. All perfect. He was thirty and I twenty. Father was anything but happy. 'You will go to America and we won't see you anymore.' He would have much preferred that I had married someone else, an acquaintance of our family. 'Fred would be a good man for you', he thought. But I did not want him. Mother supported me; we were almost like sisters: 'I would go also! In Switzerland you do not have prospects. America would be a way out. There you could further your education and do something.'

"And one day Phil wrote that he would fetch me, he wanted to marry me." The wedding took place in September 1946 at Madonna del Sasso – at the Catholic pilgrimage church of the Franciscans – although Margrit was a Protestant. "Phil did not speak Italian. We agreed on a sign when he had to say 'si', yes. It worked. We were married, made lots of pictures in front of the church and drove by car to Locarno to the hotel Du Lac. My uncle from Schaffhausen was there, my aunt from Zurich, my relatives from St. Gallen. And most of them couldn't quite understand the world: Margrit marries an American?!"

For several years Margrit and her husband led the nomad life of an army couple. In 1946 the young couple was transferred to Esslingen. "Germany was destroyed, devasted. There were no residences for American women. But at least my Swiss passport allowed me to live officially in the officers' quarters with my husband. We had one room and shared the bath with another officer. At five o'clock there was supper in the canteen. The food was terrible, all from cans. After six thirty the 'shadow-plants of the night' appeared in the barracks. All the officers somehow had women who came for the night and left again at six in the morning. Officially there was to be no 'fraternization between Germans and Americans.' One night I went to the bathroom and saw a beautiful girl sitting in the bathtub. Her name was Charlotte, she said, and that she was with lieutenant Gebhart. She couldn't believe that I was truly married to an American officer. 'You are in luck, you don't have leave in the morning!'"

Although she loved Phil Biever very much and had happy times with him, Margrit often felt like a captive. "I was not allowed to go anywhere except to the Officers' Club. In the letters I wrote home I never said how I was really doing. At home they had advised against my plans. We were transferred to Mosbach and by train passed all those stations that looked like skeletons. Everything was bombed out, was off limits. The German women who were working in the army quarters were the only ties I had to the outside world. I often sat in the kitchen and talked with Frau Hey. She had four sons: 'One is in captivity, I don't know where, two were killed in the war. Max is still at home – but if there is going to be a war against the Russians, I will have to give him up also.' Incredible! I will never forget those words."

During these years Margrit lived out of a suitcase. "Actually I had no real place for myself. Soon we were transferred to Nuremberg, just at the time when the war trials were on and Nazis of high rank committed suicide. Occasionally I took the train home. As soon as I was over the border in Basel I could breathe more easily again."

Phil was transferred to America, to an Igloo Ordnance Depot in the Badlands of South Dakota. "One hundred and fifty kilometers from the nearest tree! There were only coalmines, no vegetation, and in winter it was cold for ten months. Summer lasted for six hot weeks and otherwise everything was frozen. But I had a good time; people were nice. I could drive around, we had many friends, ate together, played bridge. I read a lot. Honestly, before I could not have imagined that one could even live in such a place. We had our own house, I felt good. Philip, our first son was born up there. In 1949 we returned with the baby to Germany. The country was totally changed and open. Suddenly you could get everything. Eschwege was the first station, only three kilometers from the Russian zone. The Russians were stealing from us. Americans were heroes. We had enough of everything – cigarettes, coffee – exchanges in kind flourished. I could interact, was interested in everything cultural, museums, theater. In 1951 I gave birth to Annie – and again we had to move. This time it was to Spokane, Washington, where our third child Phoebe was born. When she was two months old, Phil was transferred to Okinawa in Japan. We five had a good time there. The children spoke Japanese when we moved to Cincinnati and finally to Puerto Rico. An eternal nomadic life!

"Suddenly my children had enough. 'We don't want to go anywhere anymore; we finally want to be at home somewhere.' Nobody wanted to move to Switzerland. My husband did not speak German. I would have loved to return to Europe. We finally decided on the Napa Valley that we knew from visiting friends. We liked the region. Napa is only fifty miles from San Francisco; it is not far to the mountains and not far to the ocean. At that time there were 17,000 inhabitants; now there are 75,000 people."

In 1960 the Bievers with the three children finally settled down. "My husband wanted to return to teaching, but meanwhile school children, he thought, had become undisciplined and fresh. He turned stockbroker, then real estate agent."

Margrit Biever was looking for a job and was employed in the family business of the Mondavi's, in the *Winery Krug* where, however, she never met Robert Mondavi in person. She earned two dollars an hour and in courses learned all about wine. She gave guided tours and sold more wine than the men who were tour guides also. "It was learning by doing for me. I was the only woman in the whole establishment. The men thought that a woman and wine was the end of the world." Margrit laughs. "But I drank Bordeaux with Papa already as a three year old – these men, however, got to know wine only as elderly gentlemen!"

In the early sixties the Mondavi brothers quarreled. Robert left the family business; part of the employees also gave notice, among them Margrit. She now had more time for painting. "One day, outdoors, when I painted in watercolors, I realized that construction was going on in a large and open space adjacent. Rumor had it that it was the place where Robert Mondavi's new winery was to rise. People who had joined him in the venture knew me, and we started talking. Thus I soon began to work as tour guide in the new winery and also got to know Robert Mondavi. I found him wonderful. He had great charm. Occasionally he joined our small group, asked about our work, and after hours drank a glass of wine with us. And one day he asked me whether I might want to become the public relations director. 'I think you have the talent for it,' he said. I was uncertain, hesitated. I had no formal training in this area, no experience. 'I'll help you...' he encouraged me." And so she accepted the job in 1968. "I did the correspondence, organized special events and wine tastings, slowly became familiar with the task." Since she also knew French, German and Italian, her work steadily increased.

"In 1969 I suggested to Robert Mondavi to organize jazz concerts on the lawn. He let me try it. 'Do it, but remember: It has to be good!' He was a perfectionist. On the first jazz evenings we had about four hundred people; today there are two thousand who don't want to miss the 'Robert Mondavi Winery Summer Music Festival'. We also always supported our local symphony. And on the many white walls, I thought, one could mount paintings. I knew painters, photographers, sculptors, and invited them. Robert Diebenkorn, one of the most accomplished artists of California, exhibited with us. The Buona Vista Social Club, Ella Fitzgerald, Harry Belafonte made their appearance." Benefit performances followed, and today they are firmly in place; they yield millions for hospitals and welfare institutions. The idea of combining wine, a good life, art, culture, and benevolence had been born, and it found a dedicated advocate in Robert Mondavi.

Gradually, the sympathy between the two was growing, too. In his biography *Harvest of Joy* Robert Mondavi wrote: "When I was around Margrit, I realized how limited my horizons were. She pushed me; she opened me; she inspired me. In fundamental ways, she also changed my way of thinking and my approach to life (...) with Margrit around I learned to loosen up and give more credence to my instincts and feelings." And Margrit adds: "My story with Robert Mondavi sounds like a soap opera. I divorced my husband Phil who died a year later. Unfortunately, that wasn't nice. He was a very fine man and a good father. But we had nothing in common anymore; he didn't want to travel or undertake anything. That was the worst for me. I was still overflowing with the love of life, felt in the midst of my life. And he was tired, tired from the life of a nomad in the army. He did not enjoy art, loved cowboy music; we simply had drifted apart." Robert Mondavi divorced as well. "We loved each other, worked wonderfully together and also wanted to be partners. That created much talk in the Napa Valley. We could not have lived together without getting married. While my own children showed understanding, his children – he had three, too – put many obstacles in my path. Now things are going very well. I married the winemaker Robert Mondavi on May 17, 1980 – in Palm Springs. It was a small wedding; we didn't want to create a commotion."

Margrit Mondavi is radiant: "I had 28 wonderful years with Bob. We never argued. We said life is too short for quarreling. He loved to travel. Earlier he had found no time for art, only the wine business had existed for him. Now we visited museums together, had season tickets to the opera in San Francisco. He said over and over again: 'I appreciate it so much!' We built our house on the hill. He wanted a pool in which he could swim daily, in any weather, also when getting old. Therefore he had it built in the living room – with a roof that can be opened above. He also wanted an elevator in the house. Just in case, for later. He was a visionary in all, and he was a good listener. Said that he could learn something from everyone. But he didn't have a great sense of humor – he didn't understand my jokes. And being from Appenzell I joked a lot."

How would she characterize herself? "I have much energy, and I'm a positive person. On the other hand, I am also a bit shy, rather hesitant when it comes to making decisions. Helpful, that too, I believe. And I am never as decisive as Bob. He always knew that's the way to go, and he would do it. Since I am alone," she stops in the middle of the sentence, "I must organize my life anew. But I want that all continues in his spirit." To this day Margrit Mondavi Biever Kellenberger maintains close ties with her sister, her brother, with cousins, and with a 100-year old uncle in Switzerland. "It is a pity that my relatives don't come to see me anymore. If one reaches 60 or 65 in Switzerland, one doesn't travel anymore." In the large kitchen she shows her Swiss corner. "From my friend Wolfram Martel of St. Gallen I receive each year the *Calendar of Appenzell*; earlier its stories were more humorous, I think.

"Switzerland: I have lived there but a quarter of my life. And yet something from that time remains in my heart. I like to travel every year to my old homeland. But I feel American through and through. The openness and freedom in this country are wonderful. I could realize my dreams. Bob told me many times, 'if you have a job that you like you don't have to work another day in your life. And then, do it as well as you can.' These were good tips from Bob. In my life I found many things that I like to do, much that gives me joy."

ANNA
CONTI
TONINI

1944

Finding Anna Conti-Tonini is not easy. Even with a GPS. A curvy, little traveled asphalt road leads some five miles up from the vineyard-rich town of Sonoma to "White Oak Court". It is a hilly region, numerous vineyards covered in dense green foliage as far as the eye can see, brown soil, and sunshine aplenty.

"Anna and I sat for eight years on the same school bench. I saw her the last time some forty-two years ago. She was a modest girl," remembers Bruno Donati, "possibly one of the last typical emigrants from the Maggia Valley to America. They were mostly men who, – searching for new opportunities, – left for California during the last century." Donati, historian, museum curator and president, searches the whereabouts in the Napa Valley of his school friend from long ago and calls her. "It was a moving and emotional call to California," he later admits.

Near the white oak on the slope above, Anna Conti-Tonini and her husband Lee are waving from the porch of their simple house built of wood. Their welcome is cordial and spontaneous in southern fashion – *buongiorno* and *welcome.*

Anna Conti-Tonini seems touched. "Suddenly, there's so much ado about me. I am not used to that," she observes modestly and leads the way to the air-conditioned house. Given the more than 95-degree heat it is welcome. "You are invited for lunch." Before she starts telling her story, the small woman with the grey hair invites to the richly set table – barbeque and pasta in basil sauce, fresh tomatoes along with a clear Chardonnay – most of it from their own garden and home made.

Anna Conti-Tonini isn't used to talking a lot and uses simple language. "When I came to California thirty-eight years ago, I did not know a single word of English. I learned it mostly from watching television." Her Ticinese accent is obvious, her English interspersed with Italian words.

On the wall in the living room hangs an oil painting *Broglio with Campanile* and another showing the core of the village of Menzonio, a hamlet some kilometers to the south. The Valle

Maggia, Anna's and Lee's common valley of origin, is firmly ensconced with the Contis. The furniture dates from the seventies, is sturdy and mainly made of wood. One would think to be in a living room in the Valle Maggia, were it not for the view of the lush garden with its peach and fig trees, its lemon grove and vines, and the hum of the airconditioner.

"Three years ago, for the first time after thirty years, I returned to the Valle Maggia. Our son Johnny had invited my husband and me. Everything at home had changed so much. For me it was not the same valley anymore. That saddened me greatly. My village Broglio, I hardly recognized it anymore. Many of the old houses stood empty. In my time they were all inhabited, although we had not even been eighty people then. Those I had known, with whom we had lived and toiled, they were not there anymore. And where were all the cows that were part of the village in my youth? I did not see a single one."

Sadness marks her face: "Broglio – at least the stone-roofed seventeenth century house of my father is still standing in the midst of the village. That's where my brother Renato lives. He is an electrician and has work in the valley. Most people had to leave. What was there to do for the young ones in the valley? Work was sparse. If one worked on a farm, all right. But there aren't that many farms any more. My brother Renato was born in 1948 as the youngest of us children; after six girls he was the sensation – finally a male heir. He is the only one who stayed at home all his life, and he has remained single."

Anna is the second youngest of the Tonini family, born at home in Broglio on April 15, 1944. "My oldest sister is thirteen years older than I am. Father was the post-office manager in the village. He distributed the few letters and newspapers to the 15 families with his *Mofa* (motor cycle), summer and winter. The post-office was open daily for only a few hours." The small salary was insufficient for the family of nine. "As many other families of the village, we had a small farm with cows and goats, pigs and chickens, being

"As many other families of the village, we had a small farm with cows and goats, pigs and chickens, being self-sufficient." (1947)

self-sufficient." Anna and her siblings were used to working from early on at home and in the fields. "Milking was a daily task, and in the summer making hay was the main task for us children. Two cuts yearly, one at the end of May when the meadows were full of flowers, the second cut in July or early August – that made sufficient fodder for our four cows. During the summer, the goats were up on the alp Rima, a good hour's walk away at a height of about 1000 meters. Already as children we carried the hay home on our backs in the *Gerla* [traditional basket worn on the back]. We had little money. But we lived well. I don't know whether there were any rich people among us at that time. Some perhaps did have a bit more than we did. So what! We never went hungry. We fed ourselves from our own vegetables, potatoes, milk, butter, and cheese."

Her eyes light up. "Fall was chestnut time; chestnuts were an important staple for winter. The bakehouse in the village, *la grà*, was for communal use. The chestnuts were dried on a large grill for three weeks on a small fire. We had to beat them by hand to remove shell and skin. The white chestnuts came into a throw-screen before they were stored in large jute sacks; cooked in hot water and eaten with sausages or cream, they were wonderful. In winter father made the best salami and prosciutto. We did not have a car. Nobody but my uncle, the teacher, owned one. We could count the cars in our valley on one hand." In the winter months there were no foreign visitors; at best people from the region visited. But I did not mind the solitude and quiet. That was my life and I loved it."

In the 1950s more and more tourists discovered the Valle Maggia in summer, especially Germans. "But they mostly passed us by, toward Fusio. We recognized them by their fine Mercedes cars. Tourists would take pictures of us. We were an attraction." Anna laughs: "I don't know how many times I was photographed carrying the *Gerla*." School for Anna was a sideshow. "But nice," she insists. "We did not know much about the world. I liked it best to be outside in nature and with the animals. The teacher called us to school by the church bell. We did not have schoolbags, just a book and a slate." In the 1950s there were twelve children in Broglio's village school, all in the same schoolroom, from first to eighth grade and with only one teacher, her uncle. "I did not mind going to school with him as teacher. He was strict with all of us, did not tolerate disobedience. We always had to sit still and to be quiet. That was hard for me. I had a fellow in my class, Bruno Donati. Throughout those years he sat next to me. We two constituted a grade. I copied from him because he understood things better than I did. I remember Bruno well. He was born in February, I in April. We got along well. Our school was a winter school – summer vacation lasted for four months; vacation for us was the time when we had the most work on the farm."

After eight years, formal education ended for Anna. "In Cevio, however, I attended a housekeeping school for nine month. To learn what I would need for keeping house – sewing, mending, cooking, cleaning." Cevio, a larger village at the foot of the Valle Maggia, was the first expanded contact of the 14-year old girl with more people. "That I could learn a profession, such a thought never crossed my mind. Father was glad that I helped him at home. I was so tied to the valley. I had everything and missed nothing."

Work, there was plenty in the motherless family. "My mother, Ida, died when I was ten, my little brother was six. Suddenly Mama was dead, from a heart attack when working in the field. A shock." Anna Conti-Tonini's voice is but a whisper, she swallows hard. "I remember my mother only vaguely, but I do remember her funeral. That sight: The whole village, a caravan in black, praying, follows her coffin to the cemetery, led by the pastor with the cross. That scene will never leave my mind or my heart. Mother was only 42 years old and left behind a widower with seven children. The whole village suffered with us, I later heard people say. I think for many years this was one of the saddest burials in the Valle Maggia."

"My mother died when I was ten, my little brother six. Suddenly Mama was dead; from a heart attack when working in the fields." (1951)

Nonnna, the grandmother helped out, as did the whole village community. "But us children, we had to take on responsibility for our selves and our animals. It was sad. But somehow life went on. I helped where I could. Without being asked I got up at five, milked the cows, went to school, and at noon I cooked together with my siblings. When father cooked there were always onions in the pasta; these I did not like. I learned to do the wash in the wash-house of the village. There was not a single washing machine in the whole valley. All used the open washhouse with its tub made of stone. At home we put the wash into hot water with a kind of soap made from ashes. We then took the heavy load with a small wagon and scrubbed it under the running cold water. Hard work. Our large family did the wash twice a week. It was dried on lines behind the house – in winter the house was always full of drying

"For Christmas we got something practical. Whatever we needed. A new pair of shoes and with it an orange, a few cookies or some chocolate, and we had a little adorned Christmas tree."

wash." Toys were an alien world for Anna and her siblings. "I had a little teddy bear, nothing more. For Christmas we got something practical. Whatever we needed. A new pair of shoes and with it an orange, a few cookies or some chocolate. At the feast of Jesu Bambino I was so happy. The atmosphere was somehow more solemn than usual. And midnight-mass in the church was – for me – the highpoint of Christmas." Churchgoing was a matter of course in the Valle Maggia. "In this mother was strict. And we continued after her death; every Sunday we went to mass at ten o'clock."

Leisure time for the Valley's young was not spectacular. "We undertook little. I never played a music instrument. I had neither the time nor the money to go to Locarno. Nor was I interested in it. With other young people I stood around the village street, talking, and gazing after boys – once in a while." Then she adds laughing, "for a short time I had a friend from the valley. But he left me for another girl before I had turned twenty. Later they married and migrated to America. And I thought, perhaps he wasn't worth it. It was a time when neither marrying nor emigration was a topic for me. Father needed me."

What about leaving the narrow valley? To break out, as dozens of women and men in the valleys of the Ticino had done who sought their luck faraway? "Sometimes I did indeed think about it. But what would father have done with all the work and without me? Thus I stayed, until my father got older and gave up the farm. He kept only one cow for the daily milk."

In August 1966 Anna is busy haymaking when a stranger takes her photo. "As happened often. It was a young man. I told my brother: 'See that German. What might he see in me?' The next day I saw the stranger again as he was fishing in the Maggia River. We started talking. He spoke good Italian, but with a foreign accent. I was shy, but the young man interested me somehow. Lee Conti – that's how he introduced himself – and his father were from California, visiting Menzonio, his father's hometown, a stone's throw from Broglio. He told me that his father had migrated in 1920 to far-away America. For a different life and work. He found both. As did his two brothers. Now, after 46 years he had come home for the first time and had taken him, his oldest son, along." A fat Maggia fish bit at the fishing line and gave him the welcome opportunity to invite Anna for supper to his relatives in Menzonio. "And thus began our story. Now Lee came almost daily to Broglio for fourteen days. We went for walks, got to know each other, fell in love. And suddenly I could imagine going with him to another land, although I had not traveled much, and knew nothing about the world. As Lee went back with his father to California he wanted to take me along and get married. But I wasn't ready yet. At that time I couldn't leave my father and brother." Soon after, Renato became gravely ill, spent months in the hospital. She looked after her aged father, and then as well after the slowly recuperating brother. And she wrote numerous love letters to faraway California. And they were always answered. "I couldn't forget Lee anymore. Finally, two years later, being 26, I made the decision to travel alone to Lee in California, and to marry him. Without actually knowing where I was going to. I simply

trusted that it would turn out all right. I loved Lee; I think – somehow I could imagine a life with him. It was a truly big step for me, a step into the unknown. I had the picture of the Golden Gate Bridge from magazines before my eyes and thought that it would be really nice to actually see it. Father was sad about my decision. But he said nothing. And many people in the village probably did not believe that I was in earnest until I actually left. For good."

Renato accompanied his sister on the bus and train to Zurich-Kloten with few pieces of luggage, some clothing. Lee had sent her the plane ticket – a kind of advance marriage gift. "I did not know a word of English and on the Swissair plane to New York the stewardesses spoke German – I didn't know that either. I don't remember anymore how I survived the trip. In New York an airport employee brought me to the plane bound for San Francisco. Once again a six hour flight to an unknown destination. And then we landed an hour late at 10 o'clock at night on the west coast of America. I was deadly afraid that nobody would be waiting for me. What then?" Of course, father and son Conti were waiting for exhausted Anna at the airport. She was incredibly relieved. It was pitch black as they drove to the Sonoma Valley. "My first impression the next day was – here everything is brown. At home everything was so green. And it was hot, my Lord, so hot. I wasn't actually homesick although I initially missed my brother and my father. But nearby there was a family from Sementina near Bellinzona; it gave me a little feeling of home. And of course my future in-laws who spoke Italian with me; and my mother-in-law who was from northern Italy. Everywhere I was introduced as Lee's future wife, not as his friend from Switzerland." Anna lived for four months in the house of Lee's parents in Sonoma. And she learned that Lee's former friend, an American, did not suit his mother at all. "Lee's parents were truly happy that their 33-year-old son had found a wife from the Valle Maggia – one from back home. They had so much wanted that for him. My mother-in-law was strict and took care that we did not sleep in the same bedroom before the wedding. That was out of the question." On 28 November 1968 the pair married in the church of Sonoma, "shortly before my visa was to expire. Nobody was there from Switzerland. That would have been far too expensive. It was all right with me. I knew I had come to stay. Lee was the right one." The wedding trip led northward up the Pacific coast. "We had four days of constant rain. It barely bothered us."

Anna did not want to become an American citizen. "I am a Swiss, am I not. Actually I feel as if I was American, but I am not. Two years ago, when I went to Switzerland, I had to get a Swiss passport, the new one. I am proud of it. Why should I ever have changed that? Some find it stupid. But Lee never urged me. He too has half of his heart in the Valle Maggia, he always says."

Lee, the unpretentious postal clerk with Swiss roots moves with his young wife into the house at "White Oak" on the hill above Sonoma – into a house which he, the skilled craftsman, had built himself – with a balcony and a large garden, in which everything grows one may desire. Right away Anna takes on the tasks of a housewife. These she knows. She is getting used to the climate and the new surroundings. In 1971 Johnny is born, daughter Carmen in 1974, Liana – the unexpected latecomer – in 1978. "The first years I spoke Italian, the dialect, with the children. But once they went to school, they wanted to be like the others, and refused to speak their mother tongue. They still understand it, if they want to. But they rarely speak it."

California is home for Anna Conti-Tonini. "In the Valle Maggia the mountains were very close by. Here I see the hills of the Napa Valley. They are not high and not as near as if to touch. In California I get up in the morning and the sun is out, and it is sunny until half past seven in the evening. Not as in the Valle Maggia where in winter we had sometimes just two to three hours of sunlight. America is truly quite a different world. And I like it. I would not want to live in Broglio anymore. No, especially since my children live here nearby. I want to get old and to die in

America. When visiting Broglio without my daughters – oh, how I missed them. Although I still have a large family in the Ticino, and Lee, too, has many relatives in Menzonio. Together we certainly have over seventy relatives in the valley. But I belong here now." Will she visit Switzerland once more? "No idea! It costs us a fortune to travel to Europe. In the almost forty years I was there only twice – the first time in 1972 with baby Johnny. Later I had my three children and no time for travel anymore. How could I have gotten away? Then Johnny took us along. He said 'they want to see you, Mama, in Valle Maggia, at your home. Come along!' We stayed for a whole month in Switzerland. Everybody was so nice to us. Sometimes we were invited twice the same day to come to eat. I did not want to disappoint anybody. Between the two families there was a constant coming and going."

There aren't many Swiss anymore in the Napa Valley. "The old generations, many from Ticino, who had come earlier, have died. We are still in contact with a family from the Valle Maggia, the Traversis, who had come here from Cevio. But the Swiss picnic that is organized every year in Sonoma is not the same as it was earlier. Years ago Swiss came from everywhere. The second and third generations don't have much contact anymore with the old home-land of their parents. In this region I am probably one of the last women from the Ticino who have stayed. My son Johnny will continue using the name Tonini. I somehow missed to register him to become a Swiss citizen. Now it is too late. He would have to pass exams, do much paperwork. He doesn't want that. He has two boys. But they are still too little to know about Switzerland."

Anna Conti-Tonini becomes pensive. "I think that I would still be farming in Broglio if I had not emigrated. I probably would not even be married. Lee is my one true love. It is hard to tell how my life would have turned out. At any rate, I am not sorry that I am here. Return to Switzerland? I would never leave my children behind! That would break my and their heart. They are living in Sonoma – all three of them. Johnny is a firefighter, Carmen is employed by an entrepreneur, and the youngest, Liana, works in an institution for problem children. The grandchildren often come up here more than once a day to visit us. I am very pleased that they call us Nonno and Nonna."

Anna Conti-Tonini's life has been one of much work; her hands say it all: "I love to work. Still now. I think I am not a lazy person. If I think about it, perhaps I would have liked to be a florist. But now I am too old. I should have thought of that earlier. Yet, if I had a profession, there would be no time to go fishing and I would have little time to gather mushrooms with Lee." For some years now Lee is retired. "Now we are almost always together. And that is good. We work a lot in the garden and make our own wine: Sauvignon Blanc and Pinot Noir. The Chardonnay we make from grapes we buy from friends. We make over a hundred bottles of our own wine a year. I help my husband; we are a good and coordinated team. When I think about it, actually, I live a life here in Sonoma that is similar to the one in the Valle Maggia. Only the animals are missing." In America Anna's passion has become camping. The attachment on Lee's truck becomes their mobile home. "When we camp, Lee and I, I always want to cook and eat at the open fire. The region around Lake Tahoe, in the mountains, I like especially. I love the mountains, the trees, and the forest. It is also wonderfully beautiful to fish up on smaller Lake Davis. Then I am really happy, with a view of the lake, of the mountains ... almost like at home."

Does she still have dreams for her life? "Not really, no... But I dream a lot during the night. Often I find myself on the mountain alp Rima, an hour steep up on foot, where our family owned a small stone house and where we kept our goats in the summer. In my dream I meet people from the Valle Maggia. I am away from home for nearly forty years now and yet, I dream of Broglio. Isn't that strange?"

Even today, Anna still has dreams about the mountain alp Rima. (1968)

Then Anna Conti-Tonini has enough. "Now I have told you all about my life. Come, I want to show you the garden. And then you must, by all means, have a piece of apple pie before you leave."

LUISE
1930
BÜRGLER
BRUHIN

"America saved my life! Without penicillin that after World War II had arrived in Switzerland from the United States, I might not have survived my ruptured appendix as a seventeen year old. Ten years later I moved to the USA. In gratitude, as it were, I spent half my life over there," she says with a smile.

In the fall of 2001, the native of the district March in canton Schwyz had returned to Switzerland with her husband Joe who was suffering severely from Parkinson's disease. Returned for good, with a few bags only. "We left almost everything in America. Crazy, isn't it? The way I had gone, the same way I came home. With a bit more clothing, many experiences – and bent over." Shortly before Christmas 2001, Joe died after a few days in the hospital. "It did go well for him in the end, my Lord! Now I visit him in the graveyard of Schübelbach. And pray every day for his soul. Since he is gone, my tears are frozen; I can't cry anymore." She turns pensive. But given her life-long practice, she quickly puts heavy thoughts aside.

An oil painting of their farm, a John Deere mini-tractor, and a doll remind her of her life in the west of the United States. The Bürgler's dairy farm was sold, belongings auctioned off. "But only once we were in Switzerland. To witness it would have broken both our hearts." The returnee from America first hesitated to talk about her life. "It was nothing special." Her sister Ida had animated her to talk about it. But before she consented, Luise asked Abbot Martin Werlen from the Benedictine Monastery Einsiedeln whom she knows and esteems. Not the least because of his "yes, do tell your story," she lets her life pass review at her kitchen table in Schübelbach. She speaks the hearty dialect of a native of central Switzerland. When things turn difficult, when emotions surge, she utters an occasional English "My God!" or "O brother!" She builds her sentences willfully. Luise still thinks American, but speaks in Swiss German. "Those years were hard." She is visibly glad to be able to live again in her native village where her roots are. During our conversations, Luise's sister comes in for an occasional look. The two of them, both widows, get along well. They have liked each other since childhood. Now in old age they enjoy living under the same roof again. "It is the fulfillment of a dream to be able to get old in Switzerland."

Luise's life was anything but a dream. As she stresses off and on, she had to push through, to struggle. Forty-four years she had lived as a farmer, wife, mother, and Swiss emigrant in the United States.

As a young woman she had had no doubt that she would remain in the March, never to leave! For some time she had been dating the son of a well to do farmer near by. "If I could get that one, that would be something. And once I could have had him, I did not want him anymore." She would be a good asset with the homestead of her father and grandfather, someone had stated. "A safety for a man's existence, that I did not want to be."

Again and again a milk inspector from the Muotathal turned up at her father's stable. "When some day he asked me whether I was soon going to marry the young farmer, I answered more in jest. 'Certainly not, I rather emigrate to America.'"

The attentive official did not forget that sentence. He took it literally, all too literally. Because when visiting many home-steads throughout the canton, he heard of an emigrant from the Muotathal who was looking for a wife for his son: Joe Bürgler, the 37-year old Swiss farmer from Ferndale in the state of Washington, wanted to marry a capable Swiss woman in order to help manage the family farm. "He made me notice him." When she met the ten years older Joe Bürgler for the first time at the end of August 1957, it wasn't love at first sight for Luise. "The tall man stepped out of a small DKW, a German car. And my first thought was: O God, he has only legs!" She somehow refused to believe that he was in Switzer-land in search of a wife. Migrate to America? Certainly not! But Joe definitely wanted that young woman from the March. "He soon declared his love for me, said over and over again that he needed me and that he wanted to marry me. If I would not go with him to

America, he would stay single. He even cried. Men should not cry. They are the strong sex. Somehow I took pity on the American. So I said yes. It had been a quick decision. He did not have to beg me on his knees." They barely saw each other alone before their wedding – only a few times at his aunt in Wollerau. "I did not want to meet him at home. What would people have said if a complete stranger had come in and out?" After forty days of dating, on October 10, 1957, Luise married in her festive folk costume of the March in the Monastery Fahr. There was never a question of a wedding in Schübelbach. "They would have torn open their mouths about us. The bans already had created much ado among the people: She has an American!"

Before emigrating, they went on a honeymoon – as a three-some – to the canton Grisons. "It was okay for me that a cousin of Joe's accompanied us as our driver. The Swiss roads were too narrow for my husband."

The family, the neighborhood, all had counseled against a hasty wedding. "You are out of your mind. How can you emigrate with a man you hardly know? How can you move to a faraway land, to complete strangers?" But she prevailed. "Perhaps I did indeed play with my life then.

"Perhaps it had to be that way ...Yes, it is true, no one said that I had won big at the lottery. Earlier, if one wanted to get rid of people, one did buy them a one-way ticket and sent them overseas. For a forever good-by. It was not that way with me. I just went. Why? I don't know."

As little as she had brought along in 2001, as little had she taken along when she emigrated: "I had sent ahead a chest full of dowry linens by boat. On All Saints day two weeks after our wedding, Joe and I flew over the Atlantic to New York. Then by an inland flight to the Pacific coast."

On the long flight the young wife kept the cap of her native costume always on her knees. "Had the plane crashed, I would have taken it with me right then and there," she observes dryly.

During the whole long flight the young wife kept the cap of her native costume on her knees.

"Arriving early in the morning on the farm a few miles outside Ferndale, a town of about 8000 people, I realized right away that I did not have good soil under my feet."

Returning however was no question for Luise Bürgler. "My head would not have allowed that." She had decided to go for this life. That counted. "For me, there is only a 'yes and no' in my life. Nothing in-between. Go or not go. And then never again mulling it over." She barely knew a word of English: "Yes, no and good morning sir. I taught myself the language. When milking, I began counting. To this day, I don't know everything perfectly. I simply picked up something from here and there. I never could attend a language class. I had to milk. But Joe learned Swiss German from me. We never talked in English with each other."

From the second day on, the Swiss immigrant was always the first in the stable and at milking. Joe had rented 80 cows and the 160-acre farm from his father. "The first winter we lived the four of us, with the in-laws. I was not the daughter-in-law but the maid. I was the last to read the newspaper although I had paid for it. I think that my in-laws begrudged me even my food. Also our bedroom was not taboo. I set a trap for them and so did verify it. They had their nose in everything." Only when they finally left the farm and moved to the village could Joe buy the farm.

For sister Ida who was staying behind, the farewell was difficult. "In her first letter at Christmas 1957 I realized that something was not right, that Luise had it hard. She had to slave away, and we at home could do nothing for her. Often we were not even able to say much about her. There were people who would have said: Now she has what she had coming to her from her grandiose delusion," reminisces Ida. Their mother, however, believed for a long time that Luise had found heaven on earth.

Luise was born on April 21, 1930, "the same day as the Queen of England, but four years later. And I was born at home, as was the custom in rural areas then. When I was born, father was 54 years old, my mother 31."

On the homestead in Schübelbach, Luise and Lisa, who is thirteen months older, grew up like twins. "On Sunday we often went to church wearing the same outfit. The small difference in age was wonderful." What Ida proposed, the younger sister did, too. "I trotted after her, be it with the carriage full of dolls to the next village or for the burial of rooster heads to the nearby forest."

It was a simple life. Besides six heads of cattle, the father had a carting business. With horse and wagon he fetched wares from a factory, in winter ice for the brewery way back in the Klöntal, and he would drive the venerable clergy in a carriage or sleigh to Siebnen.

Her school years fell in the times of World War II. "We often had lessons outdoors under a pear tree or at the edge of the woods. One can hardly call this school, can one? The schoolhouse was mostly occupied by the military." While Ida liked to go on vacation once in a while to relatives in Cantons Glarus or Zurich, Luise loved it most to stay home and help her father in the stable. "At the age of nine already I knew how to milk and spread dung."

The irregular primary school years were for Luise a bother, and secondary school was not given even a thought. "For that I wasn't smart enough!"

At fifteen she went to work in a factory, a spinning mill. "At that time all of us young people went to work in a factory." Luise was part of the morning shift. "From 5 o'clock in the morning it meant standing for eight hours and to transfer threads from a roll onto a large weaving spool. I got 50 cents per hour. My largest paycheck was 125 francs for two weeks. I could always put away money. Nowadays they earn lots of money but don't save anything!"

A ruptured appendix at age 17 greatly endangered her life. But thanks to antibiotics, she survived. "After that there was again to be factory work, and I had to help at home besides. But a neighbor gave me the idea to look for professional schooling. To be a farmwoman was my life's goal anyway."

Luise Bürgler spent spring and summer of 1951 in the school for farmwomen at the Monastery Fahr. "It was so far away from home. That was something indeed, heaven knows! And the nuns – my experience with nuns in primary school had not been good. To this day I remember getting the cane from them." But in Fahr everything was to be different. "I had a unique time. I was not homesick. Fahr had become a second home for me. There I learned what was later to become important for me: gardening, cooking, managing the household and the farm. But I could not bring myself to kill geese, ducks, and chickens, my good Lord. With me all animals may die of old age. I am not for slaughtering." As a trained farmwoman she returned home. And when father Joseph Bruhin became ill in 1952 and died that fall, it was a matter of course that the unmarried daughter would manage the farm together with her mother. "My father wasn't anymore. I thought the world was coming to an end."

Life has not made Luise Bürgler bitter. To the contrary. Her youthful manner is serene. The longer she talks at her kitchen table, the more colorful her portrayals become. She gets excited while she pours out her memories. And yet, she remains cool, objective. Again and again she can laugh at herself. Her roundish face has few wrinkles. She needs neither hearing aid nor glasses. But she moves painfully with a cane, walks heavily bent over, her spine is contorted. Every step causes visible pain.

"My husband Joe was actually always good to me," insists Luise Bürgler. "Really. He simply married too late. With his forty years he was too tied to his family. His five siblings were constantly controlling. From the start they couldn't stand me. I was an interloper. And Joe did not have the courage to stand up for us. I never said a lot, I was there merely by marriage. But sometimes I did ask myself why in the world the father-in-law had wanted a wife for his son. If I had known that I would marry also difficult relatives ... oh brother! I suffered terribly from homesickness. Again and again there were times when I plunged very deeply. Once I wanted to know from a physician whether there were pills against homesickness. Unfortunately not, he said, only the good Lord can help. In the hayloft I made a sweater for my nephew Pirmin that in the end was washed by my tears. I cried a lot in America, until I was all cried out. Sometimes I even pitied my mother-in-law, Marie Dorothee Lüönd. She had been brought to America from Ecce Homo near Sattel by her much older husband who in 1903 had emigrated from the Muotathal. She too was always homesick. Only after one of her seven children had died was she not drawn back to Switzerland anymore."

Although she paid a heavy price for her passion of being a farmwoman, Luise Bürgler was also a good deal in her element on the American farm. "How I liked our Holsteiners – the cattle, the calves and the milk cows. And work on the farm, milking especially. For days I drove the tractor on the fields of the farm. The region around Ferndale is incredibly beautiful; it's open, but also hilly and green, and near the ocean. I love the wide sea."

After six years Luise went back to Switzerland for the first time. "Later Joe always had reservations and didn't want to let me go. He was afraid that some day I might not return." She invested her paternal inheritance. "I bought land. Land directly on the ocean. I loved that. I also bought a two-family home, later a piece of land on an island that had the form of Switzerland. I wanted even to build a restaurant there and to manage it myself. Crazy, isn't it! In the end I sold everything again with good profit."

All her life, she was a partner of her husband and a co-worker on the farm. Together they could manage a middle-sized farm. She remained forever faithful to her Joe. "I endured him; really, I also was fond of him, even while off and on I would have liked to give him away for a piece of cheese!"

She never wanted to become an American. "I have the Swiss passport – all those years I felt being an alien, I was an immigrant woman. After me no other immigrant was staying as long in the region. Many came and went. It is not as it was before. Anyway, now I will never again go over there. I can telephone my son every week." She would have really liked having her own children. "I didn't get any. Perhaps it was better that way." She did not give up though and looked for a child to adopt. "On the evening before Thanksgiving 1966, we could fetch our 1-year old Joey at his foster parents. That he threw his little arms around my neck right away made the start very much easier."

Joey grew up as a single child in the midst of nature, cows, apple pies, cheesecakes, and Swiss German. "He saw how hard we had to struggle. To our great astonishment he volunteered after his school years for the military. He became a computer specialist and as a sub-officer of the U.S. Navy dove for twenty years into the depths of the Atlantic and Pacific waters. Only three people of the United States knew where the U-boat of 175 men was moving. I still remember very well how we were allowed to telegraph only good news into the depth of the ocean so he would not get upset."

Three times the Bürglers were forced to start anew with their farmstead. "In the 1980s everything had become too much for us. We put our cattle with our neighbors, sold a part of them with a heavy heart, but kept the house and stables and went to Switzerland for a year. The stay in the homeland was to last from March to March. We sent Joey to school in Schübelbach. But before Christmas my husband was again drawn to the West. We took over the neglected farmstead again, bought cattle, and let them out on the pastures. "When chopping wood, my husband had a bad accident. For months, a trapped nerve in his back prevented him from work. Again we were forced to sell and to start the cattle herd again at a later point. And in the nineties we were both in a bad car accident. Healing took a lot of time, and work stopped. But we did it a third time, though with much effort, and together we got the farm to prosper again."

Luise fought, stood her ground – also when confronted with a false move by the hospital of Ferndale. "After many a kidney colic my physician advised an operation. Already on the operating table

I still fought with the physician about which kidney was to be taken out, the left or the right one. Luckily the narcosis had not yet worked when I realized that he put the knife on the wrong side. Imagine that! I was right of course. From the pain I knew all too well that it was the left one. After another x-ray it was clear! For a long time I could not forgive my physician."

The farmwoman knew free time only from hearsay. But there were often possibilities for interesting encounters. Some friendships formed over the years. She had only few contacts with Swiss women and men. "I was very distrustful, trusted only a few. Best I liked the Indians in the near-by Lummi reservation." She became friends not only with the chief, and brought him vegetables and fruit from her garden. She also met often with the older women of the tribe. She admired their magnificent hand woven cloth and had clothing made of it. "Joe and I attended mass mostly in the Catholic Church on the reservation. We liked it far better. Anyhow, the Indians – they were most obliging people, simple, joyful, and cordial. All that we immigrants now claim as our own had once belonged to them."

"Now you must also think of yourself." She heard that phrase from a physician for the first time when she brought her deathly ill husband to the hospital in Lachen, canton Schwyz. "That was wholly new for me. That I really had to learn at my age."

At the Ziegelhof in Schübelbach Luise is still the first getting up in the morning, also the first who puts out the light in her room at eight o'clock in the evening, "to save electricity. I can pray in the dark. I do not tell anybody when I get up. It is very early. First I must pray again, for Joe and to all the saints, so they will be there when I die. And for those I had met when I was at the Monastery Fahr. And to Saint Meinrad – he has already helped me so much – and not the least for the poor souls. They need it above all.

"Then I may go to the stable, to the cattle of my nephew Armin, to feed the animals, to clean up. I simply sit down in-between if my back hurts. The 18 milk cows, 15 cattle, and 15 calves are my joy.

"Were I to live my life over again, I would do many things differently. But there is no beginning anymore, only an end. I would certainly never again migrate to America. Perhaps I would become a nurse or even a veterinarian here in Switzerland. I assisted the veterinarians at all operations on our farm."

And at the end of our conversation Luise Bürgler-Bruhin mentions in passing: "I still have kept some 20 hectares [about 50 acres] of land that borders on the farm. Much forest. It is wonderful there. There is a hill where one could build houses. I will sell the property only when they give me what I want for it. Otherwise my son may sell it later. I don't need much anymore to live," Luise Bürgler-Bruhin dryly observes – proving once more that she is very much in command of her life.

THEY WENT BEFORE

Four Historical Portraits

In the eighteenth and nineteenth centuries some four hundred thousand Swiss moved permanently or for some time to regions now part of the United States.[1] Although about half of them were women, records by or about them beyond mere mention are relatively sparse and have received only occasional attention. Yet like the men, these immigrant women experienced the joys and hardships of the journey, mostly taking care of children of all ages under trying circumstances and at times being with child or giving birth on the way. With their husbands, they took on the arduous task of re-establishing home, farm or business in lands that were quite other in climate, soil, and vegetation and, also, belonged to indigenous peoples who defended them to the last against the property-hungry and violence-prone invaders. Sickness and death were common, sparing neither old nor young, parents or children, events that emigrant accounts chronicle predictably often.[2] What follows, portrays experiences of two eighteenth and two nineteenth century emigrant women of Swiss origin on the basis of accidentally preserved fragments that show their lives were as ordinary and unique as those of their twentieth century sisters.

Two eighteenth century accounts

In the first half of the 18th century mainly two regions of the British colonies vied for settlers, one called Carolina, the other Pennsylvania. Jean Pierre Purry (1675–1736) of Neuchâtel, Switzerland, had turned from wine merchant to emigration entrepreneur.[3] He proposed to the Dutch East India Company to settle a colony either in South Australia or in South Africa, but without success. Also in France his proposals fell on deaf ears. But the British Board of Trade was well disposed towards his plan of establishing a buffer colony on the southern Atlantic coast of North America between the French in the lower Mississippi Valley and the Spanish in Florida to the south. In 1730 Carolina had become a crown colony and Purry eventually received a land grant of 48,000 acres. He planned to build a town on the Yamassee Bluff on the north side of the Savannah River some 30 miles west of what became Savannah and to bring some 1200 Swiss to the projected town of Purrysburg and its environs. His pamphlet *The Now in the New World Merrily and Without Homesickness Living Swiss*, with cleverly shortened and probably some spurious letters of emigrants especially in the German version, promised prospective settlers a paradisiacal world of milk and honey.

The other region was promoted by William Penn (1644–1718) to whom in 1680 "by the good Providence of God a country in America" had been given by the British crown in payment of a debt.[4] He too recruited settlers in person and by pamphlets. In the end some 58 accounts and broadsides "in English, Dutch, German, and French" carried the message to people of Western Europe.[5] Penn's enterprise was religiously inspired, and the advertisements were honest and stressed that his domain would provide full "Liberty to all People to worship Almighty God, according to their Faith and Perswasion."[6] For prospective emigrants it was less than easy to decide whom they should believe. They as well as governmental authorities were keen, therefore, to receive direct and reliable news from either of the regions through trustworthy letters, occasional visitors, or returnees. But news could take a good year to reach their destination, travel experiences depended largely on luck varying from tolerable to horrendous, and conditions in the new land changed swiftly and made reports often dated. The emigration of a group of 1734 to which Esther Werndli belonged, and of Anna Thommen and her family, who left Switzerland in 1736, highlight the quandary whether emigrants should choose Carolina or Pennsylvania.

ESTHER
WERNDLI
GOTSCHI

Many documents exist that touch the life of Esther Werndli, but her authentic voice is audible from two extant letters only. These, however, intimate how she viewed her emigration and the features of the world in which she was to spend the second part of her life.[7]

A Pastor's Wife

Esther Werndli hailed from a family of Zurich of modest means and was baptized in the Grossmünster, the city's main church, on 26 January 1688.[8] Nothing is known about her youth, but she was apparently schooled to be a teacher. In her letter, written about 1736, she lamented: "My state is very abject, my profession counts for nothing in this country. I cannot teach school here because nobody will take me in" (110). On 24 June 1710 Esther Werndli married the ordained cleric Moritz Götschi, son of a fountain maker, who had been baptized in Zurich's St. Peter's Church on 26 September 1686. In 1702 he had begun his studies at the Carolinum, a school for future theologians, and was ordained on 1 April 1710 as a cleric of Zurich's State Church. Since many vied for a regular position, Götschi was not chosen before 1712 to serve as deacon in the parish of Berneck. It was basically a teaching position and he was bound to teach children's catechism classes also in neighboring Widnau.

Esther Werndli's husband seems to have had a pugnacious temperament. When in 1720 a dispute about the duties of a deacon at Berneck erupted, he involved himself in the controversy and became a target of sharp critique. He was accused of lacking in punctuality, teaching ability, and the fulfillment of duties. He was declared to be stubborn, intolerant of critique, and proud, being given to "much boasting and demonstrating his learning, in ostentatiously showing his precious pocket watch etc. which greatly offends peasants and lords alike."[9] By that time the position of pastor had opened at Salez in the Rheintal of canton St. Gallen, and Moritz Götschi, though the youngest of seven applicants, was chosen on 19 October 1720. But the position was not attractive. The people of the parish were of modest means, the dues that the pastor had to collect himself rather meager, so that the family needed to keep cattle in order to make ends meet.

During the years at Berneck, Esther Werndli had become the mother of five children. Anna was born in 1711, Barbara was baptized 2 February 1715, and Esther was born about 1717. Two sons followed; Johann Heinrich was baptized 4 March 1718 and Rudolph 30 October 1719. In Salez three more children were born. Beat was baptized 18 September 1721, Moritz 20 October 1723, and Magdalena 5 August 1725.[10] As in Berneck, also in Salez dissatisfaction with Pastor Götschi's pastoral care arose. He did not tolerate criticism, his sermons were rambling, at times delivered also with uncalled for passion, and his demands of people unreasonable. In 1724 he had introduced an hour of catechetical instruction before the regular church service and, by occasionally extending it, made people wait in front of the church. He could not get along with the bailiff, the representative of Zurich's government. An official visitation showed that the complaints were not without foundation, but in consideration of the large family and meager income neither recall nor punishment followed.

Early in 1731 43-year old Esther Werndli suffered a first misfortune. It became known that 24-year old Barbara Rüdisühli from the nearby hamlet Frümsen who had been a maid in the Götschi household, had given birth to an illegitimate son whose father was Moritz Götschi. The bailiff immediately suspended him, on 3 February he was formally deposed and stricken from the ministerial rolls, and the family had to leave the parsonage before Easter. In his plight Esther Werndli's husband behaved wildly. He was reported "to cry loudly and to scream ... that he was damned, that he was not a man but a dog, and that he should be beheaded."[11] Zurich's magistrates found it necessary to dispatch an emissary to Salez to bring Götschi to the city. There he had to face the ecclesiastical and secular authorities and was imprisoned.

It was a hard blow for the family, and Esther Werndli had to seek public aid. It was demanded that 16-year old Barbara look for a position as a maid like her older sister. The 13-year old Henry, 12-year old Rudolf, "10-year old Beat" and "8-year old Moritz" were brought to the orphanage, and only 6-year old Magdalena could stay with her mother. After his release Moritz Götschi tried to support the family by giving private lessons, but the income was insufficient to feed the family. Even the children's clothing had to be provided by public aid. How Esther Werndli endured her threefold misfortune – the trespass and deposing of her husband, the commitment of their children to the orphanage, the poverty and dependence on aid – seems nowhere documented, but soon another misfortune was to burden her.

Departure

In the early 1730s Jean Pierre Purry's advertising campaign for his settlement in the English province of South Carolina was at its height. In July 1734 his pamphlet *The Now in the New World Happily and Without Homesickness Living Swiss* that described his lands in glowing terms was sold for three shillings and had also reached the countryside.[12] In a move to Carolina Moritz Götschi saw an opportunity to start anew and perhaps to gain back his status in the new land. His wife, however, seems to have abhorred emigration. In her letters she not only praised Zurich's world, but also condemned leaving the homeland. May her experiences, she wrote, be "an example to all people, be they clerical or secular, with such a rebellious rabble who leave the country against the will of my gracious lords, who are justly smitten by God with contumaciousness and blindness" (108). And again: "Beseech therefore all the people in my fatherland not wantonly to disobey my gracious lords' decree and not to plunge body and soul into misery" (111). The Zurich authorities strove to stop Purry's campaign only hesitantly until bad news trickled in from Carolina.

They allowed Moritz Götschi and also the people who gathered around him to leave for the Promised Land. On Monday 9 October 1734 some 240 to 270 people left Zurich on three boats in order to reach Basel and then Rotterdam by traveling down the Rhine. Later some more groups joined the emigrants in Basel while others went on foot through France.[13] What Esther Werndli may have felt when she saw her husband saying a prayer at departure surrounded by the emigrants and numerous onlookers! An eyewitness reported some sad scenes: "It was pitiful to see how children would gladly have left their parents, had they only been able to stay here; ... that wives fainted in pain because they had been forced by their husbands to depart; as one occasionally also spotted men who felt quite miserable because their wives had not been easily coaxed into leaving."[14]

In Basel the emigrants met with serious disappointment. The rumor that from there on they would travel free of charge proved to be false. Moving down the Rhine, furthermore, proved to be costly since they had to contract repeatedly for the next leg of their journey. Also hostile French and imperial troops threatened the travelers. On the boats they lacked space, were exposed to rain and cold, and had to spend nights in the open. Fights erupted easily, in part because Moritz Götschi let himself be regaled in homes during halts and was suspected of pocketing money given in support of the emigrants. An eyewitness who was less than well disposed towards Götschi further reported that also Esther Werndli fought with her husband, that "she was cursing and swearing at him, and one morning even tore the stick out of his hands and treated his back with it so that he wanted to leave, but the children screamed and begged him to stay."[15] On 28 October 1734 four couples among the emigrants were married in Neuwied, among them Anna Götschi whose groom was Hans Konrad Wirz (1706–1763) who later became a teacher and pastor.[16] The emigrants rejected however the offer of the Count of Neuwied to settle on his lands. When they reached Rotterdam, they had to endure a long and costly wait

It was there that Moritz Götschi received a message from a Mr. Schobinger of St. Gallen that he was to go immediately to The Hague, which he did in the company of his son-in-law Hans Konrad Wirz while his family stayed in Rotterdam. It seems that he had hoped to get free passage to England, but was rebuffed by the British embassy. He was counseled, however, to meet with Antistes Felss, the leader of the Dutch Reformed Church who told him on leaving: "For six years we have been looking for a man to organize the churches in Pennsylvania. ... Divine Providence has sent you to us. I shall have a call made out for you, by which you shall be superintendent-general over the whole state of Pennsylvania. ... You will have an income of 2000 gulden a year till the organization is completed."[17] How Esther Werndli may have received such news? Suddenly her husband had not only been restored to the ministry, but also been called to high ecclesiastical office and been promised a decent income, although it would not be in Carolina, but in Pennsylvania. Perhaps this turn of events made leaving the homeland more acceptable, although the ocean journey lay still ahead. Her husband immediately wrote to Reverend Johann Baptiste Ott (d. 1744) in Zurich in order to obtain the necessary testimonials for him. Most of the emigrants also agreed to move to Penn's province instead of Purry's colony.

On 24 February 1735 the emigrants were finally able to leave Rotterdam on the boat Mercury, captained by William Wilson. They reached Cowes at the southern end of the Isle of Wight in two days where more victuals as well as medicines were bought. The crossing lasted 12 weeks and was beset by storms; food and water were bad, but Philadelphia was finally reached on May 28. "After an indescribably unlucky voyage" (108), the arrival was for

Esther Werndli certainly a relief, although "everything has been used up on the most abominable trip" (112) and in her view there was "no hope for salvation across the abominable sea" (111). On the day of arrival the Elders of the Reformed parish of Philadelphia came to visit Moritz Götschi on the boat. They were pleased, as the son Heinrich Götschi reported, with the charge his father had been given at The Hague, and they welcomed him as their pastor. The next day they came again to bring him and Esther Werndli to their future residence where numerous people had assembled to greet them. But as soon as Moritz Götschi was on land he became so weak that he had to be carried on a chair to the house. On arrival he asked to lie down, but since there were many people on the ground floor he was to be brought upstairs to a quiet room, but expired in the middle of the stairs. On the third day he was buried after a solemn service in the cemetery of the Presbyterian church.[18]

Partial view of Philadelphia, after an engraving of George Heap, 1754.

The Widow

How did Esther Werndli endure this third great misfortune? Just when a new day in her life seemed to have arrived, her hopes were shattered again. In the letters she did not deal with the event, but merely observed that "we almost fared as our gracious lord and other faithful people truly foretold, especially to our late father since his great toil and care for the godless people is ill rewarded" (108). And further: "As to myself, I am the most wretched creature among all of them and the poorest of all human beings" (110). As she had been in Zurich, she was again deprived of her children: "Esterli and Mari Babli are earning a livelihood here and there with spinning," she wrote, "the three younger lads are indentured until they are 21 years old," that is 16-year old Rudolf, 14 -year old Beat, and 13-year old Moritz; only 10-year old Magdalena was still with her (110). About herself she lamented: "My sight and hearing have been badly weakened on the sea, and I cannot describe what I and my family ... had to go through on the voyage, and what

I have to go through in this country. ... I would gladly suffer temporal hunger and thirst in my fatherland, and work my fingers to the bone, if only I could once more enjoy the church and the holy sacraments, then I would gladly die" (112). Now "I must spend my life in utter misery and be pushed from one miserable shelter to the other" (110). Yet not only was poverty again her lot, but she was also gripped by a deep aversion towards the new surroundings in which she could not discover anything good.

But Johann Heinrich, her 18-year old son, seems soon to have embarked on his career. Like his father, he had begun his studies at the Carolinum in Zurich to prepare for the ministry, but had to give them up after eight months and emigrate. Neither his brief studies nor his youth prevented him, however, to serve as preacher in several parishes and soon also to baptize, celebrate the Lord's Supper, and marry people without license from the ecclesiastical authorities of the Netherlands. He also adapted his name to those of the pastors in the Dutch Reformed Church, which he later joined, and called himself John Henry Goetschius (1718–1774). In her first letter his mother worried: "I don't know how it will go with Heinrich since he has to travel far for preaching his homilies, needs many shoes and clothes for it, which he cannot afford because of low pay. When the late father's clothes are worn out, he will then have to go near naked, I am much afraid" (111). His career was to turn out stormy like that of his father. He was a fervent partisan of the Pietist wing of the Dutch Reformed persuasion, saw himself as "a watchman on Zion's towers and walls," and he castigated his opponents for "their old rotten and stinking routine religion." He was often embroiled in bitter confrontation and ignored the jurisdiction of the Dutch ecclesiastical authorities. His ministry, therefore, has been appraised differently. [19]

The Reformed church of Schraalenburgh where Esther Werndli's son John Henry Goetschius preached.

Esther Werndli found everything in her new surroundings abhorrent. "In winter it is cold here beyond measure" she complained, "and in summer warm beyond measure, more than in Switzerland, so that many people faint with heat." But not only

Philadelphia's first German-Reformed church.

the climate was hard to take, "One has to live very poorly here with food and drink; bread is very coarse; … a measure of wine is three guilders." Also "clothes [were] terribly bad and dear, so you cannot get them." Also the mix of people was intolerable. "There were so many languages, English, Swedish, North Welsh, High German, Low German, Dutch. There are many *nigger*; they are sold here in groups as slaves for life. The native heathens live among us, are very abominable people, brown, real godless heathens. They beat each other dead like dogs, go naked, painted with red, green and yellow colors, rings on ears and noses, *summa* I fear them much" (109). And the young people: "They can become nothing but heathens. The young know nothing about God, therefore are terribly disobedient to their parents. When they are 18 years old, their parents may tell them nothing anymore; therefore many parents must sigh in sorrow over those that corrupt their children, as I had myself, alas! to find out, too, besides all my other misfortunes" (110).

"As to the spiritual," Esther Werndli thought, there was an even "much greater misery." Many of the Swiss immigrants had "fallen off to all sorts of sects because of the lack of the word of God, so that the people must waste away miserably in body and especially in soul" (109). There are even "people in the country, when I ask them whether their children are baptized, they say, what's the use, the pigs aren't baptized either, yet they grow. Just think of how I must feel among those people." Thus "we must be miserably ashamed of our nakedness, particularly in face of other religions which despise us scornfully and must well-nigh succumb in misery" (112). She had to endure such "misery mostly among the Anabaptists who will, to my sorrow, taunt me with how their forefathers in Zurich were persecuted and killed and driven out. … It is like a sword in my bones when they revile me every day and say, where is your religion which you take for your God?" (110). In sum, Esther Werndli could not find anything good in this new land, "among so many religions, Reformed, Lautrans [Lutherans]

Catholic, Quacrans [Quakers], Menanists [Mennonites], Pietists, Sibentägren [Sabbatists], Tumblers [Dunkers], Atheists, also those that call themselves nothing, that believe no religion, no worship, no churches, no schools, even no God, no devil, no heaven, no hell. ... This land is a house of refuge for banished sects, a shelter for all evil-doers in Europe, a confounded Babel, a repository for all unclean spirits, a dwelling place of devils, a first world Sodom" (109).

Might Esther Werndli's views eventually have softened? There seem to be no sources that give news about her later life or about her death. She became, however, the mother of a large progeny, among which there were people of outstanding talent, whose success perhaps would have comforted her.[20]

ANNA
THOMMEN
WISTER

1720

On 28 April 1736 sixteen-year-old Anna Thommen of Walden-burg in today's canton Basel-Landschaft boarded with her family and other emigrants a Rhine-boat in the city of Basel, destined to bring them to Rotterdam. There they would take the ship *Princess Augusta*, captained by Samuel Merchant and bound for Philadelphia in the British province of Pennsylvania.[21] Anna left no known account of the journey, but her older brother Hans Jacob wrote that it had been "very dangerous, difficult, and boring and costly." It was also long. "One estimates from Basel to Rotterdam 180 hours," he reported. "From Rotterdam to Filadelfia 1400 hours. We spent 12 weeks in the big boat on the ocean ... and arrived in Philadelphia on September 15. We had to endure almost every kind of sickness on the ocean. It is very unpleasant as to eating and drinking. ... There is much remorse on this wearisome journey, especially for those with small children."[22]

With young Anna (1720–1778) the Thommen family counted eight adults and a child, and consisted of her mother Margaretha (1681–1742), born Rickenbacher, and her father Durs (1679–1749); her sister Catharina (1702–1742); her brother Martin (1704–?) with his wife Barbara (1700–?), born Mohler and their son Johannes (1730–?); and her brothers Hans Jacob (1708–1739) and Durs, Jr. (1711–1775).[23] Anna's family was quite well to do. The sale of the farm had netted 3,497 Basel pounds on which an emigration tax of 310 pounds had to be paid.[24] What then drove the family to leave their homeland and move to Penn's province? Anna's father answered that question on 29 December 1735, when he stated his reasons for wanting to leave in a petition to the bailiff of Walden-burg, the Basel government's representative. They included high interest rates, his and his wife's advanced age, and their sons and daughters facing the erosion of the value of their property and eventual poverty.[25]

The Power of Pietism

But matters were less straightforward. Shortly after arrival in Philadelphia, Anna's father sent a report to "my beloved Reverend Mr. Candidate Annoni." In 1743 Anna herself wrote a letter to him, her "beloved friend."[26] Hieronymus Annoni (1697–1770) was the son of a prominent government official who had studied for the ministry. But he was to accept only hesitantly his first pastorate in Waldenburg, Anna's home parish, in 1739, and not before he had undertaken extensive journeys in search of genuine Christian communities abroad. He was to become a leading proponent of Pietism that had arisen in the early decades of the 18th century also in the churches of Switzerland.[27] Pietists stressed personal heartfelt devotion rather than assent to proper doctrine and viewed baptism less as a rite guaranteeing salvation than as a signature of experienced inner conversion. They also believed that each person was immediate to God, and they gathered in so-called collegia pietatis, assemblies of piety, which the opponents contemptuously called conventicles. Pastors like Annoni promoted them, others viewed them as doctrinally suspect, leading people to avoid regular church services and criticize the clergy. In these special meetings Pietists sang hymns, studied scripture, and shared religious experience. Formal theological learning, age, status, and gender counted little. Some of them became "Separatists" in that they rejected the established Christian churches.[28]

When in 1732 ecclesiastical officials asked Reformed pastors to turn in written reports "as to Pietism or rather Separatism," Pastor Gürtler of Anna's parish Waldenburg observed: "Thank God, as far as he knew, no so such dangerous conventicles had been held in his parish, also that no such person who might give cause for such separatism had ascended his pulpit." Yet he did have to mention three of his parishioners, among them Anna's mother Margareth and her sister Catharina. They went to church only "from time to time," stayed away from the Lord's Supper, and they had "also attended assiduously such conventicles." When asked about it, they offered "all kinds of reasons to excuse themselves because of their behavior," most however did not make the mark with him.[29] Years later Catharina's death notice was to state: "She was a loving soul and had suffered much persecution for God's sake already in Switzerland."[30] Finally, a passage in the *Chronicon Ephratense*, the chronicle of the Ephrata Cloister, that deals especially with Anna, states: "That is what a pious minister in Switzerland, Lucius by name, had told them about taking leave, namely that there were many sects in the country they were going to, therefore they should join the most despised."[31] Lucius referred to Samuel Lutz (1674–1750), a noted preacher, author, and pastor of the Bernese Reformed Church. He was a leading, but controversial proponent of the Pietist agenda and often in conflict with the authorities of the established church.[32] The Thommen family's ties to Pastors Lutz and Annoni intimate that Anna and other members of her family had been deeply touched by Pietism, the main reason for their move.

Getting Settled

In Philadelphia, where Anna's family seemed to have stayed for some weeks, she met the brothers Caspar (1696–1752) and Johannes (1708–1789) Wister.[33] They hailed from near Heidelberg in Germany, had arrived in Philadelphia in 1720 and 1727 respectively, where they became wealthy, Caspar by establishing glass works and Johannes by the wine trade. In his October 1737 account about conditions in Pennsylvania, which Anna's father had promised the Basel authorities, he remarked: "If someone would want to report or write to me, one may write to Philadelphia in [care] of Caspar Wister or Johannes Wister, there I will receive it reliably." He also mentioned that "I have taken up a place of 350 acres with 2 houses and barns," also with sundry animals and goods, for which he had paid "360 pounds, that is as much as 2700 pounds Basel currency." The family had settled in a place called "Quitopahilla, 80 miles from Philadelphia" or, as Hans Jacob wrote, "22 hours from Filadelfia in Kanastangen [Conestoga]." For those who were tempted to believe Purry's claims, Hans Jacob added: "There is in Carolina quite rotten land, no good crops grow there, one must have wheat from Pensilvania, otherwise they have no decent bread save pumpernickel."[34]

In 1737 the region, in which the Thommens settled, was in ferment. "I cannot describe it to you earnestly enough," Anna wrote to Reverend Annoni in 1743, "it would take too many words, how an unusual turn of mind and community was born out of the witness of God's Holy Spirit."[35] The religious awakening movement centered on Georg Conrad Beissel (1691–1768), a former baker from Eberbach on the Neckar in Germany, who had become an ardent radical Pietist.[36] He had arrived in Boston in 1720, went to Germantown near Philadelphia, then west to live as a hermit, but was followed by other seekers. Around 1732 he settled on the Cocalico Creek in the Conestoga region and by Anna's arrival in 1737 had gathered the solitary women and men under his spiritual leadership into a monastic community that came to be known as Ephrata. He lived however by himself and pursued a unique theological understanding and way of life, while the community was divided into a group of solitary Sisters and Brothers, married householders, and the Zionitic brotherhood.[37]

Anna "was the first in the [Thommen] family among the elect," the *Chronicon* states, "and entered the Sisters' convent in the bloom of youth."[38] Soon her mother Margaretha and her Sister Catharina followed, while her brother Hans Jacob joined the Zionitic Brotherhood. Her father stayed on his farm and, Anna wrote, he is "happy in this country and lives quite solitary and secluded near Ephrata. He is very close and dear to me because he, too, loves righteousness and is at one with the communion of the saints." But her "brothers in the flesh," Martin and Durs, had unfortunately "separated from our community," she reported, "but they are not against it either. I am of the hope that they too might change. But alas, what is there to say. The foolishness of man in these our times is so great that almost nobody asks about God anymore, and quite everybody lives in the security of the flesh." In the same letter, however, Anna had to inform Reverend Annoni, that she was the only one left in the cloister since "3 have died. First Hans Jacob died in the 6th month Ano 1739, and after that Catrina in the year 1742, also in the 6th month, and half a year later, in the 12th month, my mother died too. As for their way of life, they were all of them very sincere ... [and] would have been much at ease in our community."[39]

The Ephrata monastery of the Sisters.

In the Sisterhood

When Anna joined the Ephrata community, she took the name Tabea, meaning 'kind'. In her letter she called herself "a humble disciple of Christ" and reported: "Some 30 of us solitary spiritual Sisters are living together in one house. Our ways and conduct are solitary, devoted to God, and [we] live secluded and detached from the world. Oh! a very great grace that something is left in this wicked times that will serve him with a pure and holy life."[40] The daily routine Anna had chosen was rigorous. The day began at 5 a.m. when the Sisters were awakened, got ready for the day, and said their first prayers. From 6 to 9 a.m. they did their assigned housework, at 9 a.m. they ate breakfast, followed by prayers until 10 o'clock, when they went again to their tasks in the house, kitchen, field, or special workroom until 5 p.m. The next hour was devoted to meditation, at 6 p.m. dinner was served, 7 to 9 p.m. was a time of study, then night rest, interrupted between 12 midnight to 2 a.m. by religious service.[41] Talking was to be kept to a minimum and work to be done quietly.

The spirituality that Sister Tabea embraced was based on Conrad Beissel's view that the body, as matter, was sundered from the divine Spirit by its needs, especially by its sexuality. The separation had been caused by the Archangel Lucifer's and later also by Adam's fall and was remedied only in Christ's crucifixion. Especially the "married state had originated in sin, and would therefore come to an end."[42] Ephrata's solitary women and men were to overcome the rule of the flesh, thus hasten humankind's redemption. The Certificate of Betrothal of the Spiritual Virgins characterized its members as uniting with the Divine, the essence of redemption: "If two are in love and become paired into one, the one may preserve the treasure and virginity of the other. The pure spirit, the dove, that has drawn me to him, has paired me with him, moved by ardent love."[43] Similarly the title page of the Sisterhood's rule, possibly created by Sister Tabea in striking calligraphy, reads: "The Rose or: The Spiritual Marriage Engagement of the Pleasant Flower at Saron with Her Heavenly Bridegroom, to Whom [She Is] Engaged for ever as Her King, Head, Husband, Lord, and Bridegroom."[44]

Habit of a Sister at the Ephhrata community.

The attire, described in the *Chronicon of the Sisterhood* that Sister Tabea was to wear for some thirty years also strove to overcome the lure of the body: "First, we have a knit gown of grey fabric, just as nature supplies it. To this gown belongs a hood of same fabric, only that it may be of coarse flaxen cloth. It is arranged as follows: it is to be deep over the face, so that the head may be covered and enveloped, from this a veil is to hang from the front and back, long enough to be caught by the waist girdle. In front under the chin there are to be two small lapels, to further hide the body." For footwear the Sisters wore "knit socks ... made like shoes," made of "thin woolen cloth or leather sole, so that our walk may be quiet and silent."[45] For the "enamoured souls in God," furthermore, "life and conduct cannot agree or conform to the world, whether it be eating and drinking, – sleeping or waking, – in clothing or other requisite things pertaining to the natural life, needing to subsist upon little." Their spiritual state demanded the "contracting to the utmost our eating and drink, sleep and waking."[46] As to their work, besides their ordinary tasks in house and field, they would pursue three special endeavors: singing, writing, and quilting. Sister Tabea was to excel in two of them.

In late 1739 or 1740 the Sisters began to turn to "Sing-Arbeit," the work of song. Thus far the "Solitary had sought self-sacrifice in hard labor," the *Chronicon* observes, "but now the Superintendent was urged by his Guide to establish higher schools, of which the singing school was the beginning."[47] Sister Tabea, "accomplished and well formed, endowed with fine natural gifts," was "an excellent singer, on which account she was of much value to the Order." In addition, "she was also fortunate in enjoying the confidence of the Superintendent, and was his right hand in the important work of the singing-school, spending many sleepless night over it."[48]

First a musical expert named Ludwig Blum, about whom little is known, conducted the school. In 1741 Beissel replaced him as choirmaster, having evolved his own musical theology, notational system, and way of singing. He thought "that natural man was from below and from earth, this high art however from above and heaven." God "took no pleasure in the blubber of he-goats and rams," he claimed, "and in the clamor of wild beasts, but truly in the praise of the godly." Singing was "to glorify the wonder of our God, to adore the Almighty with songs of love and praise, performed in the manner of angelic choirs and thrones." It was, in short, "a noble and paradisiacal art."[49]

Initially only the Sisters were engaged in the craft, and Beissel turned out to be an impatient instructor, scolding them at times for hours. When the sisters had enough of his tirades, they sent Sister Tabea, "who was bold enough for such a mission," to tell him "that they would break off all connection with the school entirely."[50]

Jerenia (Father Peaceful) in Ephhrata. Vignette on the title page of the "Christian ABC".

It appears that the confrontation alienated Tabea from Beissel. Perhaps hastened also by the loss of her sister Catharina and her mother Margaretha, she fell in love with a Daniel Scheibly whom the Brethren had invited to Ephrata after having paid his ship's fare in Philadelphia. They exchanged secret letters and Tabea promised to marry Daniel. At the wedding ceremony to be performed by a householder, Beissel called Anna, now dressed as a matron, aside "and took her again under his protection." She returned to her cell. "To atone for the scandal she had caused, she shed many tears of fervent repentance" and received the new name Anastasia, "One risen from the dead."[51] She also inspired the other Sisters again to submit to Beissel's guidance and secretly trained them in singing. One day they "appeared in the meeting and sang the hymn 'God, We Come to Meet Thee,' with five voices, which was so well received in the Settlement, that everyone had his name entered for the choir, so one did not know who should perform the outside work."[52] Sister Anastasia also composed the hymn "How is the Lord so Kind, and Faithfully Delights our Heart" and set it to music in five parts.[53]

From the singing-work blossomed a second major effort: The singers needed texts and scores. Beissel's numerous hymns and those of others needed to be copied. Therefore a transcribing room became exclusively used for copying music. William M. Fahnestock observed that "Hundreds of volumes, each containing five or six hundred pieces, were transferred from book to book, with as much accuracy, and almost as much neatness as if done with a graver."[54] The Lutheran minister Israel Acrelius, who visited Ephrata in September 1753, reported that visitors "attest to the sweetness, beauty, the lilting cadence and rhythm of the hymns and chorals." He saw especially the younger Sisters "doing a wonderful amount of work" in copying musical notebooks. Among them Sister Anastasia's own, partly illuminated Choral Book has been preserved.[55] She and a Sister Iphigenia were "the principal ornamental writers," as Fahnestock claimed, who was quite familiar with Ephrata; "they left a large folio volume of sample alphabets of various sizes and style, which are both elegant and curious, exhibiting the most patient application."[56] The capital letters were adorned not only with elaborate orna-

The letter O of the Alphabet in Gothic script attributed to Sister Anastasia.

mentation, but also with human figures. The O, for instance, "suggests Anastasia's vision of Beissel being crowned with the Holy Spirit beneath the form of a dove."[57]

Return to the World

On 6 July 1768, Georg Conrad Beissel died. On 29 August the "honorable Virgin and Sister Anastasia honored his passing with a love-feast," at which a hymn of praise of Ephrata's leader was performed. But then Sister Anastasia began to travel and gradually lost touch with her community. Although Beissel had "often warned the solitary against the outward church," the *Chronicon* observed, "because it usually produced husbands and wives," she now made ever more "church visitations, and her friendly disposition drew everyone toward her, so that her fellow-combatants were little noticed aside of her. This stirred up envy within them, and they mockingly called her Court Cavalier." Alas, her natural gifts had remained "unsanctified."[58] Details about Anna's emerging relationship with the wine merchant and Quaker Johannes Wister, whom she had first met on arrival in Philadelphia 35 years before, remain unknown, except that on 27 August 1771, Anna became his third wife. She died seven years later at age 58 and was buried in the Quaker cemetery.[59] Her path from Waldenburg to Ephrata and finally to Philadelphia had been shaped by deep piety as well as by remarkable achievement.

Two nineteenth century accounts

In the history of the United States the 19th century was a century of conquest and replacement. In region after region the indigenous peoples were decimated by war, by the destruction of their economic base, and by expulsions westward across the Mississippi river. After 1860, however, the new nation claimed all territory from the Mississippi to the Pacific, having made war in 1847 also on Mexico that had claimed sovereignty over the southwest and the Pacific coast all the way to the north. The survivors of the wars against the indigenous peoples were forced onto reservations consisting of largely undesirable lands. The conquered territories were filled as soon as possible with white people who arrived mainly from the eastern Atlantic states and a good many also from Europe who established farms and businesses, villages and towns. Among them were also Swiss, exemplified by the story of two immigrant women.

ELISABETH
HABERSTICH
BIGLER

1816

It was a unique sight. In the cemetery of the small town of Sigel in southern Illinois a woman stood at an open grave, surrounded by her twelve children – the older ones accompanied by their spouses and their offspring – as well as by relatives and neighbors. The woman's name was Elisabeth Bigler.[60] She was dressed in her Sunday best, an authentic Bernese attire called *Tracht*, and, in the absence of a minister, spoke in German words of farewell from her husband who had died at age 60 on 22 March 1866 (8). The couple, as well as their first eight children, hailed from Ried, part of Worb, near the city of Bern, where the Bigler family had owned a stately farm. The Haberstichs, native of Oberentfelden, canton Aargau, were also well off and had lived nearby.[61]

Elisabeth Haberstich was born on 9 December 1816 and by the mid-1830s had grown into a beautiful woman with large blue eyes and long light brown hair. In her teens she was sent to a *Damenschule*, a finishing school, where she learned French, the art of cooking, and ways of proper entertaining. She had lost her mother early, and her father had remarried. The family was prosperous, and Elisabeth had the help of maids. "She never had to comb her long hair before she came to America," family lore reported. "Her maid always did that. On the last day before they left Switzerland, her maids pleaded for the honor of being the last to dress the hair of their beloved mistress before she left for America" (9). Elisabeth had a younger brother named Samuel Haberstich (1821–1872) who later in life turned to writing under the name of Arthur Bitter. Once he wrote to his sister that a volume of his poems had been published, a daughter remembered her mother proudly announcing (11).[62] In 1834 at age 19 Elisabeth Haberstich married the farmer Christian Bigler, born in 1806. During the next 14 years she gave birth to six sons and two daughters: Christian Jr. in 1836, Friedrich in 1838, Johannes in 1839, Anna Elisabeth in 1841, Rosina in 1842, Gottlieb in 1844 (?), August in 1846, and Samuel in 1847.[63]

In 1848 the Biglers decided to emigrate to the United States since Christian and Emily Haberstich Bigler "wanted to be able to give each of the six sons a farm" (2). That goal was difficult to achieve in Switzerland where available land was scarce and expensive, but possible in the United States where war on the original inhabitants and the expulsion of their survivors had "opened" large tracts of land to whites that the government sold them at a low price.[64] Perhaps there were other reasons for the Biglers leaving their homeland. In the fall of 1847 a Swiss civil war had brought the secularist liberal movement to power that intended to install a central government in place of the centuries-old league of states.[65]

Elisabeth Haberstich Bigler was a devout member of the established Reformed Church. "Often in the evening as the family sat around the table in the lamp light," a daughter reminisced, "brother Samuel would read aloud from the German Bible." Before meals grace was said: "Komm, Herr Jesu, sei unser Gast, und segne, was du uns bescheret hast;" and after the meal: "Danket dem Herrn, denn er ist freundlich, und seine Güte währet ewiglich" (13).[66] One night daughter Emilie "woke up to hear a voice outside. There in the moonlight stood her mother, dressed in her Swiss national [Bernese] costume, which she wore only for important occasions, telling God what it was like to have seven dry wells and no water. She was praying for rain" (15). Elisabeth Haberstich learned little English, German remained the family's everyday language that she wanted the children to speak properly, and she steadfastly followed her Bernese ways.

The Biglers had left Bern in 1848 with nine trunks and boxes for a French port, most likely Le Havre, where they embarked for New York. No account of their journey has come to light, except some

Route from New York to Chicago via the Great Lakes in 1837.

details that were told in the family: "Just as they were about to board the ship, Elizabeth Bigler noticed that little Johann was missing. The ship was due to sail soon and after an anxious consultation it was agreed that Christian Bigler would retrace their steps. If he failed to find the boy, Elizabeth and the children would go on; Christian and the boy would take the next ship. They remembered that all the children were together when they crossed a certain bridge. Returning, Christian found the little boy huddled in a corner, his tear-stained face showing that he had cried himself to sleep. When Christian arrived at the dock with Johann, there was a joyful reunion." Some trouble also happened at sea so that all passengers had "to transfer to another vessel in mid-ocean. The Bigler family made it safely, but the heavy trunk containing the family silver and copper-bottomed kettles went down. ... Elizabeth Bigler – for all her days – mourned the loss of their silver" (2).

From New York the family moved west, most likely by boat up the Hudson to Albany, from there via the Erie Canal, Lake Ontario, and Lake Erie to Cleveland where perhaps they met the well-to-do sculptor Johann Bigler, originally also from Bern.[67] From there they went overland to Bluffton in Allen County, Ohio,[68] some 75 miles southwest of Sandusky. It was laid out in 1837, after the Shawnee people had been driven away in 1832, and in 1850 the settlement counted about a dozen families.[69] The Biglers stayed there for some years only and around 1852 moved to Leyden Township near Chicago in Cook County Illinois.[70] There, Elisabeth Haberstich Bigler had four more children: Louisa, ca. 1853, Albert in 1854, Emily in 1857, and Laura in 1860 (115–116).

In Leyden Township the Biglers attended St. John's United Evangelical Church of Addison in Du Page County where the Swiss Ulrich Möcklin served as pastor since 1850 and baptized Elisabeth's second to last child Emilie in 1857. Planning in 1868 to return to Switzerland, he became ill and died in 1869. The Swiss Peter Lehmann followed Ulrich Möcklin as pastor and served the congregation until 1880.[71] Little is known about family events in

Birth and baptismal certificate of Lina Emilie Bigler of 15 March 1857.

Leyden Township. The daughter Emilie remembered, however, that in the 1850s there "were still some Indians living in the Leyden Township area, but they were peaceful, living in the woods near the Des Plaines River. Sometimes on a clear cold night, the Bigler children could hear the songs and laughter of the Indians as they danced and played on the frozen surface of the river" (5). By a fraudulent treaty the indigenous Osakiwug and Meshkwakihug nations had to surrender all their lands in present-day Illinois and were forced to leave for regions west of the Mississippi. The indigenous people, led by the resistance leader whom the whites called Black Hawk (1767–1838), fought the forced removal ordered in 1828 by the government. An American army, however, defeated the indigenous troops in two battles in 1832. Also the other people, the Potawatomi, were forced to cede their homeland by a treaty imposed in 1833, and some of them held their last dance in what is now Chicago in 1835.[72]

The first Reformed Church of Addison, Illinois, consecrated 7 October 1849.

In 1864 the Bigler family moved once more, this time to the town of Sigel in Shelby County in southern Illinois where land could be purchased less expensively. The family bought a farm on 12 October 1864, but Christian Bigler's health began to decline and he passed away on 22 March 1866. Elisabeth Haberstich Bigler would spend 36 more years in Sigel to bring up her 12-year old son Albert who would live there to age 97, 9-year old Emilie, and 6-year old Laura. She remained devoted to the proper ways she had learned in Switzerland and imparted them to her children, as this story highlights: "On a particularly cold winter day Emilie hung out the wash which froze on the clothline. ... In a hurry to finish the job, Emilie hung the things on the line just as she picked them out of the basket. ... When her mother looked out and saw the wash hung in such disorder she was quite upset. While she agreed with Emilie that the day was cold, she felt that there was only one way to do the job and that was to do it right. ... So she told Emilie to go out, take down the wash and hang it the way she had been taught" (14).

Elisabeth Haberstich Bigler died on 1 May 1902. Throughout her life she remained fully committed to her Bernese ways and was "serene and uncomplaining" (19). She was the mother of fourteen children, of whom eleven reached adulthood, and she had more than forty-two grandchildren. In the memory of her offspring she lives on as a woman of unusual strength, sunny disposition, and total dedication to her family.

LOUISE
GUILLERMIN
DUPERTUIS

On Friday 18 April 1889 in the late afternoon Louise Guillermin Dupertuis, age 41, boarded a train bound for Le Havre with her husband Henri-Louis (1852–1925) and their nine children in order to emigrate to the United States.[73] She was born on 27 January 1848, got married on 19 September 1876 at Chavannes-sur-Ollon and, like her husband, had joined the Salvation Army. Samuel, the oldest of the children, was 12 years old when they left, the youngest Paul Herbert nine months.[74] The emigrants reached Le Havre on 19 April, boarded the ship *S.S. Burgoyne* and reached New York on Friday 25 April.[75] The next evening they took the train for Rochester,[76] located some 60 miles southwest of Wichita in Kingman County, Kansas.[77] There Louise and her family stayed for nine days at the house of Louis Gonceth, a cousin of her husband,[78] then moved to a rented farm some miles distant.

The family of Louise and Henri-Louis Guillermin-Dupertuis in April 1889.

In Kansas

In her first letter dated 26 May 1889 to her sister Élise (1851–1931),[79] who like Louise was a gifted painter, the emigrant reported that they were living in a sodhouse with two rooms; one served as kitchen, the other as bedroom, and they had only the most basic furniture. When she accidentally came across pictures of their chalet *Vers les Cloux* above Ollon she wrote: "My heart failed me." But she found comfort in admiring the flowers such as morning glories, Jacob's armor, violets and little mallows with red blossoms. Henri "planted 25 acres of corn. We have also planted some castor beans, melons, beans, and sugar-cane to make molasses; then a nice piece of potatoes." They could get butter, grease, and sugar in a shop at Rochester some miles distant. On Sunday they were guests at the Gonceths where they also held a religious

A Kansas sod dwelling.

service. They had also bought a pig for 45 francs, and Louise baked bread daily which at first, she found less than easy (21–24). In many of the subsequent letters Louise tried to convince her sister, who remained single, to join them. "How happy I would be to see you arrive some fine day," she wrote on 29 June 1889; she could "teach the children in English and French, because I certainly would not want them to become little wild horses like I have seen around here" (25). Louise's hope was never to be fulfilled. She found the land to be "immense, not flat, but with little ridges of hills, but it is nonetheless the same thing as far as one can go, which appears always to infinity." There were no fleas but bugs and flies, so that one needed mosquito nets (26). On 29 August Louise confessed to her sister that she felt incredibly tired and was expecting her tenth child. "I know what your are going to complain to me, you could never refrain from saying that it is a bit my own fault. Oh well, since the job is done, it's necessary to go to the end, but it's no less troublesome. All food is repugnant to me except cakes, and fruit, too. You can imagine, I make a fine sight" (54).

Map of Rochester and Calista, ca. 1890.

But already another region beckoned, the so-called Indian Territory, which was far to the south of Rochester. On 22 April 1889 part of an area that was situated between lands assigned in the 1830s to American Indian peoples who had been forcibly driven west, was opened by the government to white settlement. "Nothing holds us back, the bait is too large," observed Louise's husband in a letter to his brother Émile in the fall of 1889 (28). For 15 dollars or 17 francs one could take possession of 140 acres of land. Henri's exploratory trip lasted a full two weeks, "but he hasn't taken land, because all the best was already taken and we think we'll stay here in this country for some time" (58). "The climate is very good here, and if we can establish ourselves here perma-nently I prefer it to going to the Indian Territory" (57). But soon the family moved to another farm about six miles away. "Here we have one of the good houses in Kingman County," observed Louise on 25 November. Four French-speaking families lived within a few miles, the land was flat and fertile, the post-office at Calista was about four miles distant and the older children could attend school and learn English. But Louise suffered from an inner void that she called "ennuy." On July 20, 1890 she wrote to Élise, "I hope that when you are here you will help me to love America, but I assure you that the more I see of it, the less I like it" (71).

In July 1890 a heat wave endangered the harvest on which the Dupertuis had to depend. They decided therefore to leave Kingman County and to move eighty miles eastward to the region of Mound Ridge in McPherson County, which was situated about 80 miles from Calista and some 40 miles north of Wichita. Because they could not find good land, they rented part of the land of the family Demielle with which they had been acquainted. An old dwelling served as kitchen, a newly constructed house made of boards served as living room and the attic as sleeping quarters for the children. "I prefer to be here than at Kingman," Louise observed in the fall of 1890, "all the same I do not find the country very beautiful. Flat, always flat, as far as the eye can see. ... For us the year will be a bit impoverished because we do not have any provisions, but it is cheaper living here than in the old place" (73–74). The region was not as remote and larger settlements easier to reach. Mound Ridge had even a nice bookshop.

Until the end of 1890 the weather was mild, but on New Year's Eve it began to rain, then the wind turned blowing from the north and brought heavy snow so that the house was surrounded by up to ten feet high snow drifts. The chickens had to be dug out of the snow since their eggs provided much needed food. "It was a terrible winter," Louise wrote on 7 April 1891. Until February the children were well, but then got scarlet fever; one-year old Hélène suffered for full six weeks from fevers, swellings, and inflammations (84). In a next letter she confessed: I am in "a country I would never love – not any more today than two years ago. ... nothing will replace for me my beautiful, my dear country" (86/ 87). She loved to spend time in the pasture among the cows and horses because

Roses painted by
Louise in 1891.

it reminded her of times spent in the Jura Mountains. "As for Indians we never see any. The troubles that happened last year occurred three hundred miles from us, and I assure you that you have had more troubles than we have. They are too few in numbers to make any large problem. But there are a few malcontents among them, and one of the chiefs, who was killed last summer by these same people; he was just giving them the idea of chasing all the whites out of America" (86).

In December 1891, for over two weeks, Louise's husband was again prospecting in Indian Territory together with French-speaking men "who want to settle among the savages, too; but don't get too frightened by this idea, because there isn't any great danger. The troubles that took place last year were quite quickly punished, and there are troops everywhere there are red skins" (96). In May the family moved for good to the Indian Territory with horse and wagon with a load of 2000 lbs. – they were on the road some fifteen days. The Indians had, she claimed, much unused land. "It's the whites who work; the redskins don't do anything – except go hunting, and they live well, because each individual, young or old, draws a big pension every three months from the government, so that if one takes their country away from them, one does not abandon them. Finally they are instructed" (102).

Louise's view reflects a then widespread claim, a tragic inversion of reality. The so-called Five Civilized Tribes of the Cherokee, Creek, Seminole, Choctaw, and Chickasaw were driven out of Georgia in the 1830s under great losses and their farms by force taken over by whites. Under military escort they were assigned lands already in the possession of trans-Mississippi indigenous peoples where they reestablished themselves. In the Civil War they were again ravaged by troops from the North and the South. After the war their territories were drastically reduced, transformed into reservations, and their previous lands opened to whites in order to transform Indian Territory into the state of Oklahoma. Especially notorious was the event of 22 April 1889, when some 50,000 settlers had made a run for the land; Henri had not been able to easily find a suitable property.[80] In December 1891, however, he rented a farm some 45 miles east of Oklahoma City to which the family moved in May in 1892.

Before their departure Louise's husband, who in Mound Ridge had preached to French-speaking settlers and on 12 April 1891 had undergone baptism again by immersion in a river (86), was chosen to be a preacher in Oklahoma for a congregation he was to form. Of course, "he'll farm for a living like in the past, because here especially in the country it is necessary for ministers to live from faith," Louise wrote on May 3, 1892 (102). The solemn ordination had been performed on 24 April by three preachers and two deacons. *"Behold, me, thus, the minister's wife,"* Louise rejoiced in English. The following day she entered a rhymed poem of twelve stanzas in French into her diary. The third begins with these words: "He must fight sin, Overturn false wisdom, Convince disbelief, he must support weakness" (106). Although Louise and Henri were affiliated with the Salvation Army, for them as adherents of the Holiness movement independence from organized religion was a primary concern. It was the experience of conversion, the experience of the certainty of salvation, and the experience of the consecration by the Holy Spirit that they perceived as crucial, not external organizational membership.[81]

In Oklahoma

In a letter dated 22 November 1892 Louise reported to her sister Élise that in May they had been on the road for eight and a half days and were now settled in the region Econtushka which was located on the south side of the North Fork of the Canadian River in the north of today's Seminole County.[82] They had immediately dug out a well, made hay for the winter, and planted two acres of wheat. Melons and beans were plentiful. A dwelling that was one big room had been constructed from boards. "It is 24 feet by 18, and has not yet any separations, which means we have space.

There's a big table for twelve people, a stove in the middle of the room, my bed in a corner with a table beside it, then a little farther my sewing machine, in another corner one of our trunks in the guise of a kitchen buffet, and the other in another place to put the linens. We have given a packing case on its side the office of shelf for our books. I have hung some oil paintings that I had. I still paint from time to time" (108). And Louise assured her sister: "I like this country very well; it's less uniform than McPherson where one saw only fences and fields at the time. Here are big forests of oak and walnut. There are up to four or five sorts of oak and then lots of little wild fruits, *meurons* [mulberries], strawberries, plums, and numerous others whose name I do not know, and which are good to eat" (108–109). The remote settlement – a three-day trip with horse and wagon from the railroad station – was called Belmont.[83] It was about nine miles to the post-office so that whoever went there, also took care of the neighbors mail. Two were French-speaking Canadian families, others hailed from Bohemia and were Moravians. "The aspect of the country also reminds me a little of western Switzerland. In the distance the horizon is bounded by forests, which reminds me of the Jura; and many spots in the oak forests make me believe that I am in the forests of Antagne and la Combe aux l'Erbois." The Indians, especially in the environs of the post-office were friendly and were "no longer what one calls savage" (109).

First the times in Belmont were difficult, Louise, who on 31 December 1892 had given birth to her eleventh child named Charles Beverly, confessed in a letter. The next year brought a rich harvest in corn, vegetables, and potatoes. They had also planted sugar cane in order to make molasses, and there were melons a plenty. "How often I would like to send you a slice. They are as big as large gourds, and pink inside and full of sweet juice" (113). They had also planted cotton that grew well, and Louise found the pale yellow blossoms to be beautiful. They could sell cotton at a good price, but had to travel some 60 miles with horse and wagon for about four days. "You travel in the middle among Indians for 18 miles," Louise reported on 11 December 1893. "You find, from time to time, encampments with huts made of tree bark or of matting. The Indians watch us go by, often they greet us quite graciously. You see some rather ugly ones, and from time to time some passable ones, but never any beautiful ones." And she admitted to Élise: "I feel better and better about being here in the middle of our forest. ... I often dream that I am in Switzerland but that I'm counting on returning here without doubt, only sometimes I dream that I don't have any more money to pay my voyage and I cry" (115). She knew, however, that the children would have received better schooling had they stayed in Switzerland (123). On occasion the family visited the Salvation Army headquarters in Oklahoma City, "but it is only too bad that they make *so much* noise. It's even worse than in Switzerland, and then I find they have so much levity" (115).

The summer of 1894 was hot and dry. The harvest seemed to be in danger, but a September rain saved much of it (124). The three older children Samuel, Louisa and Lina went to Texas to pick cotton where they could earn half a dollar a day. Samuel decided to stay on in Solana, Texas, for six months where he could get 12 dollars a month while the two daughters took jobs in Oklahoma City. Louise herself took care of some one hundred chickens, the eggs of which she could sell, two ducks, two geese, eight pigs and two good cows. In 1895 the harvest was again meager. At the end of May there was hardly a sign of what had been planted (132). But then the summer turned out well and the harvest was plentiful. In the fall, however, the children Samuel, Marguerite, and Henri suffered from fever for weeks, and Samuel seemed to be near death, as Louise reported on 13 November 1895. She and her husband Henri prayed with him to accept the inevitable, but he gradually recovered (137). On 12 April 1896 Louise wrote to Élise: "I want to take a moment to write to you; it's not that I work a lot, but thousands of little cares take up my time. The girls make the meals and do the washing up and the work in the fields that requires women's help, but besides that I am constantly busy, whether it's [looking] after my chickens or it's the calves to take care of, or so many other things, not to mention repairing the pants of my six boys" (141).

In the summer, however, tornadoes threatened the land and devastated the region of St. Louis (143). In 1897 the Mississippi flooded thousands of acres so that many people perished. "The times are serious," Louise observed on April 10, "isn't it true one receives news of troubles everywhere? The Black Death in the Indies, and the famine; the Famine in Africa; the noises of war everywhere, oh, how we need to keep ourselves ready" (150). Also fevers continued to plague the family so that in the fall of 1896 und spring of 1897 four and five of the family were simultaneously ill, perhaps with malaria. For a time Henri could not tolerate the sun which immediately led to a severe headache and fever. Louise herself suffered from feverish shivers. In April 1897 a tornado had devastated a village only 20 miles distant, twenty people had lost their lives, between thirty and forty had been injured (149).

On 6 January or February 1898 an itinerant preacher of the Holiness movement published an account of his twelve-day stay with the Dupertuis family. "There are thirteen in the family," he wrote. "They speak and sing in French as their native tongue, all of them fairly well. Two little ones are not yet of an age to be accountable. I found all the rest but one already converted. Six of them were sanctified before I met them. The father and oldest boy, who is nearly twenty-one years of age, are preachers. ... At family prayer the father reads a lesson from his Testament in French, then delivers a talk to the family. The oldest son then leads prayer, and one by one according to age lead prayer, till all except the two little ones have led. Then the mother leads, then the father. ... Sometimes a touching verse is sung, while kneeling at the close of prayers." Although the home was small, the preacher explained, it was one of the most comfortable he had ever entered. They also had an organ, and perhaps six of the family could play it. He concluded: "If Switzerland can send over any more like them, our country will do well to give them room. They live their religion daily, in the cotton field as well as in meeting. I told the father that he is the richest man I ever saw, and so he is" (151–152).[84]

In Washington

The uncertainty of harvests, the vagaries of the weather, destructive storms, and recurrent fevers drove Henri and Louise Dupertuis to move north to a better climate. In 1899, Louise observed, "you would have said that all the fevers of the universe had had a rendez-vous" at Belmont (171). Henri sought advice from many people and decided on a move to the state of Washington on the northern Pacific coast.[85] "We are two thousand miles from Oklahoma," Louise reported in a letter of 11 December 1899. "To tell you the wisdom, patience and perseverance that Henri had to bring this enterprise to a good conclusion would take me a volume. First he wrote to all parts of Washington to get information about the country and also the best route to take" (171). The journey, which cost three thousand dollars, went from Oklahoma via Kansas through the states of Colorado, Utah, and Oregon.[86] At a public auction the Dupertuis had sold their provisions, animals, and household goods for about three thousand dollars that allowed them to rent a house and farmland in Adna.[87] It was located about six miles west of Chehalis[88], which is situated south of Olympia on the river of the same name. The rent they received from their property in Oklahoma and the income of the older children who took on paid work enabled the family to make it through the first months. Louise confessed to her sister in a letter of 17 January 1900: "I can say that it was a trial for me to leave that place where we had experienced such happy days together, and I am not yet over the pain that it gave me; luckily I am the only one in the family like me" (172). While in Kansas, the children of Louise and Henri had been still small or entering adolescence, but already helped in the house and on the farm. In Oklahoma the older ones had started to earn money and contribute to purchasing the farm, in Washington they became mature adults, married, had their own children and pursued their own occupations. Samuel and the daughters Lina and Marguerite, for instance, decided to join the cadres of the Salvation Army, a step that proved to have been unhappy for Samuel who was at Portland in the Military School of the Salvation Army, but later also did some Methodist ministry studies at Puget Sound University. Lina caught a throat ailment from which she suffered for months, and both became disillusioned. The children "know quite well," Louise commented on 2 April 1902, "that we never approved, completely approved, that they join the [Salvation] Army. ... We know well that in all the churches are imperfections. I believe that one is better off as we are. Henri and I and you also, being affiliated with nothing but Jesus" (203). True religiosity consisted in personal experience and in daily practiced piety. "We are happy because we are all children of God from the oldest to the youngest," Louise explained to Élise. "I wish you could drop in on us between five and six o'clock in the morning, just before breakfast we have our family devotions, and every one except Charles and Arthur prays in turn. We pray for our friends, our relatives in Switzerland; we pray for each other, for those who are going to school, for those who are going to work in the wood, for those who are staying home. So, feeling we are in the hands of God, we each go to our work" (199).

When Samuel was in Portland in the Salvation Army School in the summer of 1901, he brought an abandoned baby to Adna. "Our little Arthur is a ray of sunshine," wrote Louise on 1 October 1901 to Élise. "He has blue eyes and a round rosy and white face and light red hair. He is big and fat and very intelligent" (196). Since her and Henri's dozen had not been complete, they decided to adopt the child as a "surplus" (197). When they bought their land in Adna, much of it remained to be cleared, and again they built a house. "I can always help Henri by holding pieces of wood or handing him tools. Our house is thirty-two feet long by sixteen feet wide, and fifteen feet high. Upstairs we have four bedrooms and down-stairs one large room and two little bedrooms. The old house that adjoins it has two rooms, a dining room and a kitchen" (195).

The place in Adna was economically well chosen. The railroad station of Chehalis was in easy reach and the town only some miles from the larger town Centralia. Eggs, potatoes, fruit and vegetables found a ready market, and the weather was more dependable than in Oklahoma (187). As to the country, Louise commented on 24 May 1901: "Everything here recalls to me so much my dear 'home' at Cretatavez or Les Cloux, but it is so far away. Nonetheless, I am very satisfied; I no longer regret having left Oklahoma, because here we have good health" (192). She and Henri could now enjoy the fruits of their incessant labor. "I can only see the hand of God that has guided and protected us in all ways, and we can well say that it is God's blessing that enriches. In fact we came to America with nine children and we did not have much money after our voyage, and now we have 260 acres of good land and we don't owe a centime besides. We can go to bed without having to expect the bill-collector at our door the next morning, or to have to borrow or steal to pay interest" (198).

Gradually, however, also the signs of age became apparent so that Louise had let others work the fields and garden. "I don't work a lot," she wrote to Élise on 19 May 1905, "only to help a little in the housekeeping, take care of my chickens, skim the milk and make butter, take care of a calf, and besides that I paint as much as I can; and some paintings!!!" Of those she mentioned were "two or three of more than 3 by two feet; on one of them are some cows in water under a big tree; another is water falling in cascades with big trees. ... On one I made a cascade taken in Oregon and on the other, Lac Léman and the immortal Dent du Midi" (236). On 12 May 1908 she wrote: "Here are what my paintings are: a box of strawberries turned over on a napkin, life size. Then, an Indian seated on a rock outcropping, nude except for a belt to hold his knife. One sees him from the back; he has a turkey feather in his hair. He is crouched before a little fire and he has the air of looking far-off in the plain, with a dreamy air; a river snakes away and loses itself in the horizon. The title is: *The Days of the Laws*, he sees that he is no longer free as before" (252). In time also painting had to cease.

Louise Guillermin Dupertuis died on 6 April 1914. That winter she had become weaker and stayed from March on with her daughter Marguerite whom she had always especially liked and who was living in Dundee in the Willamette Valley southwest of Portland. When the daughter realized that her mother became weaker, she alerted her father who looked after the farm in Adna and also her siblings. Besides Marguerite her father, Samuel, Lina, and Paul were present at Louise's passing. Her life's path had meant repeated new beginnings at different places, which proved to be especially burdensome for someone like her who liked stability and the known surroundings. But in unity with her husband a deep faith had given her the strength to master the challenges of their migrations and the numerous daily tasks her large family demanded.

Endnotes

1. A global survey of emigration from Switzerland is Leo Schelbert, "Swiss Diaspora," in: *Encyclopedia of Diasporas*, Vol. 1 (New York: KluwerAcademic/Plenum Publishers, 2004), 296–307; on British North America and the United States, 303–304.

2. For a sampling of experiential varieties see Leo Schelbert, *America Experienced. Eighteenth and Nineteenth Century Accounts of Swiss Immigrants*. Translated by Hedwig Rappolt. Rockport, Maine: Picton Press, 1996, paperback edition 2004.

3. See Verner Crane, "Purry, Jean Pierre," *Dictionary of American Biography* 15 (1935), 270–271.

4. William Penn, "Some Account of the Province of Pennsylvania," in Albert C. Myers, ed. *Narratives of Early Pennsylvania, West New Jersey, and Delaware 1630–1707*), 202; ibid. 211–215 an abstract of the king's patent.

5. See Julius Friedrich Sachse, "Literature to Induce German Emigration," *The Pennsylvania-German Society: Proceedings and Addresses*, 7 (Philadelphia: Published by the Society, 1897), 175–198; 201–256 give 56 facsimile reproduction of title pages.

6. Myers, ed. *Narratives*, 276.

7. The letters are reproduced in *America Experienced*, 108–112. Numbers in parentheses after quotations from Werndli's letters refer to that edition.

8. Main data are taken from Hans Ulrich Pfister, " Zürcher Auswanderung nach Amerika 1734/35– die Reisegruppe um Moritz Götschi," *Zürcher Taschenbuch 1986* (Zürich 1985): 45–99; genealogical data on the members of the emigrant group pp. 87–99; on the Götschis, p. 91.

9. Quoted in Pfister, "Zürcher Auswanderung," 47.

10. Ibid. 91.

11. Quotation ibid. 49.

12. Ibid. 50.

13. Ibid. 81–82; Pfister lists 333 emigrants by name. About 30 traveled through France, reached Calais in 24 days, London in a day and a half, and after eight days sailed for Charleston where they arrived on 7 February 1735 while the main group was still waiting for a boat in Rotterdam; ibid. 59–60.

14. Quoted from *Neue Nachricht Alter und Neuer Merckwürdigkeiten* (1734); reprinted in Leo Schelbert, *Einführung in die schweizerische Auswanderungsgeschichte der Neuzeit* (Zürich: Stäubli, 1976), 273–274.

15. *Der Hinckende Bott von Carolina. Oder Ludwig Webers von Wallisellen Beschreibung seiner Reise von Zürich gen Rotterdam, mit derjenigen Gesellschaft, welche neulich aus dem Schweizerland in Carolinam zu ziehen gedachte* (Zürich, bey Jacob Lindinner, 1735). Quoted in Pfister, "Zürcher Auswanderung,", 63.

16. Charles H. Glatfelter, *Pastors and People. German Lutheran and Reformed Churches in the Pennsylvania Field*. Vol. 1: 1717–1793 (Breinigsville, Pennsylvania: The Pennsylvania German Society, 1980), 166–167.

17. Quoted by James I. Good, *History of the Reformed Church in the United States 1725–1792* (Reading, Pennsylvania: Daniel Miller, 1899), 177–178.

18. Ibid. 181–182; based on Johann Heinrich Götschi's letter of 21 July 1735 to Deacon Werdmüller in Zurich. See also *Hoch-Obrigkeitliches begönstigtes Frag- und Anzeigungs-Blätlein von Basel* bey Johann Burckhardt im Berichthaus, XIX, Dienstags den 8. May Anno 1736, "Wenige Merckwürdigkeiten (A Few Interesting Items)".

[19] Randall Balmer, "John Henry Goetschius and the Unknown God: Eighteenth-Century Pietism in the Middle Colonies," *The Pennsylvania Magazine of History and Biography* 113 (October 1989), 575–608, presents Götschi's sermon printed in Dutch as translated into English by Lisbeth Fontijn. His study *A Perfect Babel of Confusion. Dutch Religion and English Culture in the Middle Colonies* (New York: Oxford, 1989), 123–127 gives a negative appraisal of Götschi; quotation from his sermon *The Unknown God*, ibid. p.127. William J. Hinke, *Ministers of the German Reformed Congregations in Pennsylvania and Other Colonies in the Eighteenth Centuries*. George W. Richards, ed. (Lancaster, Pennsylvania: Rudisill, 1951), 306–311, offers a positive view as does Glatfelter, Pastors and People, 46–47 and Georg H. Genzmer, "Goetschius, John Henry," *Dictionary of American Biography* 7 (1931), 357–358. Donald F. Durnbaugh, "Goetschius, John Henry," *American National Biography* 9 (1999), rather follows Balmer.

[20] Anna Wirz-Götschi as well as the sons had large families and numerous descendants; perhaps the most noted was Percy Goetschius (1853–1943), music theorist, a descendant of John Henry Goetschius; for 17 year he was professor at the Stuttgart Royal Conservatory in Germany, then taught at the New England Conservatory of Music and also at what became the Julliard School of Music in New York. He authored influential textbooks and in retirement edited the 43 volumes of the Analytic Symphony Series. See Howard Hanson, "Goetschius, Percy," *Dictionary of American Biography*, Supplement Three: 1941–1945 (1973), 308–310.

[21] The portrait of Anna Thommen is largely derived from Leo Schelbert, "On the Power of Pietism: A Documentary of the Thommens of Schaefferstown," *Historic Schaefferstown Record* 17 (July – October 1983): 42–74.

[22] Ibid. 49.

[23] Ibid. pp. 66–69, with genealogical sources.

[24] Ibid. 47.

[25] Ibid. 48, the bailiff's report to the Basel authorities.

[26] Ibid. 50, 59.

[27] A recent biography is Hildegard Ganter-Schlee, *Hieronymus Annoni* (1697–1770). Liestal: Verlag des Kantons Basel-Landschaft, 2001. On his travels see Johannes Burkardt, Hildegard Gantner-Schlee und Michael Knieriem, eds. *Dem rechten Glauben auf der Spur: Eine Bildungsreise durch das Elsass, die Niederlande, Böhmen und Deutschland. Das Reisetagebuch des Hieronymus Annoni von 1736*. Zürich: Theologischer Verlag Zürich, 2006.

[28] Martin Schmidt distinguishes five forms of the movement; see his article "Pietismus" in: *Die Religion in Geschichte und Gegenwart* 5 (Tübingen 1961), 373–381. A valuable collection of sources is Peter C. Erb, ed. *Pietists. Selected Writings*. New York: Paulist Press, 1983.

[29] Schelbert, "On the Power of Pietism," 49.

[30] Julius Friedrich Sachse, *The German Sectarians of Pennsylvania 1700–1800*, vol. 2 (Philadelphia: Printed for the Author, 1900), 487.

[31] Lamech [Jacob Gaas] and Agrippa [Peter Miller], *Chronicon Ephratense. A History of the Community of Seventh Day Baptists at Ephrata, Lancaster County, Pennsylvania*. Translated by J. Max Hark (New York: Burt Franklin, 1889; reprint 1972), 164.

[32] See J. Jürgen Seidel, "Lutz," in: *Biographisch-Bibliographisches Kirchenlexikon*, 5 (1993), cols. 488–490, with a list of Lutz's writings and of secondary titles.

[33] See Gerald W. R. Ward, "Wistar, Caspar," *American National Biography* 23 (1999), 699–700. On Johannes Wister see Albert C. Myers, ed. *Sally Wister's Journal* (Philadelphia: Ferris & Leach, 1902), 9–11. Their last name in Germany was Wüster, anglicized to Wistar or Wister.

34 "On the Power of Pietism, " 55, 56, 51.

35 Ibid. 59.

36 See Jobie E. Riley, "Beissel, Johann Conrad," *The Brethren Encyclopedia* 1 (1983), 112–113; John B. Frantz, "Beissel, Johann Konrad," *American National Biography* 2 (1999): 484–486.

37 For a sketch of the religious outlook of these four partly antagonistic elements see Wendy Everham, "Johann Konrad Beissels Leben und Theologie: Versuch eines Grundverständnisses," *Eberbacher Geschichtsblatt* 90 (1991): 55–67; and Leo Schelbert, "Die Ausformung von Konrad Beissels Ephrata Gemeinschaft im Widerstreit geistlicher Traditionen, 1735–1745," ibid. 41–54. An authoritative study is Jeff Bach, *Voices of the Turteldoves. The Sacred World of Ephrata.* University Park, Pennsylvania: The Pennsylvania State University Press, 2003. The "Bibliographical Essay" provides an indispensable and up-to-date guide. The book lacks an alphabetized bibliography and an index, and the critique of Sachse's pioneering work seems overdrawn.

38 *Chronicon Ephratense*, 164.

39 Schelbert, "On the Power of Pietism," 60, 59.

40 Ibid. 59.

41 Sachse, *Sectarians* 2, 185–186.

42 Paul S. Leinbach, "Beissel," *Dictionary of American Biography,* 2 (1929), 142.

43 Sachse, *Sectarians*, 1, 167.

44 Ibid. 179, facsimile in German.

45 Ibid. 191, based on the *Chronicon of the Sisterhood* which is not published. It was transcribed by Julius Friedrich Sachse, and copies of his typescript were deposited in some libraries, among them the William L. Clement Library in Ann Arbor, Michigan; pp. 58–69 of the typescript describe in detail the evolution of the attire and its winter and summer use. Sachse, *Sectarians* 2, pp. 176–306, translated key passages of this *Chronicon* into English; the document is more devotional in character than the *Chronicon Ephratense* and offers only limited historical detail. Sister Tabea is not mentioned since she had left the community.

46 Sachse, *Sectarians*, 2, 193, 194.

47 *Chronicon*, 160.

48 Ibid. 164.

49 My translation from the German, based on facsimile reproduced in Julius Friedrich Sachse, *The Music of the Ephrata Cloister, also Conrad Beissel's Treatise on Music as Set Forth in a Preface to the Turtel-Taube of 1747* (Lancaster: Printed for the Author, 1903; reprint AMS Press, 1971), 60–61, 79; see ibid. "Beissel's Apology for Sacred Song,", 24–26. The manner of singing is controversial. See for instance, Lloyd G. Blakely, "Johann [Georg] Conrad Beissel and the Music of the Ephrata Cloister," *Journal of Research in Music Education* 15,2 (Summer 1967), 120–138, a critical assessment; Blakely is overly critical of Sachse who offers the main passages in facsimile.

50 *Chronicon*, 163.

51 Ibid. 163–164.

52 Ibid. 164.

53 Sachse, *Sectarians*, 2, 146–147, in Anastasia's and in modern notation; text translated from the German.

54 Quoted in Felix Reichmann and Eugene E. Doll, *Ephrata as Seen by Contemporaries.* The Pennsylvania Folklore Society 17 (Allentown, Pennsylvania: Schlechter's, 1953), 170. For a list of hymnals see Bach, *Voices*, 215–216.

[55] John J. Stoudt, *Pennsylvania Folk-Art. An Interpretation* (Allentown, Pennsylvania: Schlechter's, 1948), 133; the work is in the Library of the Moravian Congregation at Lititz, Pennsylvania.

[56] Quoted ibid. 135.

[57] See illustration from ibid. 147; comment by Alderfer, *Ephrata Commune*, 126.

[58] *Chronicon*, 164.

[59] See W. F. Leach, "Genealogies of Old Philadelphia Families," Published in the *Sunday North American*, 3 "Wister"; copy in Pennsylvania Historical Society; on the Wisters see above footnote 33.

[60] This portrait is based on Ruth Harbecke Jewett, *The Swiss Connection. The lives and times of Frederick Joss and Emily Bigler Joss and their descendants.* Chicago: Privately printed, 1983. Numbers in the text refer to this richly illustrated type-written work. – An abbreviated version in Swiss *American Historical Society Newsletter* 21,3 (November 1985): 3–47. The story deals mainly with Elisabeth Haberstich Bigler's daughter Emily (1857–1949) who was born in Leyden Township, Illinois, and had told the details, used by Ruth Harbecke Jewett, to her own children.

[61] See "Bigler" and "Haberstich", *Historisch-Biographisches Lexikon der Schweiz* 2 (1924), 243 and 4 (1927), 32.

[62] See ibid. 4 (1927), 32; it was possibly the book *Erzählungen, Novellen und Gedichte* (1864–1865).

[63] Jewett, *Swiss Connection*, 19–20; 112–116 much additional genealogical detail.

[64] In American historiography the conquest is called "contact," "expansion," "westward movement," or "the moving frontier," thus semantically hiding human agency. For an overview see Ray Allen Billington, with James B. Hedges, *Westward Expansion. A History of the American Frontier.* 4th edition. New York: Macmillan, 1974.

[65] An overview is Joachim Remak, *A Very Civil War. The Swiss Sonderbund War of 1847.* Boulder, Colorado: Westview Press, 1993. The ideological issues are explored by Oliver Zimmer, *A Contested Nation. History, Memory and Nationalism in Switzerland, 1761–1891.* Cambridge: Cambridge University Press, 2003.

[66] "Come, Lord Jesus, be our guest, and bless what you have gifted us. Amen." And: "Thank the Lord, because he is kind, and his kindness lasts forever. Amen."

[67] See Adelrich Steinach, *Swiss Colonists in 19th Century America.* Reprint of 1889 edition of *Geschichte und Leben der Schweizer Kolonien in den Vereinigten Staaten von Nord-Amerika*, with a new Introduction in English and four new Indexes by Urspeter Schelbert (Camden, Maine: Picton Press, 1995), 204.

[68] A description of that route is "Journal einer Reise: Von New York nach Chicago im Jahre 1837," edited by Leo Schelbert and transcribed by Martin Steinmann, *Basler Zeitschrift für Geschichte und Altertumskunde* 87 (1987): 95–118.

[69] See Simeon D. Fess, *Ohio. A Four-Volume Reference Library.* Vol. 3: *Historical Gazetteer of Ohio* (Chicago: The Lewis Publishing Company, 1937), 416–422.

[70] Leyden Township includes the communities of Elmwood Park, River Grove, Franklin Park, Schiller Park and portions of Norridge, Park Ridge, Rosemont and Northlake. It was heavily peopled by German-speaking immigrants. A poll of 8 June 1855 given in the newspaper *Press* concerning a prohibition measure counted 8 votes for and 66 against it; see Weston A. Goodspeed and Daniel D. Healy, *History of Cook County*, Vol. 1 (Chicago: The Goodspeed Historical Association, 1909), 262.

[71] See Fran Horn, "Peter Möcklin and Peter Lehmann, Pastors of St. John's United Evangelical Church of Addison, Illinois," *Swiss American Historical Society Review* 36, No. 3 (November 2000): 31–33.

[72] A racist eyewitness account of John D. Caton is reprinted in Ulrich Danckers and Jane Meredith, *A Compendium of the Early History of Chicago to the Year 1835 when the Indians left* (River Forest, Illinois: Early Chicago Incorporated, 1999), 46–49.

[73] The sketch is based on Jeremy Dupertuis Bangs, *Swiss Sisters Separated. Pioneer Life in Kansas, Oklahoma, and Washington 1889–1914 of Louise Guillermin Dupertuis to Her Sister Élise, the Painter*. Rockport, Maine: Picton Press, 2008. Besides some 125 letters of Louise, the book contains also the report of her husband Henri about his exploratory trip to Oklahoma, a number of letters of the children, of Élise, and of relatives. – The numbers given after quotations refer to *Swiss Sisters*.

[74] Ibid. pp. 445–496 genealogical data for the families Guillermin, Dulex, and Dupertuis; pp. 471–472 data on the family of Louise and Henri. The children's birth dates are: Samuel, 18 July 1877; Louise, 4 July 1878; Lina 12 February 1880; Marguerite 22 July 1881; Méry 20 January 1883; Jean 1 April 1884; Daniel 11 June 1885; Henri 11 December 1886; Paul Herbert 4 July 1888; Hélène 7 December 1889 in Rochester, Kansas; Charles Beverly 31 December 1892 in Belmont, Oklahoma. (In 1901 Louise and Henri adopted Charles Arthur Levins who later used the name Dupertuis.)

[75] Samuel wrote a short account of the journey, ibid. 24. Except for seasickness it went well.

[76] Rochester was a train stop and a post-office. In 1898 the place was renamed Zenda, supposedly after the novel *The Prisoner of Zenda* of Anthony Hope (1863–1933). In 1990 Zenda counted 96 inhabitants. See John Rydjord, *Kansas Place-Names* (Norman, Oklahoma: University of Oklahoma Press, 1972), 140; and Samuel B. Cohen, ed. *The Columbia Gazetteer of the World*, Vol. 3 (New York: Columbia University Press, 1998), 3560.

[77] The county was named after the lawyer Samuel A. Kingman (1818–1904), laid out in 1872 and juridically established in 1874. See D. W. Wilder, *The Annals of Kansas*, 1541–1885. New Edition (Topeka, Kansas: Kansas Publishing House, 1886), 635. On Samuel Kingman see Todd Roberts, ed. "Diary of Samuel Kingman at Indian Treaty in 1865," *Kansas Historical Quarterly* 1, 5 (1932): 442–450.

[78] Bangs, *Swiss Sisters*, 447. L. Gonceth hailed from Aigle, Ct. Vaud, Switzerland.

[79] Ibid. 33–47, eleven reproductions in color of Élise's and eight of Louise's works.

[80] See Arrell M. Gibson, *The History of Oklahoma*. New Edition (Norman, Oklahoma: University of Oklahoma Press, 1984), 77–103 for an overview. The expulsion of indigenous peoples from what became the state of Kansas see H. Craig Miner and William E. Unrau, *The End of Indian Kansas. A Study of Cultural Revolution*, 1854–1887. Lawrence, Kansas: University Press of Kansas, 1990.

[81] The Holiness Movement derives from Methodism that stresses religion as experience. The Salvation Army and the Church of the Nazarene are two of the main organizations representing the Holiness religious tradition. See William C. Kostlevy, *Historical Dictionary of the Holiness Movement* (Lanham, Maryland: The Scarecrow Press, 2001), 224–226 on the Salvation Army and 56–61 on the Church of the Nazarene.

[82] See John W. Morris, Charles Goins, and Edwin McReynolds, *Historical Atlas of Oklahoma* (Norman, Oklahoma: University of Oklahoma Press, 1985), map 44 with legend. In 1866 the Seminole, who had been forced in the 1830s to settle in that region, were forced again to sell their land to the government for about 15 cents an acre and to buy from the Creek nation 200,000 acres for 50 cents an acre.

[83] It was apparently mainly a post-office; today the region is sparsely settled and has oilfields.

[84] Bangs quotes the *Holiness Advocate* 1889; the report was either in the January or February issue.

[85] On the history of the region see Robert E. Ficken, *Washington Territory*. Pullman, Washington: Washington State University Press, 2002 and *Washington State. The Inaugural Decade 1998–1899*. Pullman, Washington: Washington State University Press, 2007.

[86] Bangs, *Swiss Sisters*, 164–170, gives daughter Mery's journal of the trip.

[87] Adna is an incorporated settlement; in the census of 2000 it had too few inhabitants to be separately enumerated.

[88] Chehalis is the name of an indigenous people which today lives on a small reservation in the northwest corner of Lewis County; see *Gale Encyclopedia of American Indian Tribes*, Vol. 4 (Detroit, Michigan: Gale, 1998), 273–275. – Lewis County had fifty to seventy five thousand acres of the best agricultural land; see Charles Miles and O. B. Sperlin, eds., *Building a State* 1899–1939. Vol. 3 (Tacoma, Washington: Washington State Historical Society, 1940), 24.

ESSAY

Women in Twentieth Century America

In the United States, as in other countries, the women's movement of the twentieth century achieved a new understanding of the nature of women and of the role they were to play in the private and public domain. Successes alternated with drawbacks, new views and demands clashed with traditional ideals, and in the movement itself divisions surfaced that weakened its force, but highlighted the complexity of feminist thought and demands. In 1920, after decades of hard struggle, the active and passive voting rights of women were anchored in the Constitution, but the understanding of woman's nature and of her assigned role remained unchanged. Her place was in the family; she was to be wife, mother, and the nurturer of children; she was to obey her husband and economically depend on him. Key positions in business and in the educational system were generally closed to her, as were university studies and professorial assignments. Leading roles in religious bodies were mostly denied her, some religious communities of women excepted, in which they served as chief officers or administrators of schools and hospitals.

The economic crisis of the 1930s intensified the situation. In the Second World War however, when men served in the armed forces, some six million women could get jobs, but they lost most of them when the men returned. In the 1950s the view became even stronger that advanced schooling was damaging to women and that active involvement in the economic and political domains ran counter to her supposed nature because it was leading to destructive competition with men. If women in significant positions did hold their own, they were often passed over for promotion; salaries were lower for the same tasks that men performed, and if women complained, they were simply dismissed. Marriage or pregnancy, furthermore, demanded the withdrawal from paid work to unpaid work in the household.

In the 1960s the women's movement regained strength, in part due to the Black Power agitation that advocated equal rights for African Americans, in part due to initiatives of the Kennedy and Johnson administrations. Formally schooled women of the middle class fought on the national level for equal rights within the given socio-political structures while radical and mostly regional groups strove for structural change and questioned institutions such as marriage and the officially proclaimed sexual morality. To highlight those changes, the position of American women between 1900 and 2000 shall be sketched as it shifted in politics, society, the economy, education, and ideology.

Politics

On the urging of the Women's Bureau of the Federal Labor Office and of women in the Democratic Party, President John F. Kennedy established a commission in 1961 that was to assess the status of American women. The report of the group, chaired by Eleanor Roosevelt (1884–1962), featured the comprehensive discrimination of women, especially in the world of work and in childcare. In 1963 Congress issued therefore the *Equal Pay Act* that demanded equal pay for equal work, but was heeded partially at best.

The following year brought further success. Howard Smith (1883–1976), the representative of Virginia in Congress and Chair of the Rules Committee, who supported women's equality but also racial discrimination, had agreed to adding an amendment to the *Civil Rights Act* of 1964 that was to outlaw the discrimination of women. The conservative wing of Congress hoped that such a step might help defeat the pending bill. But efforts of women like Martha Griffith (1912–2003), a Representative of Michigan, and of President Lyndon B. Johnson proved effective and anchored women's equality in the law. Yet the federal commission, charged with labor issues, remained inactive and showed little interest in dealing with submitted complaints. When in October 1966 the third National Conference of State Commissions concerned with women's issues rejected the proposals of women's groups, twenty-eight women, among them Betty Friedan (1921–2006) and Martha Griffith, founded NOW, the National Organization for Women, which made the political participation of women one of its primary goals.

Despite the achievement of active and passive voting rights, women's progress in the political domain remained limited. Their presence in state and federal legislatures as well as in the executive branches rarely went beyond tokenism. In April 1917 Jeannette Pickering Rankin (1880–1973) was the first woman elected by the State of Montana to the federal House of Representatives. For the first time President Franklin D. Roosevelt appointed a woman to the Cabinet when in 1933 he chose Frances Perkins (1880–1965) as Secretary of Labor. In 1972 Texas elected Barbara Jordan (1936–1996) as the first African American congresswoman. In 1975, however, no women served in the Senate and only 19 among the 475 Representatives in the House. In 1991 there were two women in the Senate and 28 in the House, in 2005 14 and 65 respectively. In 1981 Sandra Day O'Connor (b. 1930) was the first woman appointed to the Supreme Court, and in 1984 Geraldine Ferraro (b. 1935) was the first woman to serve as Vice-presidential candidate, chosen by the Democratic Party. But two years before, the deadline for the ERA, the constitutional Equal Rights Amendment, had lapsed that Congress had approved in 1972; only 35 instead of the needed 38 states had ratified it. In 1993 Ruth Bader Ginsburg (b. 1933), who in the 1970s had won five out of the six cases she defended before the Supreme Court, became one of its members. In the same year President Bill Clinton appointed Janet Reno (b. 1938) as Attorney General, Madeleine Korbel Albright (b. 1937) as the first woman to serve as Secretary of State, and his wife Hillary Clinton (b. 1947) as chair of a special commission charged with health care reform. In 2000 she was elected senator of the State of New York and in 2008 narrowly lost the Democratic nomination for President.

Society

In the 19th century industrialization and urbanization significantly diminished the household economy in which all members of a family had a role to play. Except on farms oriented toward subsistence, the tasks of women were narrowed to the private sphere of the family and were ideologically sealed by a sentimental cult of domesticity. By marriage a woman changed from the authority of the father to that of the husband. Various states prohibited her to keep her maiden name, and single or widowed women had difficulty in obtaining loans. At the work place lewd remarks, unwanted touching, pornographic pictures, sexual advances, and the exchange of privileges for sexual favors were tolerated.

In the 1960s the women's movement strove for change by various means. Consciousness-raising groups were formed in which women could share their experience at home and at work, in marriage and sexual life, in birth control and childcare. Special places of refuge were established for mistreated and raped women who could receive legal, medical, and psychological aid. Also confrontational steps were taken. In 1968, for instance, radical feminists of New York crowned a Miss Sheep America on the occasion of the Miss America contest that they branded as a kind of cattle show. They set up "freedom garbage cans" into which they hurled curlers, artificial eyelashes, bras, corsets and high-heeled shoes. They organized sit-ins in restaurants that refused to serve women if not accompanied by a man. When on 26 August 1970 some 10,000 women took part in "marches for equality" in New York that were undertaken also in other cities, they ignored the police directive to stay on the sidewalks and filled the whole of Fifth Avenue. Women also exposed sexist language.

The distinction Miss and Mrs. was abolished in favor of Ms., chairman and spokesman became chairperson and spokesperson, fireman firefighter, and many more such transformations were insisted upon. Opponents labeled such efforts contemptuously as "political correctness."

Significant change was also sought in the sexual domain. In the early 20th century contraception was prohibited in the United States. When in 1916 Margret Sanger (1879–1966) opened the first birth control clinic in Brooklyn, she was prosecuted and jailed, but in 1921 the National League for Birth Control was nevertheless organized. Initially opposed by most denominations, the Episcopal Church was the first to advocate birth control and was followed by most Protestant groups. When in 1961 the first birth control pill, in the making since the 1920s, was released, the Supreme Court decided in 1965, that information about means of birth control and their distribution to married couples was legal; in 1972 the decision was extended to unmarried adults, and in 1977 to minors. The cohabitation of unmarried couples became accepted, by 1970 marriages had decreased by 30 and divorces increased by 40 percent, while about a third of children were born to legally non-married couples.

Since the mid-19th century, laws of most states demanded that a woman complete a pregnancy and that abortion was punishable by law. In 1973, however, the Supreme Court decided in Roe versus Wade that in the first trimester of pregnancy the decision to bear a child was – on the basis of her right to privacy – an exclusive right of the woman. This decision continues to be attacked. Since the 1980s it has been weakened by the Supreme Court itself. In 1989 and 1992 it granted states the right to regulate issues connected with pregnancy. But the decision itself has survived, although it is consistently weakened also by occasional regulatory intrusions of a hostile federal executive. By the early 20th century, prostitution had become illegal in all states except Nevada, thus the exploitation and mistreatment of women active in the sex trade increased, falling ever more into criminal hands. In the 1990s computer- and telephone sex as well as massage parlors and striptease shows expanded the commercialization of sexuality. After 1970 the feminist movement that initially had rejected the rights and concerns of lesbian women began to acknowledge and support them and vigorously battled the deeply rooted homophobia in American society.

In the religious domain the social position of women also changed. In 1963 Madelyn Murray O'Hair (1919–1995) founded the American Society of Atheists and led the fight against mandatory Bible reading and prayer in public schools. In 1970 two Lutheran Churches accepted the ordination of women, in 1972 Sally J. Priesand became the first female rabbi, in 1974 Selena Fox founded the Church of the Wicca Circle that strives to revitalize goddess worship. In 1976 the Synod of the Episcopal Church that in 1972 had rejected the ordination of women priests, reversed its position and admitted women also to the office of bishop. In 1980 the United Methodist Church was the first to ordain a woman, Marjorie S. Matthews (1916–1986), as bishop, and in 1988 Barbara Clementine Harris (b. 1930), an African American civil rights activist, became a bishop in the Episcopal Diocese of the State of Massachusetts. Also in the Catholic Church the role of women in pastoral care and in the liturgy expanded after the Second Vatican Council (1962–1965), although in only a subservient manner.

Two personalities may highlight the opposite stances American women have espoused. On the Right Phyllis Schlafly (b. 1924) advocates the maintenance or return to the prior social order. She worked for the defeat of the constitutional Equal Rights Amendment and founded the Eagle Forum with about 80,000 members by the year 2000 that hopes to overthrow Roe versus Wade. She supports instead tax cuts for the wealthy, military build-up, and parental supervision of schools. Her column appears in about a hundred newspapers and her talk show is being aired on about 200 radio stations. She claims that the institution of the family is being undermined and that soon women might be forced to use the same public facilities as men and might lose the right of a husband's economic support. On the Left stands Shulamith Firestone (b. 1945), author of the *Dialectic of Sex: The Case for Feminist Revolution*, published in 1970. In 1967 she had founded the women's group *Chicago Westside*, then three other organizations in New York City whose ideological orientation, however, she soon found inadequate. In contrast to the Marxist Emma Goldman (1869–1940), who viewed the nuclear family as the main cause of woman's plight, Firestone identified biology as the main culprit. She advocated in vitro fertilization and the maturing of embryos in artificial wombs that would free woman from the bondage of maternity.

Economy

The discrimination of women was especially evident in the economic domain. Her work in the family was unpaid and she remained financially dependent on the husband. In 1900 5.3 percent of women were gainfully employed, in 1950 30 percent and in 2000 47 percent. In 1960 about 30 percent of women worked in industry, in 2000 about 14 percent, but by then some 80 percent of the employed women worked in the service industry; the change resulted from the shift of the American economy from a production to a service industry. Today women find themselves in positions of low pay mainly in retail, health care, secretarial work, care of infants and the elderly in nursing homes. According to *Fortune 500* only 5 percent of those holding top positions in leading firms were women.

In 1998 about 70 percent of women had part-time jobs and as many a yearly income below $25,000. About 40 percent belonged to a union as opposed to 19 percent in 1960. About 28 percent did not receive a pension, 25 percent had no health benefits, 33 percent got no paid sick leave, and 74 percent no childcare supplement. Lowly paid women were forced, therefore, to spend some 35 percent of their income on childcare. According to a recent study of Aviva Wittenberg-Cox, the protection of the working family in the United States is "worldwide one of the worst." In contrast to 65 countries, there is no paid paternity leave. The right to nurse a baby during work hours, a given in 107 countries, is not guaranteed. Paid sick leave, instituted by 145 countries, exists partially only, and the length of the workweek and the permissible maximum demand of overtime is not regulated. In 137 countries employers are obligated to grant yearly paid vacation time to their employees, but not in the United States. Black women, often a family's main breadwinners, are especially burdened by lacking protection at the workplace.

On the other hand, sexist employment conditions like those of stewardesses, who had to be less than 25 years of age and unmarried, were abolished. In applications for employment sexual discrimination is prohibited, pension rights for women have been regulated, and conditions of getting credit have been made equal for women and men. The protection of pregnant women who are employed has been strengthened and sexual harassment made punishable. Class action suits against discrimination on the basis of sex have been successful such as in 1992 against State Farm Insurance and in 2007 against Morgan Stanley and Walmart. But the so-called glass-ceiling remains real, the influence of the old boys' network strong, and the over-demands in high managerial positions widespread, so that women in such positions are hardly able to combine their career with having children.

Education
In the 19th century several women's colleges like Mt. Holyoke, Vassar, and Smith were founded while the education of Catholic young women was in the hands of nuns. In 1900 about 15 percent of women enjoyed higher formal education, but had few career possibilities. "Normal" women married, supported their husbands, and had children. Access to law, medicine and theology or to

political and educational leadership was basically closed to a woman. In public discourse the question was seriously debated whether formal education equal to that of men might be harmful. After 1910 colleges introduced quotas in order to limit the number of female students. At the same time a curriculum in home econo - mics was being developed in order to rationalize family manage- ment and thereby improve society. Unmarried women were mainly engaged in nursing and social work or in kindergartens and primary schools. In the early years of the twentieth century women earned about 6 percent of the doctorates, in the 1930s about 16 and in the 1950s 10 percent. In 1970 78 percent of women had finished high school and 22 percent had earned a college degree.

The next decade brought changes. In 1970 the Association of Law Schools disallowed discrimination on the basis of sex in the acceptance of applications as well as in employment and place- ment so that in 1972 women represented 12 percent of law school students. In the same year Title IX of the *Civil Rights Act* prohibited the selection of applicants on the basis of sex in all institutions that received federal money. By 1980 half of college students were women, and they equally received stipends or loans. In 2000 88 percent of women had completed High School and 33 percent earned a college degree. They received 57 percent of the awarded college diplomas and 35 percent of the doctorates. But women were only 30 percent of university faculties, on average earned only 88 percent of the salaries of their male colleagues, and they were often disadvantaged in promotions. The average salary a college graduate might expect was $36,559 for women and $51,400 for men, lower in part because women chose predominantly programs in the humanities and social sciences. In the academic year 1991–92, for instance, 47 percent of the doctorates earned by women were in those fields, 13.3 percent in computer science, and 9.6 in engineering. In 1998 13 women and 19 men received presti- gious Rhodes Scholarships to Oxford University that until 1977 had been granted only to men.

Of importance was the introduction of women's studies programs that initially were politically, then increasingly academically oriented. They derived from the awareness that the significance of women in the past had been ignored or shortchanged in all human disciplines, and that male experience was interpreted as normative. The first women studies program was instituted in 1970 at the University of San Diego, in 1975 there were already some 150 such programs and in 1980 about 300. In 1972 the academic journal *Feminist Studies* was founded, in 1977 the National Women's Studies Association established. By the end of the 20th century more than 700 institutions of higher learning offered women's studies courses, and at major universities students could earn a bachelor, masters or Ph.D. degree in the field. Programs strove not only to deal with correcting the record, but also to present a holistic view of human society and history. In such endeavors "gender," understood as the social construction of the meaning of sexual difference, was not elevated to an autonomous category, but it was stressed that human reality was to be explored in relation to women and men from a perspective of equivalence. Androcentric assumptions and claims had to be exposed as falsifying reality and as a damaging suppression and devaluation of female experience and achievement. In the 1990s right-wing circles sharply critiqued women's studies programs, not in the least because they were interdisciplinary in approach and based on the epistemological assumption that all human knowledge was subjective, shaped by ideologies of dominance, and neither value free nor value neutral.

Ideology

Until the 1960s the understanding of women was marked by widespread stereotypical prejudice. In comparison to men who were supposedly rational, strong-willed and mathematically and mechanically gifted, women were supposed to be the "weaker" sex. They were emotional, unsteady, weak-willed, morally unreliable and intellectually less malleable. The biblical story of creation and of the primal woman Eve as temptress and cause of a universally inherited sinfulness was taught in churches and schools as unquestionable truth. It anchored the claimed inferiority of women in religiously based archetypal imagery. Since numerous religious groups of the United States are biblically oriented and proclaim the Bible's "inerrancy" as the literal word of God, they influence also the secular mind.

In the 1940s the popularized and widely disseminated ideas of Sigmund Freud (1856–1939) further deepened the negative view of woman. He had claimed that her psychological evolution was essentially different from that of men and was rooted in her unique sexuality. He also suggested that feminist women were suffering from penis envy. Betty Friedan's book *The Feminine Mystique*, published in 1963, sharply attacked Freud's theses as well as the traditional view of woman's nature and place, and it energized the feminist movement. With *Le deuxième sexe* of Simone de Beauvoir (1908–1986) published in 1949, and *Frauen im Laufgitter* of Iris von Roten (1917–1990) issued in 1958, Friedan's book became a classic expression of feminist thought. She rejected the claim that women found their fulfillment in children and in the social status and achievement of the husband. With other feminists, Friedan, who viewed the issues mainly from the perspective of the white middle and upper class, demanded that all occupations and educational fields had to be equally accessible to women and men and that household tasks and the bringing up of children were to be shared equally between husband and wife.

Also in theology feminist thought fundamentally challenged current assumptions. The biblical studies of Elisabeth Schüssler Fiorenza (b. 1938), then Professor of New Testament Studies and Theology at Notre Dame University, exposed many of the traditional interpretations of biblical texts as androcentric constructions, especially in her work of 1984, titled *In Memory of Her: A Feminist Theological Reconstruction of Christian Origins*. Rosemary

Radford Ruether (b. 1936) offered in her book *Sexism and God-Talk: A Feminist Theology*, published in 1983, and in *Gaia and God: An Ecofeminist Theology of Earth Healing* of 1992, a new ecologically grounded theological outlook. Mary Daly (b. 1928–2009), who had studied scholastic theology at the University of Fribourg in Switzerland, took the Catholic Church hierarchy to task for contributing to the oppression of women in her book published in 1968 and again in 1975 and 1985, titled *The Church and the Second Sex*. In works like *Gyn/Ecology: The Metaethics of Radical Feminism*, first published in 1978, she fully distanced herself from Christianity and interpreted it as a tradition that was hopelessly enmeshed in a system of male dominance. The theologian Sally McFague (b. 1933), Professor of Theology at Vanderbilt University in Nashville, Tennessee, offered new ways of theological thinking in studies such as the book *Models of God: Theology for an Ecological, Nuclear Age,* published in 1987. With exquisite sensitivity and in dialogue with tradition she juxtaposes the metaphors of God as Lord, Judge, and Fountain of Grace to the metaphors of God as mother, lover, and friend and explores their profound theological and spiritual impact.

The future will reveal how far the measures taken and the new understandings gained will continue to transform society. Undoubtedly, the feminist movement has achieved much in all fields of endeavor. Today American women have been able to become a powerful force in the nation's political, social, economic and educational arenas. Nevertheless, although gender equality has become part of the law, the achievements of the women's movement are not secure. Groups that reject them – partly led by women and influenced by a clergy obsessed with issues of sexual morality – view the changes achieved not only as destructive of the social fabric but also as morally flawed and ungodly. The more they see their most cherished claims threatened by legal decisions and social practice, the more they seem to become determined to protect and, if possible, to reintroduce previous views.

Thus the path to full equality is still long, especially because gender relations are shaped not only by the difference of sex but also by the realities of race, ethnicity, and a wide divergence of income levels – the American form of class. In the light of what has been achieved, a vigilant optimism seems therefore to be called for so that progress toward true equality will continue.

Bibliographical Note

The titles given below are merely a selection of some basic works that contain numerous further bibliographical data.

Surveys

Glenda Riley, *Inventing the American Woman. An Inclusive History.* Second edition. Vol. 2: *Since 1877.* Wheeling, Illinois: Harlan Davidson, 1995. [Each of the five chronologically divided chapters contains extensive bibliographical lists.]

Angela M. Howard & Frances Kavenik, eds. *Handbook of American Women's History.* Second Edition. Thousand Oaks, California: Sage Publications, 2000. [The signed thematic and biographical entries offer each bibliographical references.]

Cheryl Toronto Kalmy, "The United States," in: *The Greenwood Encyclopedia of Women's Issues Worldwide.* Lynn Walter, Editor-in-Chief. Vol. 5: *North America and the Caribbean*, Cheryl Toronto Kalmy, Editor (Westport, Connecticut: Greenwood Press, 2003), 329–351. [The surveys are according to nations and each entry has the same structure that allows the comparing of American data with those from other nations.]

Doris Weatherford, ed. *A History of Women in the United States: State-by State Reference.* 4 vols. Danbury, Connecticut: Grolier Academic Reference, 2004. [The work offers nine thematic chronological overviews, parallel constructed surveys for each of the fifty states that include biographical entries and timelines, a chronology, primary sources, and a statistical and bibliographical section.]

Documentaries

Winston E. Langley and Vivian C. Fox, eds. *Women's Rights in the United States. A Documentary History.* Westport, Connecticut: Greenwood Press, 1994. [The volume contains mainly public documents. Numbers 83–125 are from the 20th century.]

Dawn Keetley and John Pettegrew, eds. *Public Women, Public Words. A Documentary History of American Feminism.* Vol. 2: *1900–1960.* Vol. 3: *1960–Present.* Lanham, Maryland: Rowman & Littlefield, 2002. [The documents, written by women, reveal the multiple and wide-ranging interests feminist women pursued.]

Biographical Dictionaries

Barbara Sicherman and Carol Hurd Green, et al., eds. *Notable American Women. The Modern Period. A Biographical Dictionary.* Cambridge, Massachusetts: The Belknap Press of Harvard University Press, 1980.

Susan Ware and Stacy Braukman, eds. *Notable American Women. A Biographical Dictionary. Completing the Twentieth Century.* Cambridge, Massachusetts: The Belknap Press of Harvard University Press, 2004. [Both volumes contain signed scholarly biographical sketches with appended bibliographies.]

Historical Monographs

Sara M. Evans. *Personal Politics: The Roots of Women's Liberation in the Civil Rights Movement and the New Left.* New York: Alfred Knopf, 1979. [The author explores the impact of the Civil Rights Movement and of the Marxist Left on the women's movement.]

Nancy Whittier, *Feminist Generations. The Persistence of the Radical Women's Movement.* Philadelphia: Temple University Press, 1995. [Columbus, Ohio, is used as a foil to demonstrate the change from reform to structural transformation in the women's movement.]

Philosophical Works

Sandra Bartky, *Femininity and Domination. Studies in the Phenomenology of Oppression.* New York: Routledge, 1990. [Seven critical essays deal with topics such as narcissism, alienation, and the experience of supposed female inferiority on the basis of various philosophical approaches.]

Routledge Encyclopedia of Philosophy, Edward Craig, editor. Vol. 3 (London: Routledge 1998): 576–628. [Eleven signed articles discuss feminism in relation to fields such as psychology, sociology, and law and offer annotated bibliographies.]

Educational Issues

Joyce Antler and Sari Knopp Biklen, eds. *Changing Education. Women as Radicals and Conservators.* Albany, New York: State University of New York Press, 1990. [Seventeen articles explore varieties of formal schooling from the perspective of women.]

Ana M. Martínez and Kristen A. Renn, eds. *Women in Higher Education. An Encyclopedia.* Santa Barbara, California: ABC–CLIO, 2002. [Nine topical chapters deal with historical and cultural aspects of feminism in higher education with special concern for non-white groups.]

Theological Aspects

June Melby Benowitz. *American Women and Religion.* Santa Barbara, California: ABC–Clio, 1998. [Besides thematic and biographical entries the book contains a valuable chronology and an extended bibliography.]

Anne M. Clifford, *Introducing Feminist Theology.* Maryknoll, New York: Orbis Books, 2001. [Six globally oriented chapters discuss topics such as forms of feminist theology, metaphors of the Divine, and women's spirituality.]

Media

Karen Kahn, ed. *Frontline Feminism* 1975–1995. *Essays from* Sojourners *First 20 Years.* San Francisco: aunt lute books, 1995. [Eight chapters offer selected articles from the journal *Sojourners* that highlight the direction of feminism during those twenty years.]

Amy Erdman Farrell. *Yours in Sisterhood. Ms. Magazine and the Promise of Popular Feminism.* Chapel Hill, North Carolina: The University of North Carolina Press, 1998. [The impact of the influential magazine on the public is critically assessed.]

Economy

Barbara R. Bergmann. *The Economic Emergence of Women.* New York: Basic Books, 1986. [A study of the role of women in the American economy.]

Josefina Figueira-McDonough and Rosemary C. Sarri. *Women at the Margins. Neglect, Punishment and Resistance.* New York: Haworth Press, 2002. [Interdisciplinary essays deal with topics such as drug addiction, teenage pregnancy and the plight of women in prisons.]

The Present

Barbara Finlay. *George W. Bush and the War on Women. Turning Back the Clock on Women's Progress.* London: ZED Books, 2006. [A carefully documented study of the Administration's measures methodically to thwart the congressionally mandated tasks relating to women's welfare by tax cuts and military expenditures.]

Aviva Wittenberg-Cox und Alison Maitland. *Why Women Mean Business. Understanding the Emergence of Our Next Economic Revolution.* Hoboken, New Jersey: Wiley, 2008. [The work written with a light touch, analyzes the current situation and offers constructive solutions.]

Acknowledgements

I thank all the people and institutions that made the realization of my dream possible:

Albert und Rita Lacher, Albert Zeller, an American sponsor, Andrea König, Anna Taylor, Annette Ringier, Annina Bosshard, Baptiste Kunz, Beat and Regula Curti, Catherina Bosshard, Doris Stump, Elena Hinshaw Fischli, Gottfried Weber, Jürg Bosshard, Katharina Neuhaus, Katja Schönbächler, Leo and Virginia Schelbert, Margot Ammann Durrer, Marianne Egli, Mirjam Weiss, Pierre Kocher, Rébecca Kunz, Ruth Jäger, Swiss Benevolent Society of Chicago, SZenario Frauenleben, Walter Graf Chiriboga

prohelvetia Schweizer Kulturstiftung

Kulturkommission
kantonschwyz

VICTORINOX

KÄLIN Druckerei Franz Kälin AG

ERNST GÖHNER STIFTUNG

Stiftung Aurea Borealis

The following have provided official sponsorship:
Swiss American Historical Society, USA
The Swiss Society of New York, USA
Musée des Suisses dans le Monde, Pregny, Switzerland

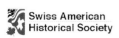
Swiss American Historical Society

Swiss Society of New York

Musée des Suisses dans le Monde
www.penthes.ch

Authors and Translators

Susann Bosshard-Kälin (1954), Egg near Einsiedeln, journalist and communications specialist, among other, projects initiator, co-editor, and co-author of spruchreif – Zeitzeuginnen aus dem Kanton Schwyz des 20. Jahrhunderts (2006), co-author of Leben im Kloster Fahr (2008).

Leo Schelbert (1929), Evanston, Illinois, a Swiss abroad, who taught American History with specialization in the history of American Immigration at the University of Illinois at Chicago from 1971 to 2003. Among his studies relating to the history of Switzerland and Swiss emigration are Einführung in die schweizerische Auswanderungsgeschichte der Neuzeit (1976), also (with Hedwig Rappolt) America Experienced. Eighteenth and Nineteenth Century Accounts of Swiss Immigrants to the United States (Picton Press, 1996, 2004.)

Annina Bosshard (1988), an America-fan, studying economics at the University of St. Gallen and daughter of Susann Bosshard-Kälin.

Translator
Marianne Burkhard, OSB, Peoria, Illinois, a Swiss abroad, who taught German Literature and Language at the University of Illinois in Urbana-Champaign (1968 – 87), then entered the Benedictine community in Nauvoo, Illinois, studied canon Law and since 1993 has been working as a Judge and Director (since 2004) of the Marriage Tribunal of the Diocese of Peoria.